THE THEATRE

Kurt Eisen is Professor of English and Associate Dean of the College of Arts and Sciences at Tennessee Tech University, USA, where he teaches world literature and drama. He is the author of *The Inner Strength of Opposites: O'Neill's Novelistic Drama and the Melodramatic Imagination* (1994). His work has appeared in *The Cambridge Companion to Eugene O'Neill* and a variety of journals, edited volumes, and reference works. He was a fellow of the National Critics Institute in 2001 and is a past president and current board member of the Eugene O'Neill Society.

THE THEATRE OF EUGENE O'NEILL

AMERICAN MODERNISM ON THE WORLD STAGE

Kurt Eisen

Series Editors: Patrick Lonergan and Kevin J. Wetmore Jr.

methuen | drama

LONDON · NEW YORK · OXFORD · NEW DELHI · SYDNEY

METHUEN DRAMA
Bloomsbury Publishing Plc
50 Bedford Square, London, WC1B 3DP, UK
1385 Broadway, New York, NY 10018, USA

BLOOMSBURY, METHUEN DRAMA and the Methuen Drama logo are
trademarks of Bloomsbury Publishing Plc

First published in Great Britain 2017
This paperback edition first published 2019

Cover design: Adriana Brioso
Cover image: David Pittsinger as O'Neill, in *A Blizzard on Marblehead* by
Kushner and Jeanine Tesori, 2011. (© Julieta Cervantes)

A catalogue record for this book is available from the British Library.

A catalog record for this book is available from the Library of Congress.

ISBN: HB: 978-1-4742-3841-0
PB: 978-1-350-11249-0
ePDF: 978-1-4742-3843-4
eBook: 978-1-4742-3842-7

Series: Critical Companions

Typeset by Deanta Global Publishing Services, Chennai, India
Printed and bound in Great Britain

To find out more about our authors and books visit www.bloomsbury.com
and sign up for our newsletters.

For Rita

CONTENTS

Contents

Contents

LIST OF ILLUSTRATIONS

LIST OF ABBREVIATIONS

CC   Dowling, Robert M. (ed.), *Critical Companion to Eugene O'Neill: A Literary Reference to His Life and Work*, 2 vols. (New York: Facts on File, 2009).

CEO   Estrin, Mark (ed.), *Conversations with Eugene O'Neill* (Jackson, MS: University of Mississippi Press, 1990).

CP1   *Complete Plays, 1913-1920*, ed. Travis Bogard (New York: Library of America, 1988).

CP2   *Complete Plays, 1920-1931*, ed. Travis Bogard (New York: Library of America, 1988).

CP3   *Complete Plays, 1932-1943*, ed. Travis Bogard (New York: Library of America, 1988).

CR   Bryer, Jackson R. and Robert M. Dowling (eds.), *Eugene O'Neill: The Contemporary Reviews* (Cambridge: Cambridge Univ. Press, 2014).

Ex   *Exorcism: A Play in One Act* (New Haven: Yale University Press, 2012).

LFA   Dowling, Robert M., *Eugene O'Neill: A Life in Four Acts* (New Haven, CT: Yale University Press, 2014).

LMC   Gelb, Arthur and Barbara Gelb, *O'Neill: Life with Monte Cristo* (New York: Applause, 2000).

SA   Sheaffer, Louis, *O'Neill: Son and Artist* (Boston: Little, Brown, 1973).

SL   Bogard, Travis, and Jackson R. Bryer, *Selected Letters of Eugene O'Neill* (New Haven, CT: Yale University Press, 1988).

SP   Sheaffer, Louis, *O'Neill: Son and Playwright* (Boston: Little, Brown, 1968).

UO   Bogard, Travis (ed.), *The Unknown O'Neill* (New Haven: Yale University Press, 1988).

PREFACE

This book considers Eugene O'Neill's plays in the context of modernity, understood here primarily as the dominant narrative of societal progress and personal fulfillment, especially in America. This narrative subsumed O'Neill himself as the Great American Playwright, but was also the target of relentless critique in his modernist dramatic art. As the following chapters attempt to show, his theatrical modernism was at its best a compelling, visceral mix of Nietzsche, Strindberg, and nostalgia; at worst, an interesting concept run amok or wrung out. Fortunately, O'Neill had the perspicacity, with time and self-understanding, to know the difference, doing his best work even after winning his profession's highest honor, the Nobel Prize.

Readers will notice that I have corralled O'Neill's plays into chapters with a particular thematic emphasis, and that many plays might aptly have been considered instead in another chapter with a different emphasis. Certainly *Desire Under the Elms* is not merely a "family play," and the Irish-Americans in *A Moon for the Misbegotten* fit readily within the discussion of masks and ethnicity of Chapter 5. Indeed, my hope is that readers will see alternative approaches that could have been taken—and thus the richness of O'Neill's art—either by extending the particular framework I've applied to particular plays or by discerning in those works something relevant, useful, or intriguing that has been only hinted at in my discussions here or perhaps excluded altogether.

Many previous scholars, cited or not hereafter, haunt the pages of any such enterprise, and O'Neillians are in my experience an especially intrepid and collegial crew. For their encouragement and support I thank Steve Bloom, Rob Dowling, and Beth Wynstra, with much appreciation also to Zander Brietzke, William Davies King, and Brenda Murphy, for their many contributions to O'Neill studies and to my own understanding of what good writing about drama should be. My four contributors—Dave, Sheila, Alex, and Katie—have my sincerest gratitude for their willing spirit and excellent work for this book.

Susan Furber and Mark Dudgeon at Bloomsbury are the kind of editorial professionals one hopes for, and likewise my boss at Tennessee

Tech University, Paul Semmes, who graciously accepts my need to sneak away from the office during business hours, within reason, to write about drama.

Finally, my dearest gratitude goes to Anna Eisen, surely the damnedest daughter in Connecticut, and to Rita Barnes, daughter of Provincetown and wife for a life.

CHAPTER 1
O'NEILL'S AMERICAN THEATRE:
MODERNISM AGAINST MODERNITY

In the summer of 1932, at the height of success following the acclaim for his monumental Civil War–era update of Greek tragedy, *Mourning Becomes Electra*, Eugene O'Neill was laboring through multiple drafts of *Days Without End*, one of his most overtly experimental plays and a forthright attempt to grapple with the problem of religious faith in the modern world. Subtitled "A Modern Miracle Play," this new work featured a split protagonist whose two warring psychological sides were played by two different actors, one of them masked and invisible to the other characters. O'Neill had established himself as a relentless theatrical experimenter, having used masks previously in *The Great God Brown*, along with a spoken-thought technique in *Strange Interlude* and expressionist staging in *The Emperor Jones*, *The Hairy Ape*, and other works. All these works dealt in varying ways with large questions of identity and alienation, all set decidedly against the grain of American triumphalism that followed the First World War just as O'Neill himself was emerging as the leading writer for the American theatre.

On the morning of September 1 he woke up with another, very different play almost fully formed in his mind. He suspended work on *Days* and quickly completed a draft of *Ah, Wilderness!*—what would become his only produced comedy. "It came on me all of a flood," he wrote to his son Eugene Jr. in November (SL 406). When it premiered at the Guild Theatre in October 1933, shortly before the opening of *Days Without End* in January, O'Neill's comedy delighted reviewers and playgoers who associated the playwright with dark themes and sometimes inscrutable stagecraft. Set on the Fourth of July, 1906, *Ah, Wilderness!* took an affectionate glance backward at the American middle-class family life in the twilight of what James Russell Lowell had nostalgically dubbed "the Fourth of July period of our history" (qtd. Kammen 1991: 254). Drawing on O'Neill's own teenage years in New London, Connecticut, as a fledgling bohemian rebel, it departed sharply from the reality of an often-troubled family life with his father, a prosperous actor, a dissolute older brother, and his unfulfilled, morphine-addicted mother. Equally remarkable was O'Neill's choice of George M. Cohan to play the father, Nat Miller. The celebrated song-and-dance man famous for such showstoppers as "Give My Regards to Broadway" and "Yankee Doodle Boy," Cohan had never performed on Broadway in a show written by someone else, and was, moreover, the very embodiment of star-centered entertainment of the commercial brand of theatre that O'Neill had so long and so pointedly disparaged. "For once O'Neill goes beyond penetrating his characters," wrote John Anderson in the *New York Evening Journal*; "here he loves them, with a nostalgic understanding of their faith and humanity" (CR 736). George Jean Nathan, the eminent critic and friend to whom O'Neill had dedicated the play, observed approvingly that O'Neill had finally eased the "arbitrary and faintly strained effort on his part to evolve a new and strange dramatic form" that was conspicuous in several of his previous works (CR 755). Most presciently, Richard Dana Skinner observed, "The whole significance of O'Neill in the theatre is lost unless we follow this continuous process," and he predicted that *Ah, Wilderness!* would be "the first of a series of plays which will give the stirring story of a man's soul in every stage of its long pilgrimage" (CR 752).

Modernism and tradition

Audiences could be forgiven in 1933 for not seeing any such continuity, and indeed, O'Neill's career had been marred by failure and missteps along with major successes. His most recent work was an adaptation of Aeschylus's *Oresteia* trilogy to Civil War–era New England, the formidable three-part tragedy *Mourning Becomes Electra*. In 1931 it had earned him the most admiring reviews of his career, and even his usual detractors acknowledged that O'Neill had made good on much of the promise evident in such works of the 1920s as *Beyond the Horizon, Desire Under the Elms, The Great God Brown*, and the similarly outsized *Strange Interlude*, and even in his critical and commercial failures *Welded, The Fountain*, and *Dynamo*.[1] Perhaps most importantly, *Mourning Becomes Electra* affirmed the pull of tradition that O'Neill felt even as he searched for new ways to flout the conventions of the commercial theatre. When O'Neill won the Nobel Prize for Literature—he remains the only American dramatist thus honored—*Mourning Becomes Electra* was the work that clinched his selection. In the 1936 award presentation speech Per Hallström praised O'Neill's innovations, but also observed, "Underneath O'Neill's fantastic love of experimenting, however, is a hint of a yearning to attain the monumental simplicity characteristic of ancient drama" ("Award Ceremony Speech"). Biographer Louis Sheaffer makes this point even more broadly, asserting that O'Neill

> was a traditionalist, despite his sympathy with advanced trends in the theater and his own urge toward experimentation. Unlike Ibsen, Shaw and other architects of the modern drama, men who rejected the standards and attitudes of the past, together with the classical models, the young American was looking both forward and back. (SP 419)

Notably, in contrast to the methods of his near-contemporary Bertolt Brecht, O'Neill's theatricality was directed not toward the possibility of societal change but as a critique of an American modernity that had failed to live up to its promise. For O'Neill, "alienation" was not a method, as in Brecht's signature "alienation effect" (*Verfrumdungseffekt*), but the essential condition of modernity that his own experiments strove to highlight.

By the time *Ah, Wilderness!* premiered in 1933, the country was also deeply in the throes of the global economic depression. O'Neill could sense an ominous epochal turn in the rise of fascism in Europe, "the prize clowning of this doleful era of moronic antics" as he called it in a letter to his son (SL 410). As an image of middle-class American family life in "a large small-town" in 1906 (CP3: 4), O'Neill's comedy was not just a fond glance backward to a simpler time or a wishfully modified version of his own youth, but an indirect critique of modernity itself in its image of American culture just before it experienced sweeping changes in art, ideology, and commerce, and before 1910 when, as in Virginia Woolf's famous (if somewhat cryptic, often misquoted) remark, "human character changed" and with it "all human relations have shifted—those between masters and servants, husbands and wives, parents and children" (1924: 4–5).

Subsequent chapters of this book will examine more specifically how political and philosophical anarchism, the new psychology of Freud and Jung, racial identity and conflict, and the rise of feminism and the New Woman, all found their way into O'Neill's drama and its representation of American modernity. The traditionalist in O'Neill saw the American family as the cohering force that could assimilate and even be improved by these new energies and ideas, as his portrait of the Millers suggests. However, for O'Neill the family was modernity's primary casualty, riven by the very mythologies that were also the source of its distinctive moral and psychological strength. The America that O'Neill constructs via the Miller family is not only a wistful version of his own past in the New London of 1906, but also a kind of model of the generational transition that tends toward stability rather than chaos. O'Neill seemed to be looking for a solid foundation beneath American modernity, highlighting "the startling difference," as he wrote to his friend and editor Saxe Commins early in 1933, "between what we Americans [once] felt about life, love, honor, morals, etc., and what we are conscious of feeling today" (Commins 1986: 136).

Youthful mentors: Nietzsche and Strindberg

In 1906 O'Neill himself was, like Richard Miller, a 17-year-old, finishing high school, about to begin what would be for him a very brief college career. Though his literary heroes at that age were also Richard's, O'Neill was decidedly more advanced both sexually and as a drinker, having been initiated by his older brother Jamie into the bars and brothels of New London, where they spent summers with their parents during break in father James's acting tours of *Monte Cristo* and other less successful shows. O'Neill himself spent much of the summer of 1906 immersed in reading Wilde, Zola, and Schopenhauer in the apartment of a local New London physician, Joseph Ganey, the hangout of "a raffish, preponderantly Irish assemblage that would have stood Richard Miller's hair on end" (LMC 199). By fall, O'Neill was off to Princeton and pursuing not the standard academic curriculum but instead, at every opportunity, "the pace that kills along the road to ruin," as he put it in his quaintly racy dedication of *Ah, Wilderness!* to his friend George Jean Nathan (CP3: 2).

While at Princeton, O'Neill began his forays into the philosophical anarchist authors whom Benjamin Tucker championed via his Unique Book Shop nearby in New York, and discovered the mind that had the strongest impact on his work, German philosopher Friedrich Nietzsche. O'Neill cited *Thus Spake Zarathustra* as having influenced him "more than any book I've ever read" and would continue to read it annually (SL 246). The mix of philosophical and political radicalism served up in Tucker's shop was a heady brew for a young man in search of alternatives to both the dulling values of mainstream America and the mundane progressivism exemplified in American politics by Woodrow Wilson, president of Princeton during O'Neill's brief stint there and later of the United States. O'Neill's association in the following decade with such Greenwich Village radicals as John Reed and Emma Goldman left a strong mark on him, but he was ultimately more interested in the moral psychology of anarchism rather than its social or political goals. "As he grew older," Brenda Murphy observes, "his youthful radicalism died away, and his devotion to Nietzsche became more intense," supplying the themes of many of his most significant plays (2005: 26). It was Nietzsche rather than Marx, Proudhon, or Bakunin who most powerfully shaped his sense of the human predicament within the modern world and who named the forces of identity and existence that interested him more than ideological questions. Likewise, as Chapter 5 demonstrates, racial and ethnic prejudice as such interested O'Neill less than the sense of alienation it induced at the heart of the American social experiment.

In this sense O'Neill participated in the "Nietzsche vogue" in America in the early twentieth century. Nietzsche's forceful attacks on religion, particularly Christianity, in favor of a new gospel of the *Übermensch* who eschews tradition and embodies new human possibilities, along with his call for a thorough "revaluation of all values" (1959: 579), carried an immediate resonance for American radicals seeking, like their more mainstream countrymen, a new boldness and ambition unfettered by reactionary traditionalism or progressivist formulas. "The sheer range of Nietzschean liberation," writes Jennifer Ratner-Rosenhagen in her study of his American influence, "could be mapped by the geography of the battles: at home against the stifling ethics and aesthetics of bourgeois parents, at the university against the sterility and scholasticism of the professors, at church against an ethics deemed purely disciplinary, and in the public square against the easy evasions of progressive thought" (2011: 49). O'Neill was drawn to Nietzsche's vision of the tragic, most fully articulated in *The Birth of Tragedy* but in some respects informing all his work and shaping his view of human existence as a clash between an "Apollonian" realm of order and reason against "Dionysian" forces that are primal, chaotic, tragic, yet ultimately creative. Notwithstanding his status as an anti-traditional iconoclast, Nietzsche represented for O'Neill the possibility of propagating the spirit of ancient tragedy in American soil.

If Nietzsche offered the vision of life as a creative struggle that inspired the young O'Neill, Swedish playwright August Strindberg, Nietzsche's contemporary and kindred spirit, served as O'Neill's primary master in the art of drama. During his six-month tuberculosis cure at Gaylord Sanatorium in 1912 and 1913, O'Neill had begun reading a full historical range of drama from classical to contemporary, including Ibsen, Shaw, and Synge (LFA 98), but would single out Strindberg as "the precursor of all modernity in our present theatre" ("Strindberg and Our Theatre" UO 387). It was shortly after his own discovery of Nietzsche that Strindberg wrote *Miss Julie* in 1888 as well as its influential preface containing his reflections on naturalism, tragedy, and modern selfhood. "I find the joy of life in its cruel and powerful struggles," Strindberg wrote in his preface, criticizing the fixed character types of the conventional stage. He argued that drama must explore the conflicts within his characters rather than just between them:

> As modern characters, living in an age of transition more hectic and hysterical than the one that preceded it, I have depicted my figures as more split and vacillating, a mixture of the old and the new. . . . My souls (characters) are conglomerates of past and present stages of culture, bits out of books and newspapers, scraps of humanity, torn shreds of once fine clothing now turned to rags, exactly as the human soul is patched together. (2007: 64–65)

In his conquest of the doomed Miss Julie, the valet Jean mixes bold ambition and craven subservience; Strindberg makes clear that even as Jean is empowered by meritocratic notions of upward mobility and other "modern ideas," he is also shackled to a quasi-medieval sense of the innate inferiority of servants, a condition that also makes him incapable of the tragic self-consciousness that Miss Julie glimpses, however pathetic her fall. In his Nobel Prize acceptance letter, O'Neill acknowledged that for him Strindberg was, "as Nietzsche remains in his sphere, the Master, still to this day more modern than any of us, still our leader" ("The Nobel Prize Acceptance Letter" UO 428). If Ibsen's work set off the shifting moral ground beneath the foundations of dramatic art, it was Strindberg who unleashed the insights of an emerging psychology in representing human relationships and the conflicted inner workings of the self. Self and society in Strindberg are presented not as rational, civil, and progressive but as fractured, irrational, and conflicted. His quest for dramatic forms commensurate with these new realities inspired much of O'Neill's work because it pioneered the expression of human consciousness on stage in terms that were intensely personal and spurred by the playwright's own trauma, and suggestive of broader fissures in the culture. It was Strindberg who, for O'Neill and other modern playwrights, offered the most compelling example of a dramatic modernism pitted against social modernity, validating the inchoate nature of personal subjectivity and trauma as a basis for a coherent dramatic art.

Modernism *contra* modernity

Elin Diamond discerns a "double optic" in Strindberg's art, a desire that audiences "respond simultaneously to the play on the stage and to the modernity bleeding through the play" (2001: 11); for O'Neill I would stress the *counter-modern* sensibility that bleeds through the overtly modernist conceits of so many of his plays. Strindberg's approach to character highlights a distinction, central to my argument here about O'Neill, between the terms *modernity* and *modernism*. The former term implies a progressive sense of historical time and, more specifically, a break from antiquity and medievalism, beginning (by historiographic convention) with the Renaissance and Reformation in Europe, followed by the Enlightenment of the seventeenth and eighteenth centuries and then by a sequence of transformational events and advancements starting in the late eighteenth century, including the French Revolution of 1789 and the Industrial Revolution that reshaped socioeconomic life in the 1800s. What emerged over this period was a fundamentally different understanding of the place of human beings in the universe, particularly as self-conscious makers of "history" and society, in contrast to what had seemed a timeless order with humanity situated within a fixed hierarchy of divinity, nature, and truth. As S. N. Eisenstadt observes, *modernity* "carried a conception of the future characterized by a number of possibilities realizable through autonomous human agency. The premises on which the social, ontological, and political order were based, and the legitimation of that order, were no longer taken for granted" (2000: 3). *Modernism*, on the other hand, was an ideological and aesthetic response to how these new possibilities had been realized in the nineteenth and early twentieth centuries, reflecting a fundamental change in the nature of experience itself amid the rapid changes of modernized, often mechanized society, frequently critical but at times celebratory of those changes.

The connection between art and society is complex and many-leveled, but in some key respects the two move in parallel, reflecting and responding to the same historical conditions: for example, the emergence of perspective in Renaissance painting as an expression of newly opened human and global spaces, and the realistic European novel of the nineteenth century as an imaginative chronicle reflecting the values of the newly dominant bourgeois family. Likewise, advances in the theatre such as highly mobile scenic machinery in the seventeenth century and dynamic stage lighting effects from lime, gas, and ultimately electricity in the late nineteenth century applied new technologies to enhance theatrical experience. However, while nearly as broad and various as the term *modernity*, cultural modernism may be seen as both an expression and a critique; modernity, so to speak, aware of itself. The excesses of logic, systems, efficiency, mobility, and mechanization, among other inherent traits, work against the possibilities of human freedom, agency, self-understanding, and spiritual fulfillment.

In his essay "What Is Enlightenment?" Michel Foucault suggests that modernity as a cultural concept is inextricable from a "countermodernity" and examines the role of nineteenth-century French poet Charles Baudelaire—another formative literary influence on the young O'Neill—in initiating a new kind of aesthetic self-awareness. Foucault invokes a passage from Baudelaire's 1863 essay, "The Painter of Modern Life," that has become a seminal document of modernism: "By 'modernity,'" Baudelaire writes, "I mean the ephemeral, the fugitive, the contingent, the half of art whose other half is the eternal and immutable" (1964: 13). Baudelaire's key insight lies in acknowledging that the most "modern" aspect of modernity is an awareness that the particular changing conditions of one's own present generates a new creative perspective. Foucault sees in this "not simply a form of relationship to the present; it is also a mode of relationship that has to be established with oneself," with the implied artistic—and, I would argue, *modernist*—challenge "to take oneself as object of a complex and difficult elaboration" (1984: 39, 41). In defining "modernity" Baudelaire thus expressed a countermodernity, in Foucault's sense, a resistance to a progressive narrative that increasingly stressed the socioeconomic, scientific, and technological advances of the nineteenth century, emphasizing the role of art in discovering within oneself the flashes of the eternal amid inchoate change.[2]

An American modernism

If Nietzsche's new gospel found receptive young minds (as well as some staunch opposition) in America like O'Neill's, American modernism diverged from its European sources in distinctive ways. The United States as a nation and culture was itself a fledgling product of modernity. In 1906 historian Henry Adams deemed the new century an era of "Multiplicity, Diversity Complexity, Anarchy, Chaos" exemplified not by any cohering faiths or traditions but by the unsettling and alluring effects of technological power (1918: 455). The "past" as such was problematic in American culture, as Van Wyck Brooks discerned in 1918, because it was not sufficiently "usable": "The present is a void, and the American writer floats in that void because the past that survives in the common mind of the present is a past without living value. But is this the only possible past? If we need another past so badly, is it inconceivable that we might discover one, that we might even invent one?" (1918: 339). This decidedly American impulse to invent a cultural tradition can be traced to the writings of Ralph Waldo Emerson, especially in such addresses as "The American Scholar" of 1837 in which he exhorts his countrymen toward an original national culture that integrates "all the ability of the time, all the contributions of the past, all the hopes of the future" (1983: 70). In this spirit, historian Daniel Singal argues for a distinction between a "bohemian" notion of American modernism as anarchic rebellion and its more purposeful "attempt to restore a sense of order to human experience under the often chaotic conditions of twentieth-century existence," adding that American modernism "most assuredly does contain a unifying principle if one knows where to look" (1987: 8). In his own brand of stage modernism, O'Neill was seeking such a unifying principle in the absence of a guiding theology or traditional values adequate to prevailing conditions of American modernity—a "usable" past in the sense that classical tragic had served as a universal perspective for human experience for an earlier time.

For O'Neill, the tragic mode had to be self-consciously reinvented for a new era in order to be true. Notwithstanding the dreadful carnage and lingering national trauma of the Civil War, there was no distinctively American tragic tradition in drama. The American stage was still dominated by the romantic melodramas typified by James O'Neill's *Monte Cristo*, but in the late nineteenth century, American producers and playwrights ventured into a more realistic mode of theatricality as advances in mechanical stage design and lighting effects coincided with a growing taste among audiences for verisimilitude in setting if not yet in theme. In 1891 the novelist and editor William Dean Howells called for a more mature American drama yet acknowledged "for a while yet we must have the romantic and the realistic mixed in the theatre," a transition he deemed "strictly in accordance with the law of evolution," prophesying:

The stage, in working free of romanticism, must carry some rags and tags of it forward in the true way; that has been the case always—in the rise from a higher to a lower form; the man on a trapeze recalls the ancestral monkey who swung by his tail from the forest tree; and the realist cannot all at once forget the romanticist. Perhaps not till the next generation shall we have the very realist. (1891: 478)

Howells knew the works of Ibsen, who had begun shaking up the European theatre in the late 1870s and whose works became available to English readers and playgoers in William Archer's translations beginning with *The Pillars of Society* in 1880. Ibsenism, like the vogue for Nietzsche, proved to be as much a cultural phenomenon of modernity as a pioneering mode of modernist dramatic art, offering a model for the progressive "law of evolution" that Howells had applied to the development of American dramatic art as it began to feature moral and societal "problems" on stage. Ibsen's shadow loomed over such American plays as James A. Herne's *Margaret Fleming* (1890), Edward Sheldon's *Salvation Nell* (1909), and *The City* by Clyde Fitch (1909), though the relative thematic boldness of these works was still eclipsed by the spectacle-oriented stage realism that captivated audiences with new stage technologies and scenic verisimilitude, and whose major exponent was David Belasco.

These early realist works carried with them a large measure of the "rags and tags," in Howells's phrase, of a formulaic romanticism in contemporary American life while affirming the virtue of artistic as well as technological progress in native dramatic art. They did not fundamentally challenge an audience's moral sensibilities or its understanding of theatre but offered an enhanced cultural product such that audiences, as J. Chris Westgate observes, could view new plays featuring prostitutes and gritty urban life such as Eugene Walter's *The Easiest Way* in 1909 as evidence of their own liberal tastes and politics,[3] but still framed in the reassuring melodramatic conventions of a clear-cut moral polarity, formulaic sentimentalism, and gratifying narrative resolution. It was the theatrically familiar power of melodrama from which O'Neill was jolted in 1907 when he journeyed into Manhattan on ten consecutive nights to see Alla Nazimova in the Moscow Art Theatre's production of Ibsen's *Hedda Gabler*, and likewise in 1911, when the Abbey Theatre brought its poetic yet antiromantic brand of stage realism from Ireland to America with works by John Millington Synge, T. C. Murray, W. B. Yeats, Lady Gregory, and others. Just as seeing Ibsen's *Hedda Gabler* had given the young O'Neill his "first conception of a modern theatre where truth might live," as he later wrote (SL 477), the Abbey Players presented him "a first glimpse" of how he might create his own version of that theatre in America (SP 205).

Melodrama as modernity

The standard narrative of O'Neill as America's greatest playwright, as Mark Hodin notes, turns on "the arrival of Eugene O'Neill in the 1920s, taking his bold dramaturgy and brash attitude as evidence of a modern break from nineteenth-century theatrical convention" while largely ignoring O'Neill's ties to its tried-and-true conventions (2014: 160).[4] In fact, critics in the 1920s and 1930s frequently noted his tendency to draw on the conventions of nineteenth-century melodrama that he absorbed from the theatrical career of his actor father, James O'Neill, best known as the star of a long-running stage adaptation of Alexandre Dumas's romance, *The Count of Monte Cristo*. Robert Benchley, typically suspicious of O'Neill's literary pretensions, expressed this view in his 1931 review of *Mourning Becomes Electra*: "In this tremendous play, he gives us not one thing that is new, and he gives us nothing to think about (unless we are just beginning to think), but he does thrill the bejeezus out of us, just as his father used to, and that is what we go to the theatre for" (CR 707). Benchley does not, however, try to account for how O'Neill reinvents the American melodramatic tradition as a synthetic modernist realism that exposes the conventions of realism as complicit in the prevailing modernity of American history and culture. O'Neill's theatrical "bejeezus" was decidedly not his father's. O'Neill also had detractors who pointed to certain melodramatic traits evident even in his seemingly most nontraditional plays, including such successful works as *Desire Under the Elm* and *Strange Interlude*. "What O'Neill did was to take Victorian melodrama and add," argues Eric Bentley, an influential critic who grappled throughout his career with a mix of antipathy and admiration for O'Neill (1987: 38).[5] The modernist techniques in his plays that seem closest to the "New Theatre" of such European visionaries as Gordon Craig should be understood not in terms of an artist constructing a signature aesthetic, or even as a writer's search for a dramatic language adequate to his personal vision; rather, they demonstrate O'Neill's sense that American modernity's unfulfilled promise could be the basis of a tragic theatrical realism.

O'Neill's rootedness in his father's theatre, which is to say the romantic American melodramatic theatre that lingered into the twentieth century, was also his strongest connection to American modernity. If his modernism denotes an innovative, experimental stage aesthetic that incorporated powerful elements of Ibsen's and Strindberg's methods, it was the melodramatic plots, characters, and effects of plays by Owen Davis,

Augustin Daly, Augustus Thomas, and other mainstays of the commercial American stage that actually constituted the contemporary aesthetic reality for theatre audiences. Melodrama, as Ben Singer argues, is the definitive theatrical mode of nineteenth-century modernity because its engaging emotional formulas reflect "an era in which logical systems-building informs most avenues of human endeavor" (2001: 22). Both escapist and normative, melodrama supplied moral and psychological archetypes that helped audiences make sense of the seismic change following the French Revolution and other upheavals of the nineteenth century. Ibsen and Strindberg unsettled audiences by exposing these archetypes as empty or illusory; however, as Mark Hodin observes, "If dramatic realism has been a stalwart critic of melodrama, then melodrama may also reveal the limits of dramatic realism and can then show . . . how *theatre* gives deeper meaning to *drama*" (2014: 170). Hodin's recuperative argument aptly describes much of O'Neill's art and its melodramatic attributes as signs of a vigorous engagement with modernity rather than a mark of weakness that some hypothetically superior artist could or should have overcome.[6]

Prophesying a modern American stage

Following Howells's example, voices calling for a new American drama were growing in the decade of the 1910s, inspired by the great European playwrights and by the visionary theatre companies of the late 1800s and early 1900s such as the Moscow Art Theatre, the Théâtre Libre in Paris, and the Abbey in Dublin, as well as theatrical innovators Gordon Craig, Max Reinhardt, and Adolph Appia. In his forward-looking 1914 study *The New Movement in Theatre*, critic Sheldon Cheney surveyed recent developments in Europe and assessed the current state of American plays and productions, including the "little theatres" springing up not only in such cities as New York, Chicago, and Boston but also at universities as in his native Berkeley, California. "What the American theatre most needs today," Cheney argued, "is *freedom*—freedom from traditional forms and conventional thought—freedom for experimentation"; Cheney maintained that this was most in evidence at "the new and broader universities that are so splendidly maintaining their place at the forefront of American progress" (1914: 192). The link Cheney draws here between artistic "freedom" and "American progress" reflects his vision of academe as an incubator of a robust national culture that would parallel its role for American science, industry, and global prominence. Yet for all his enthusiasm for university and noncommercial theatres, Cheney also believed that "the work which the experimental theatres are doing will not be fully effective until it reaches the larger audiences of the commercial playhouses. . . . What must happen is this: the Broadway theatre will adopt the ideals of the art theatres" (1914: 193).

Having recently published (at his father's expense) a volume of five short plays, O'Neill was encouraged by the eminent critic and friend of his father, Clayton Hamilton, to enroll in George Pierce Baker's two-year playwriting course at Harvard known as English 47. When O'Neill wrote to Baker in July 1914, he declared his desire "to be an artist or nothing" with the clear implication that the "nothing" he meant to avoid was to be merely "a mediocre journey-man playwright" for the commercial stage (SL 26). Baker's course, first offered at Harvard in 1905, was the prototype of the university playwriting workshop and part of the larger movement seeking to treat the playwright as a literary artist. Like Cheney and Baker, Hamilton believed American audiences were ready for a new kind of theatrical experience showcasing the art of the playwright rather than the producer. "The trouble with most ineffective plays," Hamilton wrote in 1909, "is that the fabricated life they set before us is less real than such similar phases of actual life as we have previously realized for ourselves. We are wearied because we have already unconsciously imagined more than the playwright professionally imagines for us" (1909: 446). In developing his distinctive dramatic vision, O'Neill would come to fulfill Baker's own ideal of the artist who pursues a "complete freedom of choice in subject and complete freedom in treatment," as Baker himself wrote in 1919 as O'Neill was about to launch his first major New York production, *Beyond the Horizon*. However, this artistic freedom, Baker continued, may be achieved only by "mingling of much out of the past and an adaptation of past practice" (1919: vi), a dependence on traditional dramaturgy that O'Neill rejected but never fully escaped.

From Harvard to Greenwich Village

As O'Neill would soon realize, Baker's dramatic aesthetic was essentially conservative in favoring the "well-made" play with its sturdy formal conventions of plot over the more immersive, atmospheric, and character-centered theatricality emerging in Europe. According to Baker, *Bound East for Cardiff*, the one-act sea play that O'Neill had written in 1914 under the title *Children of the Sea* shortly before enrolling at Harvard, was evidence of O'Neill's talent but not really "a play at all" (SP 296). Declining the second year of Baker's course, O'Neill returned instead to New York in the fall of 1915. He had misspent several months of his post-Princeton youth there, and upon returning continued preparing to be "an artist or nothing" by drinking with street toughs and anarchists in such notorious dives as the Golden Swan, also known as the Hell Hole and later immortalized in the settings of *Anna Christie* and *The Iceman Cometh*. He also read Nietzsche, delved into Eastern philosophy, and, according to Robert M. Dowling, used a "nearly year-long hiatus in playwriting to methodically train his mind to think like a dramatist" (LFA 121), presumably beyond any lessons he had taken from Baker.

Like many restless Americans he was drawn to bohemian Greenwich Village, where urban American modernism was brewing in the salons, cafés, galleries, and public squares of lower Manhattan. Hippolyte Havel, the Czech expatriate anarchist later portrayed as Hugo Kalmar in *The Iceman Cometh*, described the Village in 1915 as a way of being more than a particular urban locale, "a spiritual zone of mind . . . the rallying point for new ideas" (1915: 34–35). The epochal International Exhibition of Modern Art in the early months of 1913, better known as the Armory Show, introduced European post-Impressionist art to the United States and thrilled the group of writers, artists, and intellectuals then frequenting the salon of Mabel Dodge on lower Fifth Avenue. In June, Dodge helped John Reed and other Village radicals organize a pageant at the old Madison Square Garden to showcase the plight of the striking Paterson silk workers, which also highlighted a new convergence of theatre and social ferment. The burgeoning of literary and journalistic publishing resisted the prosperity that would emerge in the era following the First World War, instead supporting radical causes at home and abroad. With its "invasion of the war-scattered artists from other worlds," Greenwich Village, as the New York *Tribune* reported glibly in November 1915, "is learning new lessons from old masters, taking on the tone of original Bohemia, acquiring the polish of European culture and even talking French" (Addington 1915: sec. 4:2). In fact, the war had the effect of generating an internationalist American modernism in the crucible of Greenwich Village, fostering an oppositional community in the urban heart of triumphal American modernity, New York City.

Energized by the Paterson strike pageant and by such companies as the Toy Theatre in Boston and the Little Theatre in Chicago, Greenwich

Villagers took up drama as a means of trying out new aesthetic ideas, new perspectives on culture and society, and new modes of collective action and creativity. The Washington Square Players had formed in New York in 1914 as an alternative to commercial theatres on Broadway. The one-act plays it produced with their lower production costs and technical demands were also "a weapon with which to win recognition and build up the histrionic capacity to tackle longer works," as critic Walter Prichard Eaton described the group (1916: xv). For a group of Greenwich Villagers summering in Provincetown on Cape Cod, the Washington Square Players were insufficiently committed to nurturing American playwrights. In 1915, led by Susan Glaspell and her husband George Cram "Jig" Cook, they formed an enthusiastic collective called the Provincetown Players. Its first two resolutions affirmed these goals, stating as the group's "primary object" that it "encourage the writing of American plays of real artistic, literary and dramatic—as opposed to Broadway—merit" and that "such plays be considered without reference to their commercial value, since this theatre is not to be run for pecuniary profit" (Kenton 2004: 27). Even more propitious for O'Neill when he joined the group in Provincetown in 1916, the playwright was no longer to be subordinate to the will of the producer or director; rather, the Players resolved, "The author shall produce the play without hindrance, according to his own ideas," selecting the cast and with all "resources of the theatre, including the volunteer staff, the actors *within and without the club willing to take part, the properties, scenery, costumes et cetera on hand . . . at the disposal of the author*" (Kenton 2004: 27, 28). The first ever production of an O'Neill play, *Bound East for Cardiff*, in 1916 in a converted fish house on a Provincetown pier, featured the playwright also as director and on stage in a very brief speaking role.

The Provincetown Players became a magnet of literary and artistic talent. The group launched the pioneering playwriting careers of O'Neill and Glaspell, while drawing contributions from such other future literary stars as Wallace Stevens, Theodore Dreiser, Djuna Barnes, and Edna St. Vincent Millay; equally important, it embodied an ideal of an experimental, visionary, even transformational theatre. Its ideals of aesthetic individual freedom and collective production, as well as the staunchly amateur spirit of what its leader Jig Cook called "the beloved community of lifegivers," explicitly countered the established practices of the commercial theatre, yet also generated internal tensions that made such an enterprise unsustainable (qtd. Sarlós 1982: 141). Despite the breakout uptown success in 1920 of the full-length *Beyond the Horizon*,

O'Neill remained committed to the Provincetown group and its artistic ideals even as he outgrew the one-act form that comprised the great part of its first five seasons in New York. Productions of O'Neill's *The Emperor Jones* in 1920 and *The Hairy Ape* in 1922 swelled the Players' subscriber list and then realized full commercial success in moving uptown, along with other of their plays, to Broadway theatres.

After Provincetown

The rifts among Jig Cook and other Provincetowners had reached a breaking point as Cook and Glaspell departed for Greece, where Cook died in 1924. "Jig Cook's fundamental error," remarks Robert K. Sarlós, "was his unwillingness to accept popular success as an indication that the experiment had profitably been completed" and his insistence on "a permanent state of revolution" (1982: 141). O'Neill joined with Provincetown stage designer Robert Edmond Jones and Kenneth Macgowan, a theatre critic and author, to form The Experimental Theatre, Inc., a name that conveys the adventurous spirit of the Provincetown while professionalizing its ambitions. Despite O'Neill's pursuit of professional success and his emergence as America's leading playwright, his disdain for the commercial theatre did not diminish, nor did his persistent testing of aesthetic and formal boundaries. From this "triumvirate" with Jones and Macgowan, as it was called informally, came some of O'Neill's most daring and successful plays of the 1920s, including *All God's Chillun' Got Wings*, *Desire Under the Elms*, and *The Great God Brown*, along with several of his most notable duds such as *Welded* and *The Fountain*, as well as *The Ancient Mariner*, an adaptation of Coleridge's poem.

This period after the demise of the Provincetown Players also established the image of O'Neill as the solitary genius, toiling in intense, even tortured isolation away from the collaborative buzz of the stage, moving restlessly from home to home ever farther from the lights of New York. As William Davies King's essay in this volume suggests, O'Neill's process of creating a definitive artistic persona was itself essential to his search for a unifying principle in his sense of modernity, a coherent self rendered in the many photographic portraits generated during his career.[7] While living in California in 1940, immersed in his two great retrospective works set in 1912, *The Iceman Cometh* and *Long Day's Journey Into Night*, O'Neill declined a plea for funds to save the Provincetown Playhouse building on Macdougal Street yet allowed himself to reminisce in terms that suggested both the lingering spirit of Jig Cook and his own growing pessimism:

> There was a theatre then in which I knew I belonged, one of guts and idealism. Now I feel out of the theatre. I dread the idea of production because I know it will be done by people who have really only one standard left, that of Broadway success. . . . The idea of an Art Theatre is more remote now, I think, than it was way back in the first decade of this century, before the Washington Square Players or the P[rovincetown] P[layers] were ever dreamed of. (SL 513–14)

In self-imposed exile from the commercial stage and with Europe embroiled in yet another, even more catastrophic global war soon to draw in the United States, O'Neill was gloomy about the prospects for American theatre and his country. "After all," he told Macgowan with his decidedly counter-progressive view of modernity, "the times *are* obviously decadent, and the condition of the theatre reflects them" (SL 514).

Journeying into the past

O'Neill therefore "surrendered himself to nostalgia," as Dowling puts it (LFA 430)—not the emotional refuge he had found previously in *Ah, Wilderness!* but the creative nostalgia that Tammy Clewell has argued is characteristic of much literary modernism, "which invokes the past not to restore it, as much as to measure and challenge the present" (2013: 6). He recognized that these two later plays should not be produced on stage immediately, that their cultural moment had not yet arrived. O'Neill pointedly deferred their production until after the war and, in the case of *Long Day's Journey*, after his own death. None of these late plays was overtly experimental in form or staging like much of his work from *The Emperor Jones* to *Days Without End*. In withdrawing from the commercial stage in the mid-1930s and then abandoning his massive American history cycle project in 1940, O'Neill had seemingly given up his own search for a new form and a new language to critique the nation's moral destiny. Publishing magnate Henry R. Luce had proclaimed "the first great American Century" in the pages of *Life* magazine (1941: 65), but O'Neill, during his much-anticipated but critically mixed return to the New York stage with the premiere of *Iceman*, reflected on this subject in one of several interviews he granted at that time. "America is due for a retribution," he said, bluntly contrary to the nation's triumphal mood in the wake of the Allies' military victory over Hitler and fascism. "There ought to be a page in the history books of the of the United States of America of all the unprovoked, criminal, unjust crimes committed and sanctioned by our government since the beginning of our history—and before that, too." He denounced "the American Dream" of enlightened progress as a hoax and called for the portraits of "our great national heroes" to "be taken out and burned" (Bowen 1946: CEO 221–22).

Iceman was the final New York premiere O'Neill would live to see. Along with *Long Day's Journey* he had completed three other plays during the war, including the one-act *Hughie* and *A Touch of the Poet*—the only finished play of the cycle. The elegiac, confessional *A Moon for the Misbegotten* was produced soon after *Iceman*, but its tryout tour in several Midwestern cities in 1947 was cut short. O'Neill's declining health no longer allowed him to write down the ideas for plays that continued to crowd his mind. A congenital tremor increasingly hindered the tiny, precise penmanship in which he had always composed his works. By 1953, when O'Neill died in a hotel suite in Boston, he had been eclipsed by younger American playwrights Tennessee Williams, Arthur Miller, Lillian Hellman, and William Inge, and rendered seemingly obsolete on the world stage by the paradigm-shifting reinventions of dramatic form and sensibility by such Europeans as Bertolt Brecht, Samuel Beckett, and Eugène Ionesco. The playwright whose heroes always struggled with the problem of belonging in modernity had in his own final years himself become a marginal figure in the Cold War culture and within the new postmodern aesthetic.

But not for long. In 1956 a revelatory revival of *Iceman* in New York and the premiere—first in Stockholm and then in New York—of *Long Day's Journey* were followed the next year by the belated arrival of *A Moon for the Misbegotten* on Broadway and in 1958 by the premiere of *A Touch of the Poet*. O'Neill's place as the preeminent American dramatist was swiftly restored as directors such as José Quintero—aptly, in the off-Broadway house Circle-in-the-Square—reframed his tragic modernist vision for a postmodern age that had grown skeptical of the grand historical "metanarratives" of modernity, in Lyotard's term. With these later plays he had clearly surpassed even those works from the 1920s and early 1930s that were deemed powerful enough in 1936 to earn him the Nobel Prize. The path of his career had featured meteoric fame if not unbroken success followed by a lengthy if productive retreat; it could now be seen as a life of artistic struggle that had culminated in the creation of some of the most durable, definitive plays of the modern stage and a legacy that resonated beyond his own body of work.

The jagged path of O'Neill's own striving as an artist has no parallel in American drama, perhaps in modern literature or theatre, yet also authorized the legitimacy of risk and failure for playwrights who followed. The plays completed and produced in his lifetime include almost as many failures as successes; indeed, his inability to complete the biggest project of his career, the American history cycle, may be seen in retrospect as a necessary precondition to the completion of the great works written from 1939 to 1943. Given its epic ambitions, the cycle was perhaps inherently doomed in its collusion with American modernity even as it tried to provide a critique of it. As subsequent chapters will explore, O'Neill had set for himself the challenge of capturing the experience of American modernity while also countering it with the more compelling reality he could create on stage and for readers of his published works. Having pursued the wistful nostalgia in *Ah, Wilderness!* and the failed experiment in *Days Without End*, O'Neill eventually came to recognize that by applying something like the classical unities in *The Iceman Cometh, Long Day's Journey*, and *A Moon for the Misbegotten*, he could more effectively confront the present as a dynamic conjunction of the past stripped of its capacity for comfort and a future closed off to easy progressive formulas or illusions of hope. O'Neill's posthumous success carries on his argument with modernity and is perhaps his greatest creation.

CHAPTER 2
A MODERNIST IN THE MAKING:
O'NEILL BEFORE BROADWAY

The early 1900s were "the happy days" of American theatre, according to Glenn Hughes, "in the sense that all forms of theatrical entertainment were booming"—commercially, that is, if not perhaps artistically (1951: 320), thus fortifying the place of the theatre industry within the mix of American modernity. Theatre companies enjoyed a large network of performance venues, with extensive regional touring circuits and a wide range of entertainments from Shakespeare to vaudeville. Its star system overshadowed its playwrights, with such native eminences as Edwin Booth, Joseph Jefferson, Maude Adams, and O'Neill's father, James, dominating the stage, with iconic Europeans such as Sarah Bernhardt and Eleonora Duse crossing the Atlantic to perform before large, admiring audiences. Meanwhile, by 1900 most American playhouses and touring companies were controlled by the profit-minded Theatrical Syndicate, which strong-armed artists who dared to attempt any measure of autonomy. Eventually the monopoly of this "unseen monster that hovered over Broadway and preyed upon theatre people," according to Brooks Atkinson (qtd. Wilson 1973: 257), was disrupted by competitors such as the Shubert brothers and by popular demand for productions like those of David Belasco, who refused to submit to Syndicate control. Yet the commercial theatrical culture that O'Neill derided as "the show shop" held sway.

It would be misleading to suggest that O'Neill appeared suddenly from the void of serious literary drama in the United States, as if conjured by more demanding audiences and the growing number of critical voices calling for a more serious brand of American theatre. Several other playwrights had taken up something like this challenge in the previous century, including Bronson Howard, Steele Mackaye, Clyde Fitch, and especially James A. Herne, whose *Shore Acres* and *Margaret Fleming* led some critics to dub him "the American Ibsen."[1] In 1906 Rachel Crothers had a major success in New York with the Ibsenesque *The Three of Us*, and O'Neill's Provincetown colleague Susan Glaspell was also innovating in theme, character, and staging in such plays as *Trifles*, *Bernice*, and *The Verge*. O'Neill is perhaps the most compelling figure around whom to build an origin story of a serious American drama, however, because he was an eminent actor's son and thus a child of the theatre industry, thoroughly rooted in the commercial theatre that he rejected, and yet ambitious to test the limits of the medium. His innovations thus had a metatheatrical force akin to that of traditional melodrama, but instead of good-versus-evil, he highlighted a theatrical art animated by a conflict of innovation against tradition—"de new dat's moiderin' de old!" as his brash hero Yank Smith declares in *The Hairy Ape* (CP2: 128). O'Neill gave the story of American drama the dauntless playwright-protagonist it had been lacking, one whose resistance to the conventions of theatre and conspicuous commitment to his own vision were essential to his art.

Just prior to the emergence of Glaspell and O'Neill, William Vaughn Moody's 1906 frontier drama *The Great Divide* had been praised by some critics as the long-awaited great American play. Its relatively daring sexual realism complemented the playwright's treatment of mythic national themes, especially the American regional conflict, as Hughes put it, between "Eastern culture and Western violence" (1951: 340). Featuring an attempted gang rape in a rowdy frontier outpost but concluding with a devout reaffirmation of marriage in a New England village, it dramatized a clash of nature and culture that was more challenging and literate than the usual melodramatic fare. "No other American play has ever gone so deep," wrote critic Walter Prichard Eaton, who saw signs in *The Great Divide* of a new and better kind of drama grounded in "the most powerful forces in human life" instead of standard dramatic formulas: "In this soul-drama externals are burned away, and primal things, becoming naked, become decent, become wonderful" (1908: 18–19). Eaton discerned in Moody, Herne, Fitch, and Crothers a more robust and modern national stage:

> These authors, then, who are bringing to bear on the problem of creating an American drama the largest amount of dramatic skill, truthful observation, intelligent reflection, and passion for reality are the ones who are keeping our drama connected with life, who are leading our stage on toward better things by making it a vital force in the community. . . . The mere scenic fidelity of Belasco seems tame, old-fashioned. (1908: 25–26)

Eaton's upbeat, progressive view of American playwriting was not shared by all, especially some leading playwrights. A very successful writer of crowd-pleasing stage potboilers in the United States, the English-born Charles Klein, in 1911 specifically blamed Nietzsche, along with Ibsen and Shaw, for what he considered an unfortunate turn against romantic idealism (and Christian values) in contemporary playwriting:

> Nietzsche was exceedingly modern. . . . The idea of self-sacrifice is uplifting, and partly through his destruction of this idea Nietzsche's influence is depressing. It is depressing also for the same reason that Ibsen's is. Ibsen shows life in its most painful relation to truth: Shaw, under a comic aspect, shows us the same thing. Pain is the prominent characteristic of all three men. And it is these three men who have driven the modern playwright into realism. ("Three Men" 1911: 14)

A victim of an all-too-real disaster when a German U-boat sank the *Lusitania* in 1915, Klein ascribed this new appetite for realism in audiences to their consuming the sordid details of modern life in their daily newspapers. Meanwhile, Klein himself had made a handsome living by pandering to American playgoers, only about one in ten of whom "can think," he judged, with perhaps a touch of cynicism; "introspection" he noted, "is non-American" ("Three Men" 1911: 14).

Even so, the influential American philosopher William James in 1890 had posited introspection to be the essence of psychological understanding and, with Emersonian conviction, declared one's own consciousness to be a bulwark against the dizzying flux of modernity, the most unshakable fact "in a world most of whose other facts have at some time tottered in the breath of philosophic doubt" (1890: 185). James thus affirmed the cohering effect of a writer's own consciousness as he eschews crowd-pleasing convention and grapples with "philosophic doubt" and other uncertainties. In the theatre especially, the reign of convention was strong. During his year in Greenwich Village after leaving Harvard, O'Neill read *The Great Divide* among many other American plays, recalling it later as "a fine play for two acts" that "falls to pieces because it has to end happily," like "practically all" American plays to that point (Crichton 1960: CEO 195). The dramatic happy ending was virtually official American doctrine, "the pursuit of happiness" having been written in 1776 into the nation's founding document; what O'Neill had learned from Strindberg in particular was that a play should ruthlessly follow the inconvenient logic of the playwright's consciousness and experience instead of the prevailing conventions of plot or typology of character. Rather than any consistent style, method, or set of themes, it was this insistence on externalized introspection that marked the O'Neillian turn in American drama.

An early "skit"

Released from the sanatorium in June 1913, his relatively mild tuberculosis cured, O'Neill began writing plays at twenty-four with a relentless productivity that would continue for the next three decades. O'Neill considered *A Wife for a Life* merely "a vaudeville skit" likely inspired by his experience touring the vaudeville circuit with James O'Neill the year before (LMC 395–96) and by his brief stint as a gold prospector in Honduras a few years before that. Such apprentice work has value primarily in the context of O'Neill's later plays, of course, but these two pieces also offer a link between the American mythic realism of Moody's *The Great Divide* and such later works by O'Neill as *Beyond the Horizon, Desire Under the Elms*, and even *The Iceman Cometh*.

A Wife, like the first two-thirds of Moody's play, is set in the Arizona desert and focuses on the effects of a troubled marriage entangled with the search for gold on the western frontier. In O'Neill's much briefer work, two prospectors, identified as the Older Man and the "younger man" Jack, sit by a campfire "on the rim of the world," as the former puts it, working out the terms by which Jack will return east to New York to "organize a company" to manage their soon-to-be lucrative mining claim (CP1: 5). Meanwhile a telegram arrives, a message for Jack from his lover in New York, who, having chastely awaited the return of her long-absent husband, is now at last summoning Jack to her. The Older Man, realizing that this faithful woman is the very wife he left behind, suppresses an urge to kill his young partner as a rival; without revealing his own connection to her, he acquiesces in a brief final soliloquy: "Greater love hath no man than this that he giveth his wife for his friend" (CP1: 11). The arrival of the telegram evokes the modern technology and commerce of New York City in direct contrast with the primitive and, as Jack sees it, "corrupt environment of a mining camp" with its "atmosphere of sordid sin and suffering" out west (CP1: 7). Jack's happy future in the east depends on the Older Man's grim, self-imposed isolation out west in the desert, alienated from love, wealth, and modernity. The noble self-sacrifice that playwright Charles Klein blamed the influence of Nietzsche for erasing in American plays is here alive and well, but O'Neill undercuts the happy ending by emphasizing the Older Man's lonely, self-absorbed brooding in the final moments.

First publication: Testing the waters

O'Neill would later disavow this very first foray into playwriting. He began to generate new plays with remarkable industry in 1913, and with a $450 subsidy from his father to the Gorham Press of Boston, O'Neill published five pieces in *Thirst and Other One-Act Plays* in 1914. In effect he was following the advice of his father's friend, critic Clayton Hamilton: "Keep your eye on life,—on life as you have seen it; and to hell with the rest!" (qtd. LFA 103). Hamilton was thinking of the young O'Neill's adventures at sea; three of the five plays, though actually written before the advice from Hamilton, feature plots with shipwrecks, an experience that O'Neill himself had not specifically faced at sea but clearly felt was compelling dramatically. In fact, none of these five early plays could be considered fully rooted in O'Neill's personal experience, but rather marked his first attempts to sort out themes and situations that interested him dramatically, including some already well established as stage motifs. O'Neill called *The Web* "the first play I ever wrote" (qtd. Floyd 1985: 21n), dismissing *A Wife for a Life* as a mere sketch for vaudeville. Not produced until many years after his death, *The Web* shifts abruptly from the desert campfire of *A Wife* to the "*squalid bedroom in the top floor of a rooming house on the lower East Side, New York*" (CP1: 15). This is not the prosperous New York imagined vaguely in the earlier play, but an urban jungle rife with criminal violence, disease, poverty, and sexual exploitation.

Urban realism had fully arrived on the New York stage in the 1908 and 1909 seasons in such plays as Edward Sheldon's *Salvation Nell* and Eugene Walter's *The Easiest Way*. These and other "sociological plays," as J. Chris Westgate calls them, combined verisimilitude in staging with "decidedly progressive attitudes about poverty, drunkenness, and prostitution that defined the misbegotten as victims of environmental and material circumstances rather than of pathological or inherent [moral] failings" (2012: 36). In O'Neill's play, Rose Thomas is a prostitute confined to her shabby room with a small child and an acute tubercular cough. She voices her plight in the broadly urban stage dialect that would mark several of O'Neill's most distinctive early plays: "Gawd! What a night! (*laughing bitterly*) What a chance I got!"

(CP1: 15). Attacked by her pimp Steve, she is rescued by a gallant fugitive, Tim Moran, who hears the commotion and bursts into her room just in time to stop him. As the police close in on Tim, he and Rose bond by sharing hard-luck tales. In the play's most telling "sociological" lines, Rose laments the futility of social progress and places the blame for her lot on the good intentions of a progressive society: "I've tried that job thing. I've looked fur decent work and I've starved at it. . . . There didn't seem to be no use. They—all the good people—they got me where I am and they're goin' to keep me there. Reform? Take it from me it can't be done. They won't let yuh do it, and that's Gawd's truth" (CP1: 21–22). After Steve sneaks back into the room from the fire escape, he shoots Tim, then slips back into the night. The police arrive, arrest Rose as Tim's murderer, and take custody of her child. According to O'Neill's stage directions, in her despair, Rose sees "*perhaps the personification of the ironic life force that has crushed her*" (CP1: 28), though nothing is offered scenically to convey such a vision to an audience. O'Neill's curtain line has an acerbic, even ominous twist, underscoring Rose's cynical take on progressive social uplift: "Mama's gone," a plainclothes policeman says to her child. "I'm your Mama now" (CP1: 28).

The key interest of both these two otherwise slight early plays, as Travis Bogard notes, is that "the significant action lies less in external events than in the psyche of the central character" (*Contour* 1988: 20). However, in other works O'Neill was also beginning to construct his signature metaphysical framework, drawing on his experience as a young man on seagoing vessels. In three of the plays included in his first published volume, he portrays a shipwrecked humanity, a microcosm of impotent modernity against the primordial and fateful backdrop of the sea. Among the first O'Neill plays to be staged by the Provincetown Players in the summer of 1916, *Thirst* is a brief allegorical piece with three characters adrift in a life raft under a relentless sun that is "*like a great angry eye of God*" (CP1: 31), beset by sharks and by their own personal desperation. An inherently mythic, mystical force, the sea for O'Neill proved a far more compelling setting than the Arizona desert or a New York tenement. Throughout his body of work, either as image or as setting, the sea served as a counterpoint to the banality of modern life on land, a palpable symbol of fate and his own distinctive version of a "great divide" between being and nothingness. O'Neill found himself also facing an aesthetic divide between traditional realism and a more adventurous stage modernism, evident in *Thirst* primarily in the internal dispute during its 1916 staging between the avant-garde painter and sculptor William Zorach, who created "a backdrop of formalized waves," and O'Neill himself, who insisted on "a sea cloth with someone wriggling around underneath it to represent the ocean," in Zorach's words (qtd. Murphy 2005: 94). According to the Provincetown hierarchy, the playwright ruled. This first staging of *Thirst* was also notable as the playwright's only appearance onstage in one of his own plays (or any play) as a key character—the West Indian Mulatto Sailor—along with Jig Cook as the Gentleman and Louise Bryant, with whom O'Neill was having an affair (despite her attachment to John Reed), as the seductive Dancer. Though Bogard judges *Thirst* to be "neither realism nor symbolism but a somewhat dismaying mixture of both," he also allows that it shows O'Neill making dramaturgical strides toward a more effective representation of the "ironic life force" that he had introduced thematically in his first two plays but had begun to convey more distinctively here in a maritime setting (*Contour* 1988: 30).

O'Neill likely took some inspiration for these early shipwreck plays from the sinking of the *Titanic* in April 1912, as Robert Richter notes in his study of O'Neill and the sea (2004: 138). A supposedly unsinkable marvel of engineering, the *Titanic* became an emblem of modernity's overreach, of the ultimate helplessness of humanity against the brute power of nature. The three survivors adrift in *Thirst* are likewise a microcosm in which O'Neill portrays the collapse of civil society. An allegory of gender, class, race, colonial politics, and madness emerges in the alternating confrontations and alliances among the Dancer, the Gentleman, and the mulatto Sailor. Initially the Gentleman and the Dancer exclude the Sailor from their provisional bond, put off by the "*monotonous negro song*" he sings to himself (CP1: 31). The Sailor calls his song "a charm" against the sharks circling the boat, but the Dancer, though claiming familiarity with the songs of many countries, can't discern its provenance or meaning, while the Gentleman declares that "the accursed humming of that nigger only makes one feel the silence more keenly" (CP1: 40). They both accuse the Sailor of hiding water and food, a delusion reflecting their sense of racial and economic superiority. The Dancer reaches her breaking point while trying to seduce the Sailor in order to gain this imagined water; rebuffed, she descends into madness, deluded that she is back performing once more on stage. In a final frenzy, she drops dead. The Sailor sees his chance to quench his overpowering thirst by drinking her blood, but the Gentleman thwarts him by pushing the Dancer's body into the water and in turn is promptly stabbed by the Sailor. In their mutual destruction—an almost exact counterimage of the resolution of *A Wife for a Life* in the desert—the two men both tumble off the boat to be devoured by sharks, leaving a "*black stain on the water*" as the Dancer's "*diamond necklace lies glittering in the blazing sunshine*" (CP1: 51).

If the doomed steamship in *Thirst* suggests a flawed modernity, the lifeboat represents something of a test of human will and conscience amid that struggle. The image of the fledgling playwright in the 1916 production knifing the wealthy and pompous Gentleman and then plunging with him into watery oblivion perhaps reflected O'Neill's own early anxieties about playwriting and commercialism, a fear that he might lose his own balance not just between conventional realism and avant-garde symbolism, as in his staging dispute with Zorach, but between theatre as business and as art. O'Neill often treated the moneyed classes with contempt or ridicule in his plays, yet this final image, however sketchily, presents an artist, a businessman, and a laborer bound together within the tenuous constructs of modern technological and civil society, all three of them ultimately meat for sharks.

Another sea play in this early volume, *Fog* continues the allegorical situation of a shipwreck primarily as a dialogue between two male characters identified as the Businessman and the Poet. As Virginia Floyd justly observes, *Fog* has "a forced, strained quality" and serves chiefly "to provide O'Neill with a vehicle to express his philosophical beliefs" (1985: 55). As in *Thirst* the situation is allegorical but relies on a more explicit ideological debate between the two main characters and the uncanny spirit of the sea itself. The "*genius of the fog*" that "*broods over everything*" in the opening stage directions (CP1: 97) is perhaps itself the most important O'Neillian trope introduced in this apprentice work, anticipating its moody presence in several of his later plays, including *Bound East for Cardiff*, *Anna Christie* and, most importantly, *Long Day's Journey Into Night*. Adrift in a lifeboat, which also contains a dead child and its silent mother who also turns out to have died, the Businessman and Poet take up such questions as fate and free will, economic justice, and one's ethical responsibility for the lives of others. As a ship responding to their distress signals steams toward them, a gigantic iceberg is revealed through the fog; the two men debate whether to call out and be saved or to remain quiet and thereby keep the ship and those on it from a fatal collision with the ice. O'Neill cuts short this dilemma by having the ship's rescue crew approach by rowboat, devising an uncanny resolution in which the rescuers claim they were guided through the fog to the drifting lifeboat by the cries of a child. Where a traditional sea melodrama might feature a thrilling rescue at sea, O'Neill chooses to highlight the sea as a mystical force conveying the voices of the dead.

Yet another one-act play with a shipwreck theme, *Warnings* is notable for O'Neill's use of a two-scene structure that juxtaposes domestic and maritime settings, a thematic pairing he would integrate more fully later in such major works as *Beyond the Horizon, Anna Christie*, and *Long Day's Journey*. The opening scene in *Warnings* is a modest Bronx family apartment, furnished with cheap, mass-produced décor and home to five children and their parents, James and Mary Knapp—the first of several plays with a husband and wife whom O'Neill gives his own parents' first names. James's livelihood is threatened when he discovers that he is going deaf and can no longer responsibly perform his job as a steamship's wireless radio operator. Again the *Titanic* looms over the action, in particular the failure of its wireless distress signals to bring aid quickly enough to avert mass death (Richter 2004: 142). O'Neill devotes the entire first scene to the family's dire financial situation; while the looming catastrophe at sea in the second scene lacks the kind of dramatic tension one might expect, it does generate the clearly intended thematic link between life at home and work at sea. O'Neill gives Mrs. Knapp and the older four children a fair number of speaking lines, emphasizing the family pressures that force the husband to persist in his seagoing job despite his dangerous condition. As his wife reminds him, a telegraph job on land had turned out badly for James: "You was too old and slow, wasn't you? Well you're older and slower than ever now and that's the only other job you're fit for" (CP1: 88). Thus, even before his hearing started to fail, he had trouble keeping up with the demands of modern technology and, in scene two aboard the steamer Knapp, now completely deaf, clings desperately to his radio as if for his very life. His personal predicament collectively dooms all aboard the ship. Overwhelmed by guilt, he grabs a revolver, shoots himself, and "*falls forward on his face on the floor before his instrument*" (CP1: 94).

The fifth piece in *Thirst and Other Plays* is situated at the opposite end of the socioeconomic spectrum from the volume's other landlocked play, *The Web*. Set in a well-appointed summer home in the Catskills, *Recklessness* marks O'Neill's first foray into the stormy marital waters explored so powerfully by his master, Strindberg. This unproduced work bears some resemblance to *Miss Julie*, particularly its illicit love affair between Mildred Baldwin, the young wife of "*a moderately wealthy man*" (CP1: 55), and their chauffeur, Fred. O'Neill musters little of Strindberg's naturalistic power, relying instead on a mix of conventional revenge plotting and deploying some modern gadgets in the staging. Mildred's husband, Arthur, a car enthusiast, discovers the affair from a note sent by his wife to her lover when the telephone by which they usually communicate malfunctions. On the false pretense that Mildred is in mortal peril from a hemorrhage, Arthur sends Fred to fetch a doctor, directing him to use a car that he secretly knows to have faulty steering. When Fred dies from the inevitable deadly crash, Mildred collapses and is taken offstage to her room, where, we learn, she revives sufficiently to pull a gun from a drawer and shoot herself, thus adding a touch of the finale of Ibsen's *Hedda Gabler* for good measure.

The Gelbs justly liken *Recklessness* to "the lurid melodramas of his father's theater" and observe that far from achieving a genuinely Strindbergian effect, O'Neill "had not yet learned to blend his own vision with what was useful from his father's theater" (LMC 405–406). In fact, the automobile seems the vengeful husband's true passion; deploying it as a sensational plot device only obscures O'Neill's ostensible focus on class difference and the amoral complacency of the wealthy as personified by Arthur. Indeed, the Baldwin home is conspicuously stocked with modern devices that threaten to upstage the characters, including three telephones, electric lighting, and an electric bell that summons the maid. Fred's plan to rise above his lowly station and support Mildred when they run off together depends on his aim to master technology by becoming an engineer; the plot device of Fred's love note to Mildred written when the garage telephone fails and then disclosing their affair to Arthur completes the picture of modern technology as pervasive, unreliable, and contrary to human happiness. In contrast to the Old Man's selfless gesture in the Arizona desert at the end of *A Wife for a Life*, the well-to-do technophile of the Catskills must have his revenge.

Trying the longer form: Two early portraits of an artist

In 1914 O'Neill also attempted his first full-length work, *Bread and Butter*, an early portrait of an artist as a young man in a predicament not unlike O'Neill's own. Aside from its length, *Bread and Butter* does not represent a step beyond the apprentice quality of his pre-Provincetown writing, but it does reveal perhaps O'Neill's own vocational anxieties in the period between his release from the sanatorium and his enrollment in Baker's playwriting course. John Brown is an aspiring painter clearly influenced by recent modernist trends in Europe but under great pressure from his prosperous, traditional-minded family to achieve commercial success. John, after holding out for several years against his father's desire that he become a lawyer or accept a retail position offered by his future father-in-law, foregoes his potential to be a great artist and marries into a staid bourgeois life. Meanwhile, his friend and fellow art student Babe Carter is both happily married—to John's own free-spirited younger sister, Bessie—and acclaimed as "one of the most promising of the younger school" of American painters, heading for Paris with Bessie to enjoy, presumably, international fame and wedded bliss (CP1: 176). Like Mildred in *Recklessness*, John shoots himself offstage with a revolver, completing O'Neill's cautionary tale of dashed dreams and artistic compromise.

As "the flip side" of this portrayal of an artist and his marriage, in Robert Dowling's phrase (CC 418), O'Neill's other pre-Harvard full-length play, *Servitude*, features a playwright and novelist named David Roylston who manages to be both prosperous and visionary. Late one night while his wife, Alice, is away with their children in the city, a beautiful young woman, Ethel Frazer, appears at their home and proclaims herself a devoted fan of Roylston's work and a true believer in his apparent "ideal of self-realization, of the duty of the individual to assert its supremacy and demand the freedom necessary for its development" (CP1: 244). The Nietzschean overtones of this ideal, along with the play's Ibsenesque image of marriage (*A Doll's House* and *The Master Builder* are clear influences), suggest that O'Neill was pondering the proper balance of a young playwright's egocentric commitment to his work and the need for support and companionship, especially in marriage. Confronting Roylston's wife, Alice, the next day and admiring her support for him, Ethel now sees the full measure of Roylston's self-absorption and scolds him for it, soon departing their home when her own husband comes seeking her there. Fully chastened, Roylston proclaims the value of self-sacrifice: "Servitude in love, love in servitude! Logos in Pan, Pan in Logos!" (CP1: 285). In O'Neillian fashion he thus complicates his affirmation with a (mostly) Greek phrase drawn with no further elaboration from Ibsen's *Emperor and Galilean* signifying a happy convergence of flesh and spirit. At the curtain, the artist and his wife affirm their mutual devotion, an ending that almost seems deliberately contrived to belie fears such as playwright Charles Klein's that moderns like Ibsen and Nietzsche had pushed drama into a darker realism and purged the ideal of personal sacrifice from the stage. In fact, O'Neill was holding on to such ideals at this point, not yet certain of his footing as a dramatist, especially of the full-length form. Taken together, *Bread and Butter* and *Recklessness* offer complementary images of artistic transcendence either through failure and death as in John Brown's pathetic death or through a kind of enlightened merging of life and art such as David and Alice Roylston achieve. He would elaborate the first effectively in *The Great God Brown* and indulge the latter motif far less successfully in *Days Without End*; in any case, he could not quite let go of his desire to portray an artist transformed by his art until he came to write his final full-length works.

Finding his voice

O'Neill had sent this script upon its completion to prominent theatrical producer George C. Tyler and "innocently expected," he admitted later, "an immediate personal reading and a reply within a week—possibly an acceptance" (qtd. LFA 107). He was already at work on the play that would become his first stage production in the crucial summer of 1916 as *Bound East for Cardiff* with his newfound colleagues in Provincetown. While serving the group's mission to foster American playwriting, this play also marked a major artistic step forward for O'Neill, a cohesive rendering of dramatic character, dialogue, milieu, and action that did not rely conspicuously on symbolic gestures, plot twists, heavy-handed irony, or a climactic suicide. The sailors gathered around their dying mate in the claustrophobic forecastle of a steamship conveyed an image of the grim undercurrents of life at sea that was not upstaged by the visual conventions of stage realism. "Very important, this play!" O'Neill would reflect many years later:

> In it can be seen—or felt—the germ of the spirit, life-attitude, etc. of all my significant future work—and it was written practically within my first half-year as a playwright, before I went to Baker, under whose influence the following year I did nothing 1/10th as original. Remember in these U.S. in 1914 *Bound East for Cardiff* was a daring innovation both in form & content. (SL 438)

Much of the play's form and content, as Bogard argues, derives not so much from the advice O'Neill received from critic Clayton Hamilton to draw on his own experience at sea but from O'Neill's inspiration from a literary source, Joseph Conrad's *The Nigger of the "Narcissus"* (1988: 39–43). The originally copyrighted title of O'Neill's play, "Children of the Sea," was also the title of the first American edition of Conrad's 1897 novel, and the two works share the central plot element of a sailor dying at sea and its effect on his shipmates. O'Neill's most important Conradian move is to feature life at sea as the dominant thematic framework. In *Thirst*, *Fog*, and *Warnings*, the sea was a useful setting for their various moral and ideological conceits, but in this play O'Neill was able, for the first time, to use setting to create a primordial sense of fate, indeed a shared sense of fate that grips the characters as well as an audience within what Foucault calls a *heterotopian* "other" space with the ship at sea its most perfect example (1986: 27). This is the first work in which O'Neill dared to invent his own method of stage exposition, an instinct that would remain evident in his varied experiments with style and explosition in later plays. In the preface to *The Nigger of the "Narcissus"* Conrad described his own similar challenge to avoid being unduly "faithful to any of the temporary formulas of his craft": "Realism, Romanticism, Naturalism, even the unofficial sentimentalism (which like the poor, is exceedingly difficult to get rid of), all these gods must, after a short period of fellowship, abandon him—even on the very threshold of the temple—to the stammerings of his conscience and to the outspoken consciousness of the difficulties of his work" (1914: xi–xii). This statement seems an almost prophetic glimpse of O'Neill's navigation through the modernist styles of the time, through the experiments of the 1920s and early 1930s to the unadorned, confessional style of his late plays, including Edmund Tyrone's moving acknowledgment of his own "stammering" as a fledgling writer.

In its experimental realism, *Bound East for Cardiff* is also alive to external circumstances of modernity, most notably the transition from the square-rigger sailing ships such as the *Charles Racine* on which O'Neill had his first taste of life at sea in 1910 to tramp steamers like the SS *Ikala*, which took O'Neill back to New York in 1911 after his knockabout period on the Buenos Aires waterfront. Like the men on Conrad's *Narcissus*, the crew of the SS *Glencairn* speak in a full range of European-English dialects while living out a combative camaraderie within the urgent and mortal bond of men at sea. "*The blast of the steamer's whistle can be heard above all the other sounds*" throughout the play (CP1: 187), a constant reminder of the ship's voyage through the fog as a kind of shared destiny connecting the men on stage to an audience. While Yank lies dying in his bunk following an accident, his shipmates carry on with music and storytelling as if keeping a pact to stave off Yank's death and the more general prospect of mortality. Meanwhile the ship's adherence to order and authority is plain throughout. The men go forth from the forecastle and return from their duties with unquestioning regularity; the play's revised title itself stresses their mission, sailing to Cardiff. In a humane gesture, Driscoll, the burly Irishman whom O'Neill based on a memorable sailor from his own final voyage as an able-bodied seaman in 1911, begs off his watch duty on deck to keep vigil with the dying Yank in the forecastle. When he revives, the men leave off their griping about the *Glencairn* as a "starvation ship" run by "owners ridin' around in carriages" (CP1: 190), now trying gamely to buoy Yank's spirits by recalling their good times together and looking ahead to more. Yank himself becomes "the centre of the ship's collective psychology," to borrow a phrase from Conrad's American edition preface (1914: v), as he dreams of the home on land that he and most of the sailors will never know. Having exhausted his rudimentary medical knowledge, the captain leaves Yank to his fate, but Driscoll keeps up his own ministrations till the very end. The real-life Driscoll, also the model for the protagonist of *The Hairy Ape*, would eventually commit suicide (see SP 335), but the Driscoll of this play bravely confronts human mortality in his fellow sailor's fate. When *Bound East* became O'Neill's first theatrical production in the summer of 1916 in Provincetown, it also helped focus the shared destiny of a crew of fledgling American theatre artists.

Meanwhile, O'Neill returned to academe in the fall of 1914, eight years after his year at Princeton; he was one of the "young rebels who wrote plays at Harvard," according to Wisner Payne Kinne, for whom Baker "may well have recalled the image of their fathers" (1954: 109).[2] In the classroom Baker downplayed new European dramaturgy and stagecraft in favor of the well-made play of the nineteenth century, a method that the professor believed, according to one of his students, "would save the would-be playwright five or ten years of mistakes" (Kinne 1954: 107). Certainly the five plays O'Neill wrote during his year under Baker are far from his strongest; only *The Sniper* and a full-length work originally titled "The Second Engineer" and later published as *The Personal Equation* (discussed in the next chapter) survive. O'Neill did not return for the second year of English 47, perhaps simply for lack of tuition money, but he had probably already gotten what he most needed: a forum for his work and a respected mentor's encouragement. "He helped us to hope," O'Neill wrote shortly after Baker's death, when "a play of any imagination, originality or integrity by an American was almost automatically barred from a hearing in our theatre" ("Open Letter" UO 420).

Among the bohemians

O'Neill's transition from drama classroom to drama collective was not direct. Following his one-year stint at Harvard training in "the science of drama-making," in Baker's own modernizing phrase (1919: iii), O'Neill spent the rest of 1915 and the first half of 1916 knocking around Greenwich Village, writing some poems but no new plays. The myth of O'Neill's single-handed creation of modern American drama has its most memorable image in Susan Glaspell's oft-quoted account of the Provincetown Players' first reading of *Bound East for Cardiff* on Cape Cod in mid-July 1916, "we knew what we were for" (1926: 195). Certainly O'Neill embodied their common aspirations, a young American writing ambitious plays against the grain of American theatre. Inspired by the plays and stagecraft of Europe, the Players offered O'Neill "virtually unlimited freedom for experimentation," according to Robert K. Sarlós, and prodded "American playwriting from mere craft into art" (1982: 161). O'Neill found his first audience in the Wharf Theatre on a pier above the Provincetown shore and then in the makeshift urban theatre at 139 Macdougal Street in Greenwich Village. The Players were creating a new audience for modernist American plays, and Jig Cook in particular pursued a utopian vision of a society united by theatre: "A whole community working together, developing unsuspected talents. The city ought to furnish the kind of audience that will cause new plays to be written" (qtd. Glaspell 1926: 193).

As O'Neill's connection to this group grew stronger, Jeff Kennedy observes, he "created for himself a curriculum that used the company as a vehicle to test the boundaries of audiences and his own writing" (2011: 177). Just before the productions of *Bound East for Cardiff* and *Thirst* in the summer of 1916 in Provincetown, O'Neill wrote a new play that would be staged in the Players' first New York season and was explicitly mindful of this new opportunity. The one-act monologue titled *Before Breakfast* featured as its only speaking character a young wife, with her husband a mostly silent interlocutor visible to the audience only as "*a sensitive hand with slender fingers*" that receives a bowl of hot water for shaving (CP1: 395). In his final effort at stage acting, O'Neill himself presented the hand of the otherwise offstage husband, an unemployed poet named Alfred Rowland. The shrewish Mrs. Rowland attacks her husband's feckless bohemian ways much as Maud Brown badgers her artist husband John in the full-length *Bread and Butter*. In both plays the young would-be artists kill themselves in the finale and their wives run off shrieking at the discovery. The key difference in these two plays is not just their length but the playwright's deliberate experiment in *Before Breakfast* to see how long an audience would put up with a lacerating Strindbergian monologue. "'How much are they going to stand before they begin to break?' he wondered," according to Provincetowner Edna Kenton's account. "He put himself on the stage in that play to find out. O'Neill didn't care about the success of the play—he cared only about the reaction of the audience to monologue, trick shocks, trick relief" (2004: 44).

More interesting is how O'Neill manages the audience's spectatorship of Mrs. Rowland's monologue while she undertakes her morning routine in the Rowlands' dingy Greenwich Village flat. She is given no first name, and her *"pinched"* eyes, *"shapeless stoutness,"* and *"characterless"* face (CP1: 391) signal an unsympathetic persona that makes her husband, though almost entirely unseen, all the more sympathetic, much as Glaspell had done with an unseen farm wife in her 1915 play *Trifles*. The more Mrs. Rowland laments her various grievances, the less appealing she becomes. Alfred's apparent unfaithfulness, his privileged background, or even the stillbirth of their child, which she mentions in her monologue, fail to generate any empathy for her. "All your friends know about your unhappy marriage," she tells him, with unwitting irony. "I know they pity you, but they don't know my side of it. They'd talk different if they did" (CP1: 398). She resists his gaze from the other room, demanding, "Don't look at me that way!" (CP1: 396), as if also defying the critical judgment of the audience, whom we can implicitly connect with Alfred's "friends." Her uncomprehending shock at his suicide makes her seem all the more emotionally narrow and self-absorbed. If O'Neill stacks the deck rather heavily against his on-stage character, he does achieve a small dramaturgical success in making the anguish of a character who never appears on stage the most compelling presence in the play.

The Provincetown group produced two to three new O'Neill plays in each of its first five New York seasons, culminating in the breakout successes of *The Emperor Jones* in 1920 and *The Hairy Ape* the following season, which immediately followed O'Neill's own recent success with the professionally produced *Beyond the Horizon*. In their debut 1916–17 season in New York, two of his pre-Provincetown works had their first staging, including *Fog* (*Thirst* had been done in Provincetown) and a work he had written for Baker's course, *The Sniper*, of interest primarily for its depiction of a contemporary event, the brutal German invasion of Belgium during the First World War, which the United States would enter formally six weeks after the play's five-day run in February 1917.

The homeless life at sea

Among the forty-eight works the Provincetown Players mounted during its first three years, seven were O'Neill's one-acters, including three more about the crew of the *Glencairn* introduced in *Bound East for Cardiff*. One of these, *In the Zone*, was dismissed by O'Neill himself years later as too "conventional" in its "stuffy, grease-paint atmosphere" and heavily dependent on conventionally "theatrical sentimentalism"; worse, it evoked little of the spirit of the sea and might have been set "just as well, if less picturesquely, in a boarding house of munitions workers" (SL 87). *In the Zone* was produced as a wartime show in 1917 by another amateur group, the Washington Square Players, formed just before the Provincetown and later reconstituted as the Theatre Guild, a groundbreaking professional company that would produce several major O'Neill plays. *In the Zone* focuses on the crew's suspicion that an aloof fellow seaman, an introverted Englishman named Smitty, may be signaling German U-boats in the vicinity; when they discover finally that the mysterious box he keeps under his bunk holds only letters from a failed marriage, his crewmates leave Smitty to his private anguish. *In the Zone* effectively conveys wartime paranoia during the period just before the United States entered the First World War and especially the imminent hazards facing a merchant ship. Its mingling of private sentimentalism and the current world crisis was highly effective with various wartime audiences, generating O'Neill's first royalties as a playwright with an eight-month vaudeville run, as if confirming the inverse link that he already presumed between artistic merit and commercial success.

At the same time, another *Glencairn* one-acter, *The Long Voyage Home*, was being offered by the Provincetown Players and advanced the more basic predicament in O'Neill's sea plays, first broached in *Bound East*, of the essential homelessness of sailors and by implication of humanity generally. Set in a *"low dive on the London water front"* (CP1: 509), it omits any mention of the war and instead focuses on the trap laid for the ship's crew by the bar's proprietor and his shady henchmen. Their villainous scheme to abduct a sailor for a notoriously cruel ship waiting to sail is represented within a larger fatalism of the sea, as their victim, Olson, is drugged and taken off to a notoriously cruel ship, foiled in his plan to escape the seafaring life and return home to his mother and a farmer's life in his native Sweden. The virtual slave labor Olson faces on his next voyage serves as an extreme illustration of the powerless and disconnected lives of O'Neill's sailors. "I only wisht I'd a mother alive to call me own," the big-hearted Driscoll laments. "I'd not be dhrunk in this divil's hole this minute, maybe" (CP1: 513). Just before he is shanghaied, Olson envisions his new life: "No more sea, no more bum grub, no more storms—yust nice work" (CP1: 517). The happy ending is likewise snatched away. The fatal pull of the sea is thus far stronger in *The Long Voyage Home* than in *In the Zone*, where O'Neill exploits wartime emotions and one sailor's personal angst rather than the crew's collective predicament at sea.

The longing for a stable home life is even more central to a play O'Neill wrote in 1917 just before writing the latter three *Glencairn* plays. *'Ile*—the old New Englander pronunciation of "oil"—is set on a whaling ship in 1895 and based on actual events. With domestic and commercial maritime values in direct conflict, *'Ile* offers a veiled early image of his own parents' marriage, dramatized more openly in his writing of *Long Day's Journey Into Night* two decades later. Captain David Keeney is determined to make a full cargo despite the pleading of his wife, Annie, who is accompanying him at sea for the first time and yearns to return to the auspiciously named "Homeport" in New England after an arduous Arctic voyage including almost a full year (as was normal practice) bound in polar ice. The crew is likewise inclined to sail home, and complain bitterly among themselves of "this dog's life, and no luck in the fishin', and the hands half starved with the food runnin' low, rotten as it is; and not a sign of him turnin' back for home!" (CP1: 492). Captain Keeney suppresses their incipient mutiny but finds it much harder to placate his increasingly desperate wife. "I wanted to see you the hero they make you out to be in Homeport," she tells him. "All I find is ice and cold— and brutality!" (CP1: 500). The captain seems to yield to her wish to give up the hunt, but when a large pod of sperm whales is spotted nearby, he abruptly departs to lead the chase, leaving Mrs. Keeney alone in her now full-blown madness to play "*wildly and discordantly*" on the organ her husband had brought aboard to make her feel more at home (CP1: 506).

In these final moments of *'Ile*, O'Neill demonstrates his preference to foreground the psychic trauma and compulsions of his characters, pushing the potentially sensational or spectacular scenic interest of the whale chase offstage. Mrs. Keeney's inability to return home is caused not by anything like the scheming villainy of the waterfront dive that dooms Olson in *The Long Voyage Home*, but by a more basic obsession with wealth and achievement that is fully entwined with modern American values. Parallels between Keeney and Melville's Captain Ahab are conspicuous, but O'Neill found his direct inspiration for *'Ile* in accounts of the arctic voyages of whaling captain John Cook of Provincetown and his wife, Viola, who accompanied him on several voyages (as did other captains' wives) and was reported to have come back from one of them with signs of mental breakdown (Richter 2004: 110– 15). O'Neill saw in Viola Cook a glimpse of his own mother and created Annie Keeney as "the earliest image of Ella O'Neill in her son's writings" (SP: 385). As with Mary Tyrone's longing for a "real home" in *Long Day's Journey* (discussed in Chapter 6), undermined by her husband James's pursuit of a prosperous career, in *'Ile* O'Neill first presents these two core modern American ideals as mutually incompatible. Moreover, they are represented as pathological, with the confining setting of the sea intensifying the conflict to the point that both of the Keeneys sink into their respective versions of madness. What would have been a liability in the commercial stage—the constrained space and limited technical resources of the Playwrights Theatre—aptly served the intensely psychological focus of this and other works by O'Neill with their often pointedly anticommercial themes.

Haunted by the primitive sea

O'Neill's last two one-act sea plays, both staged by the Players late in 1918, likewise explore madness and alienation as shaped by the primal forces of the seagoing life that O'Neill set in conspicuous contrast with the rational, normalizing forces of modernity. The shipwreck motif of *Where the Cross Is Made* glances back to *Thirst* but is also thematically continuous with *'Ile* in following the obsessive madness of a sea captain after his return home to the coast of California. Captain Bartlett now haunts a room at the top of the family home, *"fitted up like the captain's cabin of a deep-sea sailing vessel"* (CP1: 695), thus inverting the situation of Mrs. Keeney, who tries to simulate her home at land aboard her husband's ship. The captain's evident madness stems from experiences while stranded on an island near Malaysia following the wreck of his ship with three members of his crew. According to the tale recounted by his son Nat, as their extreme privation drove them toward cannibalism, the captain and his stranded men discover two chests filled with what Nat calls "the stuff of dreams" (CP1: 699). A crudely drawn map of the alleged treasure's location on the island represents the captain's legacy to his son, himself a casualty of the sea having lost an arm to the seagoing life forced on him by his father. Nat has summoned a local psychiatric doctor to determine "all the facts—just that, facts!" to confirm Captain Bartlett's delusional madness and convey him to an insane asylum (CP1: 696). However, Nat himself soon comes to believe in the reality of the buried treasure despite the rationalist protestations of the doctor and Nat's sister.

The play suggests that the desire to believe is itself a hard human fact: "The root of belief is in you, too!" Nat tells the doctor who also becomes intrigued by the story of treasure, in spite of himself (CP1: 699). In effect, Nat is also pressing the audience and its assumptions about belief and reality, a challenge brought out in the eerie staging. As the captain's three now-dead shipmates appear carrying two wooden chests, the stage is awash in "*a dense green glow . . . as of great depths of the sea faintly penetrated by light*" (CP1: 709). These barefoot apparitions have "*slimy strands of seaweed*" in their hair and skin that "*in the green light has the suggestion of decomposition*" as "*their bodies sway limply, nervelessly, rhythmically as if to the pulse of long swells of the deep sea*" (CP1: 710). The audience of '*Ile* serves as shocked witness to the visual and aural spectacle of the Keeneys' mutual madness in '*Ile*, but in *Where the Cross Is Made*, the audience is immersed in the common delusion of father and son as O'Neill inverts the normative reality, excluding the doctor and the sister from what seems most real to the main characters and the audience itself in the theatrical experience. O'Neill resisted pleas by the director and other company members to not use actors to represent the dead sailors and to present them instead as phantasms in the minds of the deranged Bartlett men. "This play presumes everyone in the play is mad but the girl [Nat's sister]," O'Neill argued. "I want to see if it's possible to make an audience go mad too. Perhaps the first rows will snicker—perhaps they won't. We'll see" (qtd. Kenton 2004: 82). New York *Tribune* critic Heywood Broun confirmed O'Neill's instincts: "We sat so close that there was little visual illusion, but the sweep of the story and the exceptional skill with which the scene of the delusion is written made us distinctly fearful of the silent dead men who walked across the stage" (1918: CR 47).

In 1920 O'Neill acknowledged to his friend Nathan that *Where the Cross Is Made* "was great fun to write, theatrically very thrilling, an amusing experiment in treating the audience as insane . . . a distorted version of a long play idea and never intended for a one-act play in my mind" (SL 130). He had abandoned the one-act form altogether by this point and would soon expand this play into a four-act version called *Gold*, produced unsuccessfully in 1921. His willingness to take risks with the Provincetown Players' adventurous subscribers—the subscription system also shielded them from censorship laws—prepared him to challenge theatregoers at larger uptown houses where the stakes were higher and the forces of American modernity, especially the theatrical formulas that reinforced it, were more entrenched.

Creating an immersive setting and atmosphere was the primary goal of O'Neill's fourth and final *Glencairn* play, *The Moon of the Caribbees*, written in 1917 and featured in the Provincetown Players' third season in December

1918. Reversing the situation of *The Long Voyage Home*, in which the ship's crew carouses in London in a waterfront dive, here they are joined aboard the ship at anchor by a group of West Indian women selling fruit, liquor, and sex. The exotic Caribbean backdrop with palm trees and a full moon reflecting on a white sand beach generate a primitivism that shares an obsession with non-western native cultures shown by many modernist visual artists, but it is the *"melancholy negro chant"* from the shore that creates the play's intended timeless ambience (CP1: 527). The modernist approach lies mainly in defying the usual emphasis on plot, but also makes visible the ruthless modernity implicit in the transient life of the working sailor, each a small player in a globalized shipping industry. The scenes aboard the tramp steamer temporarily reverse the standard imperial-colonial hierarchy; it is the native women who supply the goods scarce for the men aboard the ship, especially some "foine rum, the rale stuff," as Driscoll proclaims it in his thick Irish brogue (CP1: 533). Throughout the play the white sailors demean the native women, even as they lust after their bodies and merchandise, with debates breaking out over whether the West Indies inhabitants are exotic cannibals or "only common niggers," as Yank—presumably the same American sailor who dies in *Bound East*—calls them as if to modernize their racial otherness (CP1: 529). In their more discreet, offstage way, even the ship's officers participate in these proceedings when two of the women—"swate little slips av things, near as white as you an' me are," as Driscoll describes them—are summoned to their quarters (CP1: 533). The momentary transformation of the ship into a brothel breaks down as the rum and sex lead to violence. The first mate expels the women, restoring the normal hierarchy by threatening to have them jailed and refusing to pay them anything for their goods or services.

A kind of prequel and Dionysian counterpart to *Bound East for Cardiff*, depicting the drunkenness, sexuality, and occasional violence recollected by the sailors in the earlier play, *The Moon of the Caribbees* again features the character Smitty from *In the Zone*. Here Smitty is shown similarly detached, alternately sinking into drunken melancholy (while fending off advances by the prettiest West Indian woman, Pearl), or sharing thoughts on life with "the Donkeyman," an engine operator with a doughty temperament unburdened by any troubled "mem'ries." The details of Smitty's introspection are not revealed, as if O'Neill deliberately wished to avoid the conventional exposition of *In the Zone*, focusing instead on the emotional effect of the natives' singing. It evokes two distinct responses: the Donkeyman's easy enjoyment of its beauty, likening it to the organ music one hears outside a church, and Smitty's troubled descent into "the beastly memories the damn thing brings up—for some reason" (CP1: 537). The play concludes as the two men say goodnight and leave the stage, but for the audience "*the haunted, saddened voice of that brooding music, faint and far-off*" continues "*like the mood of the moonlight made audible*" (CP1: 544).

Whatever his personal angst, Smitty provides an onstage proxy, argues Joel Pfister, for the educated, middle-class audiences coming down to Greenwich Village for an authentic art experience and to see their own modern anxieties played out by this "self-consuming psychological tourist acting out his inner drama" among hardier shipmates whom Pfister calls "psychological primitives . . . scripted to 'live' in the machine" (1995: 115). O'Neill himself regarded the previous Smitty of *In the Zone* as artificially "magnified into a hero who attracts our sentimental sympathy," whereas in *The Moon* "we get the perspective to judge him" and can see him more critically as "much more out of harmony with truth, much less in tune with beauty, than the honest vulgarity of his mates." For O'Neill no particular character but "the spirit of the sea" itself was "the hero" of *The Moon of the Caribbees* (SL 87). O'Neill thus succeeds in representing the sea as a counterforce to modernity by means of modernist staging rather than primarily through dialogue or plot, as in his first sea plays such as *Thirst* or even the previous *Glencairn* plays.

As important as O'Neill considered *The Moon of the Caribbees*—"an attempt to achieve a higher plane of bigger, finer values"—its production late in 1918 also exposed the technical and production limitations of the Provincetown Playhouse as well as the formal constraints of the one-act form as his ambition grew to convey theatrically "the impelling, inscrutable forces behind life" (SL 87). Sarlós observes that the offstage "crooning" from the island was highly effective in this initial staging of the play, but the detailed "scene descriptions were not complemented by the cardboard settings, nor was serious thought given to ethnically accurate casting, and white amateurs in blackface played the West Indian girls" (1982: 101). The casting issue would be addressed forthrightly the next year in *The Dreamy Kid*, the first of O'Neill's two plays for the Provincetown's 1919–20 season in which all four characters are African American and all performed this time by black actors. As discussed in Chapter 5 (and Katie N. Johnson's essay in the "Critical Perspectives" section), the group's production of *The Emperor Jones* the following year featured a major lead role for an African American actor as well as Jig Cook's ambitious experimental set, a landmark for O'Neill, the Players, and American theatre generally.

Staging suicide

O'Neill's second play for the Provincetown season of 1919–20 proved to be his last effort in the one-act form until the close of his writing career more than two decades later. Several of his previous works had concluded with suicides, successful and otherwise, including *Bread and Butter*, *Recklessness*, *Now I Ask You* (discussed in Chapter 4), and *Before Breakfast*, but *Exorcism* occupies a unique place in O'Neill's body of work as the only script he tried to suppress after it was staged; he personally rounded up all the known copies after its two-week run. The play's narrative draws directly from O'Neill's sordid divorce in 1911 from Kathleen Jenkins (mother of his first child, Eugene O'Neill, Jr.), which required a documented act of infidelity under New York state law, and the intense guilt leading to his suicide attempt by an overdose of Veronal pills. In 1914 O'Neill wrote a play on a similar theme called *Abortion*, unproduced in his lifetime. Set on a college campus, not unlike the Princeton which O'Neill attended in 1906, its privileged student-athlete hero, Jack Townsend, learns that the local working-class girl he impregnated has died undergoing the abortion he paid for. Overcome with guilt, in a sensational if predictable ending Jack shoots himself. *Exorcism* is far closer to a confessional drama in drawing more openly on the particulars of O'Neill's dalliance with Kathleen and subsequent marriage to her, though like *Abortion* it foregrounds the protagonist's guilt and self-punishment.

The handful of extant reviews of the Provincetown production of *Exorcism* in spring 1919 and a concise contemporaneous entry in O'Neill's notebook provided the most detailed information about *Exorcism* until the chance discovery of a typescript in 2011. Biographers were intrigued by O'Neill's motives for trying to expunge the play from his *oeuvre* and speculated that it might contain important hints about the links between his life and his art. In his note to the publication of the recovered typescript in *The New Yorker* in October 2011, John Lahr called *Exorcism* "the tipping point—the moment in O'Neill's tortured life when he gave up the romance of death for the romance of art" (2011: 73). *Exorcism* offers a glimpse of his far greater achievements in *Long Day's Journey* and especially *Iceman* in its lower-Manhattan dive setting and derelict characters; its suppression is only the most extreme example of O'Neill's desire to control the self-revelatory aspects of his art, also evident in his withholding of *Long Day's Journey* from publication during his lifetime.

The recovered script of *Exorcism* also reveals problems in structure and tone that suggest O'Neill's thematic and theatrical ambitions had outgrown the one-act form, especially as a vehicle for exploring the kind of intensely personal trauma on which he based the play. In contrast to the seamless atmospherics of *The Moon of the Caribbees*, along with plenty of background exposition, O'Neill inserts a curtain drop midway through *Exorcism*, just after its young protagonist Ned Malloy has swallowed the lethal pills. As the curtain rises Ned is regaining consciousness, having been rescued when his roommates discovered him near death and rushed him to the hospital. His widowed father, a prosperous merchant, insists that Ned return home to his forgiving wife and take up his job again at the Malloy family firm, an image of home life (as noted in Chapter 6) that departs from O'Neill's own family experience and the consenting role that Kathleen's family played in the contrivance of O'Neill being caught, per the requirements of divorce law, with a prostitute.[3] Seeming to consent to his father's wishes, Ned instead takes up an offer of farm work and a fresh start out west, declaring, "New leaf be damned." He declares "It's a new book without a leaf of the old left in it. The Past is finally cremated. I feel reborn, I tell you! I've had a bath! I've been to confession! My sins are forgiven me! . . . So here's looking forward to the new life, reform or no reform, as long as it's new" (Ex 55). This counter-tragic declaration must have seemed to O'Neill a willful, unearned affirmation of "the new life" that, according to the credo of progressive modernity is always within reach—even to failed suicides. More convincingly, the "new book" that Ned proclaims, as I have argued elsewhere, hints strongly at "O'Neill's own modernist determination to leave behind traditional artistic forms and to pursue newer, bolder experiments" in longer plays (Eisen 2012: 124).

After the revolution

Critical acclaim for his first Broadway production, the full-length *Beyond the Horizon* (discussed at length in Chapter 6), signaled O'Neill's coming of age as a playwright when it was produced early in 1920. Heywood Broun, who had been reviewing O'Neill's work in "various little alley theaters" since the first New York production of *Bound East for Cardiff* in 1916, predicted this first commercial production—a series of matinees and then regular evening performances—would be seen as the playwright's "dramatic birth" (CR 62). O'Neill won his first Pulitzer Prize for this play in 1920, and the production of *The Emperor Jones* later that year would signal the demise of the Provincetown Players as a home base for O'Neill when it moved uptown after seven weeks in Greenwich Village followed by a national tour. "To go uptown with our first success," Edna Kenton recalled, "was higher honor than to stay downtown with our experiments . . . we were a little drunk with the wine of applause and we lost our balance and fell" (2004: 141). Their resistance to American modernity as cultural outsiders had launched O'Neill's career but was in a sense swallowed up by the very commercial pressures they had scorned, and the Players themselves became part of the larger progress narrative of American culture. As the doors of Broadway opened to him in the 1920s, O'Neill found himself in the middle of the commercial terrain he hated but whose production resources he needed, and was soon to become its leading figure. Realizing that the Provincetowners' revolutionary and communitarian ideals were impossible to sustain in modern America, he nonetheless undertook to make his new, larger audiences recognize the tragic implications of this fact.

CHAPTER 3
TRAGEDY AND THE
POSTREVOLUTIONARY CONDITION

By the early twentieth century, rapid changes in the institutions and cultural demographics of the United States were unsettling any semblance of a coherent national identity, however nostalgic or illusory, even as the doctrines of social progressivism began to shape mainstream political discourse, seeing an accelerated pace of change in modern life as desirable in itself. As the influential progressive thinker Herbert Croly wrote in 1909, "The increased momentum of American life, both in its particles and its mass . . . is the beginning, the only possible beginning, of a better life for the people as individuals and for society" (14). Croly and other progressives favored reform—"the improvement and the intensification of existing human relations"—over revolutionary action, which they considered inimical to the national democratic institutions on which progress depended (1909: 210). Radical contributors to *The Masses*, however, including several with ties to the Provincetown Players, joined leaders of such labor groups as the Industrial Workers of the World in rejecting incrementalist reform in favor of a bolder, radically democratic revolution in socioeconomic life, convinced that capitalism itself must be overturned to fulfill America's special role within the larger promise of global modernity. Against this modernity, as Jackson Lears notes, a counter-modern sentiment emerged in America, "rooted in longings to recapture an elusive 'real life' in a culture evaporating into unreality" (1981: 32). As an aesthetic expression of contrary forces, modernist art and thought, according to Malcolm Bradbury and James McFarlane, offered

> an extraordinary compound of the futuristic and the nihilistic, the revolutionary and the conservative, the naturalistic and the symbolistic, the romantic and the classical . . . a celebration of the technological age and a condemnation of it; an excited acceptance of the belief that the old régimes of culture were over, and a deep despairing in the face of that fear. (Bradbury and McFarlane 1991: 46)

In grappling with this mix of contraries, O'Neill gave shape to the special nature of American modernist tragedy as the mirror of a national culture torn between its progressive, even utopian instincts and the anxious nostalgia for a stable, meaningful past that seemed to have been sacrificed on the altar of materialist progress.

O'Neill admired the commitment of his revolutionary friends but considered their goal—saving humanity from itself, as he saw it—a futile enterprise. Unlike the radical poses he struck in his early poetry, however sincerely, O'Neill's work for the stage resisted the prospect of any fundamental change in the human condition. He rejected many established theatrical conventions not because they were traditional as such—he admired the masterly stage acting of his father's era—but where they seemed facile, formulaic, or blocks to self-expression. "Where, two centuries earlier, revolutionaries focused their attention on authoritarian governments," writes Anne E. Fernald, "in the early twentieth century, writers focused on the persistence of authoritative thinking in social custom and familial structure. Texts that question tradition as it is lived play an absolutely central role in making tradition visible" (2007: 165). For O'Neill, the internationalism pioneered by the European stage offered an idiom for his critique of modern America, yet he could never fully abandon the "discursive tradition," in Fernald's phrase, of the American theatre he grew up with. For O'Neill the primary flaw of the American theatre was not so much its artificial language, emotional stridency, or contrived plots, but its pandering to audience expectation and sentiment.

The Village banner of social revolution would be carried into the postwar years by John Reed, Max Eastman, Mary Heaton Vorse, Dorothy Day, Hippolyte Havel, and especially Emma Goldman, the iconic feminist anarchist, along with her lifelong collaborator Alexander Berkman. Like his early mentor Benjamin Tucker, O'Neill was by inclination a philosophical rather than a social anarchist like Goldman and Berkman; accordingly, his own work as a dramatist expressed a highly individual sensibility and would not affirm Goldman's belief in drama as "the vehicle which is really making history, disseminating radical thought in ranks not otherwise to be reached" (1911: 249–50). Several of O'Neill's strong female characters are based largely or in part on Goldman, most notably Olga Tarnov of his 1914 play *The Personal Equation* and Rosa Parritt—though not fully a "character" in that she does not appear onstage—in *The Iceman Cometh*, written twenty-five years later. O'Neill could likewise never embrace his Provincetown collaborator Jig Cook's goal of creating a socialist utopia that would extend into the world beyond the amateur-communitarian operation of the Provincetown Players. He was especially wary of overtly political plays, as he wrote to fellow playwright Mike Gold in 1926: "My quarrel with propaganda in the theatre is that it's such damned unconvincing propaganda," and playwrights should "let that life live itself without comment" (SL 206). Yet he would also acknowledge in an admiring letter to Berkman the next year, "It is not so hard to write what one feels as truth. It is damned hard to live it!" (SL 233). The elements of philosophical anarchism "permeate the full canon of O'Neill's plays," as Dowling observes (CC 703), reflecting not a revolutionary vision but a sympathetic iconoclasm in its image of society constructed of many sustaining if illusory narratives—"pipe dreams," in the recurring motif of *The Iceman Cometh*—that are connective rather than collective, not a revolutionary movement so much as the "hopeless hope" that generates tragic consciousness from its inescapable dialectic of ambition and despair.

Youthful revolutionary verse and drama

In the verse he printed in the New London *Telegraph* during his brief stint in 1912 as a newspaper man, O'Neill displayed revolutionary impulses that seem directed more toward outraging readers than charting any radical commitments. Frederick Latimer, the *Telegraph* editor and the model for Nat Miller in *Ah, Wilderness!*, claimed early recognition of O'Neill's gifts and called him "the most stubborn and irreconcilable social rebel that I had ever met" (qtd. Bowen 1946: 208). Several of these poems are barbed critiques of progressive ideals that mask the greed and egotism of financiers. "The Waterways Convention, A Study in Prophecy" features a vainglorious municipal leader who "sketched with rare prophetic sureness / The New London, of the future" a modern metropolis bustling with commerce, urban transportation, new office buildings, and even a stock exchange (*Poems* 5). By 1914 O'Neill's poems reflected the urgency of the antiwar movement. The pro-labor "Fratricide" appeared in the New York *Call*, an organ of the Socialist Party, its concluding lines echoing the period's bold revolutionary tone: "Comrades, awaken to new birth! / New values on the tables write! . . . And cry: 'All workers on the earth / Are brothers and WE WILL NOT FIGHT!'" (*Poems* 46). In 1917, having emerged as a forceful new voice on the stage among the radicals in Greenwich Village, O'Neill published "The Submarine" in *The Masses*, capturing that journal's distinctive blend of topical socialism and free individual expression in its opening lines: "My soul is a submarine. / My aspirations are torpedoes" to destroy the "Rust-eaten, grimy galleons of commerce" steaming along its surface, while affirming the beauty of the sea and vowing to "lurk / Menacingly / In green depths" (*Poems* 88). This hostility toward commerce carried over explicitly into O'Neill's earliest plays. In his self-published 1914 volume, the clash between the Poet and the Man of Business in *Fog* extends this theme from his poetry. The four *Glencairn* plays likewise reflect O'Neill's strong empathy for the laboring class over those who exploit them at sea and on shore. O'Neill tries his hand at political satire in *The Movie Man*, also written in 1914 and the first script he pitched to the Provincetown Players. The satire goes no further than exposing how easily revolutionary ideals can be undermined by American commercialism but shows O'Neill's suspicion of such ideals even in his earliest writing for the stage.

O'Neill's second full-length play offers his most straightforward image of revolution and its tragic potential. Written as "The Second Engineer" in 1915 to fulfill a requirement in Baker's course, *The Personal Equation* reflects not only O'Neill's inexperience with plot construction—Baker himself judged that his talented pupil could not yet "manage the longer forms" (qtd. Floyd 1985: 96)—but also his ambivalence in representing revolutionary agency as dramatic art. Its direct depiction of anarchist revolution reveals a skepticism toward ideologically driven action and an interest in anarchist radicals as flawed individuals rather than in their principles or actions as such. Indeed, the revised title, a term describing the variability in astronomers' measurements, had been adopted by American psychologists and social scientists, including William James and Thorstein Veblen, to describe variation in individual perception as an obstacle to certitude in the human sciences (Canales 2010: 40–42). The phrase likely appealed to O'Neill as capturing the contrast between his goal in Baker's class to master the "science" of dramatic writing while also developing his own distinctive voice and perspective.

The play's somewhat ungainly plot concerns a group of anarchists belonging to "the International Workers of the Earth," a thinly veiled version of the Industrial Workers of the World founded in 1905 and known as the "Wobblies." They scheme to dynamite the engines of the SS *San Francisco* of the Ocean Steamship Company, with the larger aim of sparking a general strike to cripple the infrastructure of western industrial commerce with the world on the brink of war. The group's strongest voice is that of the Russian-born Olga Tarnov, one of O'Neill's most dominant female characters.

"Think of what it would mean, that strike," Olga declares, envisioning a complete shutdown of the modern world. "No electricity, no cars, no trains, no steamers, the factories dark and deserted, no newspapers, no wireless, nothing . . . if they wanted war, they would have to fight it themselves" (CP1: 320). Her lover, the young Tom Perkins, is their lead saboteur, but to perform the deed he must confront his father, Thomas, the ship's second engineer (originally O'Neill's title character), a widower with a quasi-mystical bond to the ship's powerful steam engines and, in spite of his meek demeanor, a fierce willingness to defend them.

In focusing on this central triangle of Olga, Tom, and Tom's father, O'Neill makes no attempt to generate audience sympathy for the radicals or the aggrieved seamen aboard the ship in the conventional way, by depicting any specific oppression or injustice they suffer. Instead, a sentimental, traditional dramatic family bond emerges within the ostensible radicalism of the action and rhetoric. In the climactic third act, the elder Perkins accidentally shoots Tom in the head, leaving him permanently brain-damaged and setting up an extended resolution in Act Four, when Olga reveals that she is pregnant with Tom's child. Meanwhile, the once-militant workers, including a key leader of the movement, turn obediently patriotic in the excitement of a national wartime emergency, abandoning their revolutionary goals as abruptly as Tom loses his brain function from the gunshot wound. Olga herself remains faithful to the cause but also makes peace with Tom's father. Her resemblance to Emma Goldman is plain as several scholars have noted (e.g., Frazer 1974: 17–22), and like her model, Olga has faith in the eventual triumph of the proletariat; however, in the play's curtain scene the now-debilitated Tom repeats Olga's final words, "Long—live—the Revolution" (CP1: 387), as a sad echo of his earlier zeal and a clear hint of the futility of revolution. As Patrick Chura observes, O'Neill's finale suggests "that the downward affiliations of radicals are only as deep as a need for personal fulfillment that is, after all, available within the parameters of a bourgeois society" (2003: 528).

Yank's personal revolution in *The Hairy Ape*

Though *The Personal Equation* was not especially daring in theme or form, it does combine O'Neill's persistent interest in ships and revolution, and foregrounds the fact that transatlantic shipping is a crucial driving force of industrial modernity. In his more compelling one-acters such as *'Ile* and the *Glencairn* plays, O'Neill explored the social microcosm of a ship's crew and authoritarian hierarchy as the conflicted spaces that Michel Foucault has dubbed *heterotopias*: "real places—places that do exist and that are formed in the very founding of society—which are something like counter-sites, a kind of effectively enacted utopia in which the real sites, all the other real sites that can be found within the culture, are simultaneously represented, contested, and inverted" (1986: 24). As Foucault also notes, somewhat romantically, "The ship is the heterotopia par excellence. In civilizations without boats, dreams dry up" (1986: 27). If the Glencairn plays as discussed in the previous chapter were O'Neill's most distinctive early realization of heterotopic drama as a convergence of various global cultures within a ship's forecastle, *The Hairy Ape* represents a more fully developed treatment of the implications of the ship as an "effectively enacted utopia" in Foucault's phrase that collapses when it makes contact with the societal forces beyond the ship. O'Neill adapts the techniques of European expressionism in creating his distinctively American protagonist; he likewise reveals his conception of the modern stage as itself a heterotopia where international voices and styles converge but, contrary to Emma Goldman's belief, where modernity can only be portrayed in its full impact and implications but not significantly changed.

In a letter to Kenneth Macgowan late in 1921, having finished a first draft of *The Hairy Ape* in "a terrific splurge of intensive labor," O'Neill explained his aims in writing what would be his final play with the original Provincetown Players company: "I have tried to dig deep in it, to probe the shadows of the soul of man bewildered by the disharmony of his primitive pride and individualism at war with the mechanistic developement [*sic*] of society" (Bryer 1982: 31–32). In creating Robert "Yank" Smith, his archetype of American masculinity in the early twentieth century, O'Neill followed up his portrait the previous year of an African American protagonist, Brutus Jones, with this portrait of a modern white America: its essential rootlessness, mechanization, and illusions of effectual agency. In a theatrical style that, as he told Macgowan, "seems to run the whole gamut from extreme naturalism to extreme expressionism," O'Neill shifts the balance toward "more of the latter than the former" (Bryer 1982: 31). He foregrounds Yank's clash with mechanistic societal forces by insisting in the play's opening stage directions that each scene "*should by no means be naturalistic*" (CP2: 121). Yank is surrounded in the stokehole below the deck by a decidedly heterotopian (if racially segregated) gathering in which "*all the civilized white races are represented*," with Yank as "*the very last word in what they are, their most highly developed individual*" (CP2: 121). This subsuming of all of white

Western civilization into one hyper-American individual summarizes the play's view of cultural teleology with O'Neill's characteristic irony.[1] Yank's self-image as a working-class *Übermensch* is undercut by the cramped, cage-like space the men occupy as *"the ceiling crushes down upon the men's heads"* (CP2: 121)—designed jointly by Cleon Throckmorton and Robert Edmond Jones in the tight quarters of the Provincetown Playhouse—and by the *"confused, inchoate uproar"* that somehow conveys *"a sort of unity, a meaning"* within the play's predominantly expressionist mode (CP2: 121). As with *The Emperor Jones*, the expressionist structure, following the "station drama" pattern developed by such German dramatists as Ernst Toller and Georg Kaiser in the late 1910s, effectively served O'Neill's purposes in showing both the fragmentation of Yank's selfhood and his quest to recover the coherent, powerful figure portrayed in the first scene.

Yank asserts this ostensibly powerful selfhood early in the play when the Irish seaman Paddy waxes nostalgic on the ideal of a more traditional seagoing life, one in harmony with the natural rhythms of the sea. His poetic recollections and Yank's response establish a stark contrast between the romance of sailing ships and the steam-driven shipping industry, juxtaposing Paddy's stereotypically poetic Irish persona and Yank's brusque Americanism. "'Twas them days men belonged to ships, not now," Paddy recalls. "'Twas them days a ship was part of the sea, and a man was part of a ship, and the sea joined all together and made it one." He confronts Yank with the definitive question of their lives in the stokehole of a steamship: "Is it a flesh and blood wheel of the engines you'd be?" (CP2: 127). Yank dismisses this as illusory, "de pipe of de past," and embraces an identity that merges completely with the elemental forces of industrial modernity:

> I'm at de bottom, get me! Dere ain't nothin' foither. I'm de end! I'm de start! I start somep'n and de woild moves! It—dat's me!—de new dat's moiderin' de old! I'm de ting in coal dat makes it boin; I'm steam and oil for de engines; I'm de ting in noise dat makes you hear it; I'm smoke and express trains and steamers and factory whistles; I'm de ting in gold dat makes it money! And I'm what makes iron into steel! Steel, dat stands for de whole ting! And I'm steel—steel—steel! (CP2: 128–29)

His mighty bluster abruptly collapses. Mildred Douglas, the daughter of the president of the Steel Trust, the ship's owner, decides to ply her undergraduate schooling in sociology by going below decks to see the gritty working class, but once there, she is repulsed by her encounter with Yank's sheer brute presence. This outcome seems to represent a triumph of Yank's Dionysian vitality, in Nietzschean terms, over the vitiated Apollonian social order represented by Mildred's world, were it not for the sudden blow to Yank's own invincibility. He "*feels himself insulted in some unknown fashion in the very heart of his pride*" (CP2: 137) and no longer has a secure place where he once ruled. In a posture recalling Rodin's famous statue, Yank tries to think ("t'ink") through his predicament as the other men tease him in a stridently modern choral voice that has "*a brazen metallic quality as if their throats were phonograph horns*" (CP2: 139).

Deeply shaken, Yank soon departs the ship on a mission of vengeance and heads straight to Fifth Avenue. O'Neill portrays the heart of fashionable American wealth in expressionistic terms that bring out a spiritual poverty: "*The general effect is of a background of magnificence cheapened and made grotesque by commercialism, a background in tawdry disharmony with the clear light and sunshine on the street itself*" (CP2: 144). Yank is accompanied into the city by the play's chief revolutionary agitator, an English shipmate named Long, who prods Yank toward political radicalism but misunderstands the more traumatic source of his unease. Home, not the workplace, was where Yank first "loined to take punishment" (CP2: 145), apparently having internalized this violent family past in craving the punishing conditions of the stokehole. Therefore, as the radical Long discovers, Yank's most urgent aim is neither social justice nor political change but a kind of existential self-recovery— acting on what Nietzsche would call his *ressentiment* by getting even with perceived oppressors, the upper-class figures strolling past him on the street like "*gaudy marionettes*" with "*something of the relentless horror of Frankensteins* [sic] *in their detached, mechanical unawareness*" (CP2: 147). After Long abandons Yank when he sees these dark impulses, Yank reprises his stokehole speech from scene one, again proclaiming himself "steel and steam and smoke and de rest of it"; however, a passerby whom he strikes with full force "*stands unmoved as if nothing had happened*" (CP2: 148–49), visually confirming Yank's alienation from what had been his source of power.

At the end of this scene the police arrive and haul Yank off to a seemingly more literal cage in a jail, though even here the staging suggests that Yank is more a prisoner of his own will than of unjust social institutions. While behind bars he learns of the Industrial Workers of the World (IWW) from the other inmates, unseen voices in adjoining cells that are "constructed like Yank's in forced perspective, reced[ing] on a slight angle into the darkness up right" with a lighting scheme that emphasizes his peculiar isolation among even the perennially isolated (Wainscott 1988: 118). One of the other prisoners reads aloud a newspaper op-ed against the IWW written by a Senator Queen who denounces the group as a scourge that "would tear down society . . . and make of our sweet and lovely civilization a shambles, a desolation where man, God's masterpiece, would soon degenerate back to the ape!" (CP2: 153). This caricature version of the IWW excites Yank's lust for vengeance against the Steel Trust's president, Mildred's father. The next scene finds him a month later in the local IWW office offering himself for the job of sabotage he assumes must be the organization's primary mission, as O'Neill himself had suggested in his portrait of labor radicals in *The Personal Equation*. Even the prospect of assassinating Mildred's father is now too mild a revenge for Yank: "I mean blow up de factory, de woiks, where he makes de steel. . . . Dat'll fix tings!" (CP2: 158). Suspecting an infiltrator, the members pitch Yank into the street. Alone, he ponders his brokenness: "I don't tick, see?—I'm a busted Ingersoll [watch], dat's what. Steel was me, and I owned de woild. Now I ain't steel, and de woild owns me" (CP2: 159). In this almost classical *anagnorisis*, or self-discovery, like a broken watch Yank finds himself out of sync with mechanized modernity and is now living Emerson's pragmatist idea of tragic experience: "It is very unhappy, but too late to be helped, the discovery we have made, that we exist. That discovery is called the Fall of Man. Ever afterwards, we suspect our instruments" (1983: 487).

Thematically and theatrically, the play's final scene at the zoo when Yank confronts the gorilla in the cage fulfills his quest to "belong" after discovering the fact of his existence, while underscoring O'Neill's notion of a tragic American modernity. With no usable past or future prospects, Yank's existence is reduced to a paralyzing "what's now," as he calls it: "I ain't on oith and I ain't in heaven, get me? I'm in de middle tryin' to separate 'em, takin' all de woist punches from bot' of 'em" (CP2: 162). The society O'Neill portrays in *The Hairy Ape* is "an objectification of the nineteenth-century concept of progress," argues Herbert Zapf, so that in Yank's predicament and ultimate demise O'Neill "deconstructs, in the medium of the drama, the ideology of progress which this model, in its uncritical application to modern reality, implies" (1988: 36, 39). Erika Rundle makes a similar point in more theatrical terms, arguing that the expressionist "station drama" structure, though linear, operates as a critique of both history and performance. In this final scene "Yank moves from a fantasy of the gorilla's glorious past as 'King of the Jungle,'" Rundle observes, "exempt from the corruptions of civilization, to a realization of his own distance from the humanist ideal"; thus, "excluded from linear paradigms of history that signify 'progress' . . . Yank turns to an episodic model of action, one where it is 'always now': performance" (2008: 116–17).

Even after being crushed by the gorilla (the actor playing this role in costume was widely praised by critics), Yank persists in performing this fallen self in his dying moments, finally embracing his identity of "Hairy Ape," a phrase capitalized like a title in the text as if to call attention to O'Neill's play itself as something, like an uncaged gorilla, that has been let loose upon the genteel theatrical world. As with Yank's quest to "belong," O'Neill has made the search for theatrical method a central concern in this play, as he seeks to move beyond the American theatre embodied by his actor father. Thus, O'Neill the playwright enacts "modernity's drama," in Elin Diamond's phrase, and the presumed success of his method justifies the play's subtitle, "A Comedy of Ancient and Modern Life in Eight Scenes": its concluding stage directions suggest comedy in asserting that in death *"perhaps, the Hairy Ape at last belongs"* (CP2: 163). This amounts to the playwright's declaration, somewhat willfully in Yank's own manner, that the modernist-expressionist method the play had found could now be said to belong in the canon of modern world drama.

If O'Neill's successes had vindicated Jig Cook and his vision of a theatrical revolution led by the Provincetown's committed band of amateurs, it also exposed the limits of that vision. With O'Neill clearly dissatisfied with his preliminary work as director of *The Hairy Ape*, Cook departed for Greece. James Light, O'Neill's friend and Cook's rival in the company, took over directing duties as rehearsals proceeded "under the watchful eye" of veteran Broadway producer-director Arthur Hopkins (Wainscott 1988: 109). Though James Robinson may overstate his case in arguing that "O'Neill's rebellion against a middle-class style of existence would end with this play" (1995: 107), the playwright's determination at this point in his career for a more professionalized company is also reflected in his more literary aspirations for his writing (as Alexander Pettit demonstrates elsewhere in this volume) rather than its value either as direct social critique or as part of a transformative communal enterprise such as the Players.

Defying empire in *Lazarus Laughed*

O'Neill benefited nonetheless from the collaborative Provincetown spirit in the production of *The Hairy Ape*. The masks used in the Fifth Avenue scene following Yank's departure from the ship were actually suggested by Provincetown costumer Blanche Hays, and helped trigger some of the experimentation in O'Neill's subsequent works. He would go on to deploy masks in the mid-1920s for symbolic and psychological purposes in *All God's Chillun Got Wings, Marco Millions*, an adaptation of Coleridge's *Ancient Mariner*, and most centrally in *The Great God Brown*, as discussed in detail later in Chapter 5. *Lazarus Laughed*, which he subtitled "A Play for an Imaginative Theatre," was his most thorough, one might say extravagant, use of masks, as well as the only work he completed during his Broadway period that has never been professionally produced. Its vision, method, and scope seemed almost deliberately beyond the production constraints of the commercial stage, leading Barrett Clark to quip that O'Neill should have called it a play for "an Imaginary Theater" (1947: 117). The fact that O'Neill himself considered *Lazarus* a great unrealized project, a utopian, even heroic attempt to transform theatricality itself, underscores the fact that he saw the theatre, or rather his own dramatic imagination, as the only potentially utopian space and thus the only effectual site of revolutionary transformation.

In a sense, Lazarus is O'Neill's most successful revolutionary, defying not only the Roman Empire but death itself. The plot of this outsize pageant-play (it calls for 400-plus distinct roles) derives from the account in the Gospel of John of a man raised from the dead. O'Neill's Lazarus gives voice to a desire to overcome the control over life and death exerted by powerful earthly regimes, here represented by the Roman Empire of Tiberius and the young emperor-to-be, Caligula. They both see in Lazarus's gospel of laughter a dangerous threat to their power because it undermines the people's fear of death on which their power depends. Yet so strong is Lazarus's example that in the final scene while Lazarus is executed by fire in a public amphitheatre, Tiberius declares his conversion to his new truth. Outraged by this seeming betrayal, Caligula kills him, but not before Tiberius declares, "Caesar is your fear of Man! I counsel you, laugh away your Caesars!" (CP2: 626). Assuming the imperial throne, Caligula, now himself torn between his lust for power and the genuine desire he also feels to follow Lazarus's teaching, makes his choice and proclaims himself "conqueror of the Daemon, Lazarus, who taught the treason that fear and death were dead! . . . A moment more and there would have been a revolution—no more Caesars" (CP2: 627). Ultimately Lazarus dies, achieving no substantive or collective change in the people, his voice trailing off, according to the rather abstract stage directions, as "*a faint dying note of laughter that rises and is lost in the sky like the flight of his soul back into the womb of Infinity*" (CP2: 628).

O'Neill's image of humanity in *Lazarus* is not especially flattering or optimistic: in the final scene both Lazarus and Caligula declare that "men forget" and that any positive transformation they may feel is temporary. Travis Bogard notes that O'Neill was responding to his colleague Kenneth Macgowan's call in *The Theatre of Tomorrow* for an American playwright who, through the use of masks and in the spirit of the ancient Greek theatre, "can create a world [on stage] which shines with exaltation and which seems—as it indeed is—a world of reality" (qtd. Bogard 1988: 287). As late as 1944, with the Second World War raging and his writing life essentially over, O'Neill pondered a resurrection of *Lazarus* scaled down with "all the pageantry of my immense 'Imaginative Theatre' stadium [taken] out" and observed a grim parallel with contemporary events: "There is also a lot of the murder madness and death realism of Tiberius and Caligula in Hitlerism— very much so!" (SL 567). O'Neill wrote *Lazarus* with the conviction that even if humanity was beyond redemption, the medium of theatre itself could offer some transcendence, a "world of reality" where revolutions might succeed according to their own theatrical power and there would be "no more Caesars," at least for a time.

Days Without End: A failed revolution of the soul

Notwithstanding his affinity for the tragic and skepticism toward any notion of human progress, *Lazarus Laughed* is evidence that O'Neill clung to the possibility that theatre itself could effect some experience of transcendence, at least for the playwright. In *Days Without End*, produced in 1934 and his last new production until 1946, O'Neill reprised some of the core themes of *Lazarus* on the more conventional scale of a Broadway drawing-room play while revisiting his own youthful fascination with radical ideology. The play's overtly Catholic ideas and symbols, and a priest as one of its major characters, signaled to some critics that O'Neill had reconciled with the faith of his youth, but as Wainscott observes more generally: "It is curious in retrospect that so many critics of O'Neill throughout his constantly vacillating, experimental career so frequently assumed that a new experiment or message indicated a trend" (1988: 276). In fact, O'Neill could no more fully reconcile himself to the past, or remain satisfied with the present—including his own most recent play—than he could believe in a progressively improvable future. "So many Revolutions there have been since the Greeks," he wrote in a letter while struggling through an early draft of *Days Without End*, "and Man's soul has grown dumber and dumber" (SL 400). As if testing this pessimism, O'Neill creates in this play a split-protagonist approach in which two actors portray the conflicting selves of a single protagonist, locked in a kind of Faust-Mephistopheles battle over the fate of his soul. John Loving is a writer struggling with an autobiographical novel that he hopes will help him resolve his metaphysical dilemmas as well as his alienation from his ailing wife, Elsa. O'Neill presents one side, "John," as the persona visible to the other characters, and "Loving" as the masked, cynical demon who undercuts John's quest for faith.

O'Neill assigns a long speech in Act One to Father Baird, the Catholic priest-mentor who reappears from the past and recounts John's quest as a more extreme version of O'Neill's own:

> First it was Atheism unadorned. Then it was Atheism wedded to Socialism. But Socialism proved too weak-kneed a mate, and the next I heard Atheism was living in free love with Anarchism, with a curse by Nietzsche to bless the union. And then came the Bolshevik dawn, and he greeted that with unholy howls of glee and wrote me he'd found a congenial home at last in the bosom of Karl Marx. . . .
> I knew Communism wouldn't hold him long—and it didn't. Soon his letters became full of pessimism, and disgust with all sociological nostrums. (CP3: 121–22).

Now, says Father Baird, following an excursion into "the defeatist mysticism of the East" and a period as "a dyed-in-the-wool mechanist" John has turned to the bourgeois ideal of home and marriage as "his last religion" (CP3: 122, 123). In the final scene, inside *"an old church"* beneath a large crucifix, a reintegrated "John Loving" celebrates wife Elsa's recovery from illness and the final defeat of his cynical "Loving" self. Echoing the affirmative message of Lazarus, he declares, "Life laughs with God's love again! Life laughs with love!" (CP3: 178, 180).

Though this ending seems to reaffirm Christianity, no play in O'Neill's canon presents a more dissonant contrast between modernist experimental methods—the split-character, masking, and the "Plot for a Novel" framework, as O'Neill dubs the first three acts—and the more traditional roots of value and morality that O'Neill was also inescapably drawn to, a contrast hinted in his subtitle for the play as a whole, "A Modern Miracle Play." The scope of John Loving's transformation is highly personal rather than broadly collective or even exemplary, however, and the stridency of his final declaration of victory over death recalls nothing so much as the tone of a more conventional hero's triumph over villainy at the end of a traditional melodrama. As I have argued elsewhere, for O'Neill the novel form offered the most comprehensive literary vehicle of modernity; John Loving's ambition to write an autobiographical novel thus represents a quest to master the personal implications of modernity by a literary means (1994: 116–23). However, for many reviewers it was stage imagery, the "low, sleek, modern designs" of Lee Simonson's sets along with the "straight lines, sharp angles, stark pictures, and almost monotonous tones" of Philip Moeller's direction and the striking image of John beneath the crucifix in the final scene, that proved more moving and persuasive than O'Neill's story line with its affirmational ending (Wainscott 1988: 276, 277). One might reasonably conclude, ironically for a playwright who sought frequently to approximate the novel form in his plays, that O'Neill's own faith in *Days Without End* lay ultimately in the power of its theatrical images rather than its literary "Plot for a Novel" frame.

A touch of the revolutionary: The American history cycle

Following the failed production of *Days Without End* in 1934, O'Neill's playwriting in fact did not suggest a personal conversion to Catholicism or an interest in religious themes in his self-exile from the stage. O'Neill turned his efforts to exploring the meaning of American history in a projected cycle that grew eventually to a plan for eleven plays spanning the period from 1754 to 1932, with the overall working title of "A Tale of Possessors Self-Disposessed." Largely destroyed by O'Neill and wife Carlotta in 1952 when his declining health made it clear that he would never complete the project, the grand cycle survives in fragments that include some notes, outlines, and one completed play, *A Touch of the Poet* (discussed at length in Chapter 5). He also left behind a lengthy, unfinished draft of what was to be the sixth play in the cycle, *More Stately Mansions*, composed in the late 1930s. Centered historically on the Panic of 1837 and its disastrous effects on the national economy, *Mansions* extends the split-persona method of *Days* by focusing on the battle over Simon Harford's mind and soul waged between his patrician Yankee mother, Deborah, and his ambitious but devoted working-class Irish wife, Sara. Like John Loving, Simon is a would-be writer. He suppresses his nobler romantic instincts in pursuing material success, succumbing to ambitions modeled on Napoleon (this comparison is made several times) in building a mercantile empire. Staged posthumously from an abridged script first in Sweden in 1962 and then in New York in 1967, the play traces O'Neill's vision of the nation's spiritual decline from its early revolutionary ideals to the grasping ambition of the mid-nineteenth century.

Though not so overtly unorthodox in its stage technique as *Days Without End* or many of his previous works, *Mansions* does feature long, often telepathic exchanges that convey Simon's internal split expressed alternately in Deborah's aristocratic fancies and the striving materialism of Sara. Simon's divided self, leading eventually to his mental breakdown, is emblematic of the cycle's overall aim to explore the conflict between America's moral idealism and its obsessive materialism. "The American wanted both all the time, still wants them," critic Walter Kerr wrote in the most insightful review of the 1967 New York production; in an image that both recalls and inverts the ending of *Days Without End*, Kerr observed that this "double want that can never be satisfied, never come to rest, is a lasting crucifixion" (1967: CR 955). Connecting this dilemma to the act of writing, O'Neill presents Simon as a would-be philosopher who had tried to work through this predicament: "There I was at night in my study trying to convince myself of the possibility of a greedless Utopia, while all day in my office I was really getting the greatest satisfaction and sense of self-fulfillment and pride out of beating my competitors in the race for power and wealth and possessions!" (CP3: 360). This leads him to envision "a frank study of the true nature of man as he really is and not as he pretends to himself to be" and "a new morality which would destroy all our present hypocritical pretences [*sic*] and virtuous lies about ourselves!" (CP3: 361). Mirroring O'Neill's own struggles with the cycle, Simon is unable to finish this grand proto-Nietzschean project and destroys it. In his final mental breakdown Simon gives up both his intellectual and his material ambitions, and retreats with Sara to the rustic cabin where she will care for him—a finale that recalls the debilitated state of the young radical Tom Perkins at the end of *The Personal Equation* and Olga's vow to care for him. In the epilogue, Sara vows to take care of Simon, telling him, "I'm your mother now, too" (CP3: 558). She concludes the play by imagining the wealth and power their sons will realize in the bourgeoning, opportunity-filled

America of the latter 1800s, but checks herself and resolves, "You'll let them be what they want to be, if it's a tramp in rags without a penny, with no estate but a ditch in the road, so long as they're happy!" (CP3: 559). This is Sara's version of her own "double want," in Kerr's phrase, a genuine selflessness that counters the material lure of modernity. She thus embodies a sustaining dynamic of the cycle itself, driving it forward while emerging intact from the wreckage it portrays in the two plays that survived O'Neill's destruction of the cycle manuscripts.

Revolution as pipe dream: *The Iceman Cometh*

O'Neill failed to complete the cycle for multiple and complex reasons, primarily his deteriorating health but also his manifest despair at the state of the world amid global economic depression and the looming Second World War. As an epic depiction of American modernity, moreover, the cycle verged on becoming complicit with the very forces it purported to criticize, a manifestation of O'Neill's own ambitions rather than a tragic expression of resistance to American overreach—the two sides of O'Neill's own conflicting and at times disabling "double want" as an artist. By 1939 O'Neill was ready to turn back to the crucial year in his own life, 1912, and thus to the period when a traditional America and a commercially driven American theatre were giving way to innovative stage methods and a critical dramaturgy that called into question the values from which previous theatrical traditions derived, including those O'Neill saw as the foundational values of America itself. The result of this retrospection would be *Long Day's Journey*, *A Moon for the Misbegotten*, and his most thorough treatment of the postrevolutionary condition, *The Iceman Cometh*.

Just before its premiere in 1946, O'Neill told an interviewer, "I'm going on the theory that the United States, instead of being the most successful country in the world, is the greatest failure. . . . Through moving as rapidly as it has, it hasn't acquired any real roots" (qtd. Wilson 1946: CEO 164). In *Iceman* O'Neill sought to reexamine the national ideals of happiness and individual freedom. The United States had just emerged triumphant from a second, even more cataclysmic world war and was therefore poised to fulfill the promise of modernity as the great democratic bulwark against totalitarianism. Foregoing both the overt experimentalism of his earlier works and the multi-play sweep of his unfinished American historical epic, in *Iceman* as well as *Long Day's Journey* O'Neill imposed the traditional dramatic unities along with a stern, self-knowing retrospection. Both are plays that expose the pretenses of American nostalgia while affirming its necessity in the distinctive construction of personal and national identity. In the dingy barroom retreat of *Iceman*, O'Neill also offers his most fully realized image of an American heterotopia where the power to dream of a glorious past and a happy tomorrow, reduced to the illusory form that O'Neill calls the "pipe dream," is also the root of its distinctively modern tragedy.

It was Ibsen who established the "life lie" as an essential feature of modern drama, explicitly in *The Wild Duck* but in various ways throughout his mature dramatic canon, and made it a defining element of the modern stage. This is the dramaturgy that mirrored Nietzsche's attacks on the idealist tradition in philosophy and impressed the young O'Neill in 1907 when he watched Alla Nazimova in *Hedda Gabler* in New York. The sodden, multifarious band of has-beens in the heterotopic "counter-site," in Foucault's useful phrase, of Harry Hope's back room in *Iceman* freely share their individual pipe dreams with anyone willing, or compelled, to listen. O'Neill could empathize so strongly with the people and milieu of this play not only because he had lived among individuals very much like them in his late youth, but because the stage reality he creates from their illusions about "tomorrow" seem to convey his own reflections on the futility of modernist experimentation and its utopian promise of artistic freedom, a foreboding that the once-inspiring divide between being an "artist" or "nothing," to cite his early statement of ambition to Professor Baker, had considerably narrowed and become even more urgent. In returning to classical unities and realistic staging with *Iceman*, O'Neill was acknowledging his own postrevolutionary temperament as a dramatist, just as the key characters of the play have grappled in various ways with and given up on the revolutionary possibilities of their lives. "The specific revolutionary pathos of the absolutely new," in Hannah Arendt's phrase (1990: 37), was never fully attainable for O'Neill in his art. The past as history and tradition weighed heavily upon his characters here and in *Long Day's Journey*, and certainly upon the playwright himself as he contemplated the state of the world and the arc of his own life and career while writing those works from 1939 to 1942 in relative isolation in the hills above Oakland, California.

Though neither expressionist nor precisely documentary, the 1946 staging of *Iceman* conveyed its characters' existential predicament while also recalling the reformist tradition of such nineteenth-century temperance dramas as *The Drunkard* and *Ten Nights in a Barroom*. O'Neill's retrospection leaves behind the overt experimentation of much of his previous work in favor of a complex realism that expresses the fully intertwined, collective fate of his characters. The setting devised by longtime collaborator Robert Edmond Jones (who also handled lighting and costumes) in the words of one reviewer "managed the miracle of making visible and at the same time expressive a sordid environment which is essential to the play but would lose its power were it merely photographic" (Gilder 1946: CR 833). Director Eddie Dowling had just played Tom Wingfield in the 1945 premiere of Tennessee Williams's breakout play *The Glass Menagerie*, with its similarly rueful take on a modernized America "lit by lightning" rather than illuminated by memory (Williams 1966: 115).

In the printed set directions, O'Neill draws on his own past to situate Harry Hope's establishment with great specificity—historically, geographically, politically, and legally. Based on the dives where the younger O'Neill drank, brooded, and once attempted the suicide depicted in *Exorcism*, the setting is a "Raines-Law hotel of the period" in the lower West Side, with room rentals and "a property sandwich in the middle of each table" to fulfill conditions of the law that allowed liquor sales "after closing hours and on Sundays" in back rooms, notwithstanding the "fleeting alarms of reform agitation" (CP3: 563). The proprietor, Harry Hope, has some lingering ties to the notorious Tammany Hall political machine that dominated New York City politics, and his premises seems a safe haven from inspectors, police, competitors, and respectable bourgeois society generally. Maritime images and metaphors recur throughout the play, and like the heterotopian spaces aboard the ships of O'Neill's earlier plays, Harry's back room is situated on the fringes of American social history, with any hint of a ship's purposeful ocean voyage enduring only in the pipe dreams of its drunken crew as they nurse identities built on past exploits and ever-deferred prospects.

The forward pressure of modernity against the characters' introverted, retrospective resistance to change and self-knowledge is a key dynamic of *Iceman*. Their pipe-dream selves depend on a mutual validation by the others; this is the internal social contract that shields them from the rapidly changing external world. When the charismatic traveling hardware salesman, Theodore Hickman, or Hickey, makes his annual visit on Harry's birthday with much anticipation, to everyone's surprise and dismay he declares they must attain true peace by unflinchingly confronting themselves and their illusions—the very reality they all wish to escape. The tragic dialectic of *Iceman* emerges from its conflict between what historian Daniel Singal identifies as the two major tendencies of American modernism represented by William James and John Dewey—individual consciousness and pragmatic social action, respectively (1987: 16–18). If Hickey embodies pragmatic reform, Larry Slade exemplifies the burden of individual consciousness. These two primary characters together generate the play's tragedy not in terms of an individual fate but as a fatal contradiction in national ideology between action and self-knowledge, and thus for O'Neill, a defining condition of modern American tragedy.

In his guise of total disengagement, Larry "de old Foolosopher," as Rocky the bartender calls him (CP3: 570), is nonetheless a kind of narrator-figure who introduces and comments upon the habitués of Harry's back room. A former anarchist revolutionary, Larry makes clear early in Act One, "I'm through with the Movement long since," elaborating in terms that summarize the playwright's own critique of contemporary humankind: "I saw men didn't want to be saved from themselves, for that would mean they'd have to give up greed, and they'll never pay that price for liberty. So I said to the world, God bless all here, and may the best man win and die of gluttony!" (CP3: 570). Larry's cynicism is revealed as a pose, masking his fundamental human empathy and, notwithstanding all his talk of welcoming death, an emotional shield for his deep fear of mortality. When the salesman Hickey arrives late in Act One, he begins pushing his salvational agenda by challenging everyone to confront his or her carefully nurtured "pipe dream" and, by rejecting it, achieve a kind of personal transcendence, not unlike the laughter of O'Neill's Lazarus. "I'm not trying to put anything over on you," he declares in his amiable salesman's manner. "It's just that I know now from experience what a lying pipe dream can do to you—and how damned relieved and contented you feel when you're rid of it," ominously comparing this remedy to "the grand feeling, like when you're sick and suffering like hell and the Doc gives you a shot in the arm and the pain goes, and you drift off" (CP3: 613). This metaphor, a reference to morphine—a narcotic favored by modern medicine—is of course far too potent for the inmates at Harry's, who prefer the old-fashioned haze of alcohol to maintain their illusions.

As if bringing closure to O'Neill's early sea plays, the heterotopian space of *Iceman* is "the last harbor," in Larry's phrase, the "Bottom of the Sea Rathskeller" where the shipwrecked inhabitants are content to live out their days (CP3: 577–78). Several are linked in codependent pairs, including former police officer Pat McGloin and Ed Mosher, the former circus man, bound together by a shared appetite for graft and grifting. Likewise, Piet Woetjoen and Cecil Lewis continue fighting their two-handed version of the Boer War with a kind of grudging affection with hints of bloodshed and the atrocities of colonial conquest. The three female characters who appear in the play are prostitutes whom the others call "tarts" to downplay the full implications of their work and to keep the men they work for, the bartenders Rocky and Chuck, from having to acknowledge their own identities as pimps. Others seem more isolated, including James Cameron, called "Jimmy Tomorrow," who embodies the pipe dream both in his indefinite postponement of taking any action and in denying the reason for his failed life: a weakness for alcohol rather than, as he claims, the cruel infidelity years ago of a fiancée. The African American Joe Mott, formerly a bigtime gambler and the play's only non-white character, in exchange for booze now submits to the lowly role of Harry's janitor and to the others' demeaning compliments about his honorary "whiteness." Willie Oban, the ex-student of law at Harvard, lives with the shame brought on by the criminal conviction of the corrupt father he once idolized, a shame that also destroys Willie's faith in himself. "A revolution deposed him, conducted by the District Attorney," Willie declares of his disgraced father with his typically mordant, besotted irony (CP3: 585), draining the word "revolution" of meaning by conflating it with the banal reformism of governmental anticorruption campaigns.

The most authentic revolutionary of the group, Hugo Kalmar, seems at first glance a caricature with "*the stamp of an alien radical, a strong resemblance to the type Anarchist as portrayed, bomb in hand, in newspaper cartoons*" (CP3: 566). Though playfully teased by them, he is treated with respect by his fellow down-and-outers because of his commitment and suffering as a political prisoner in Europe. At first confirming the stereotype by blurting out radical catchphrases, Hugo becomes increasingly dour as Hickey's program of reform proceeds toward its ruthless conclusion. Hickey's zeal spurs the dark side of his own revolutionary aspirations, a bourgeois and even cruelly autocratic self hidden beneath his proletarian empathies. Hugo's fondest dreams of a revolutionary utopia become a nightmarish dystopian terror for "our little Robespierre," as Lewis calls him (CP3: 615). "I cannot sleep!" Hugo cries, a grim vision descending on him late in the play. "Always there is blood beneath the willow trees! I hate it and I am afraid!" (CP3: 680).

Like Hugo, the young Don Parritt is an ex-revolutionary, but was raised to it by his radical-anarchist mother, Rosa. His rejection of her life and agenda amounts to a filial rather than a political conflict, as he feels her commitment to "the Movement" always took precedence over her commitment to her son. Parritt gradually works up to his confession of having betrayed his mother, who also happens to be Larry Slade's former lover and fellow anarchist. Based on the real-life informant Donald Vose, who in 1914 turned on his mother, Gertie Vose, and her west coast anarchist comrades,[2] Parritt threatens the comfortably deactivated state of Larry's own revolutionary commitment by forcing Larry to take responsibility for his past. Larry can dismiss revolution as a pipe dream but not his emotional connection to Rosa and the sense of personal failure he continues to feel, heightened by Parritt's arrival. Parritt offers various motives for his own rejection of the anarchism, all of them a dodge, especially the supposed surge of nativist patriotism inspired by his "studying American history": "I saw that all the ideas behind the Movement came from a lot of Russians like Bakunin and Kropotkin and were meant for Europe, but we didn't need them here in a democracy where we were free already" (CP3: 636). The begged question of being "free already," as a self-justifying dodge from Parritt, seems a direct dig at the triumphal smugness of an American audience fresh from victory in war rather than a patriotic stance as such. When Parritt admits finally that he betrayed Rosa not from principle but from his resentment, even hatred, of "the great incorruptible Mother of the Revolution, whose only child is the Proletariat" (CP3: 704), Larry is finally shaken from his detached presumption of being "free already" and takes action, directing Parritt to take his own life as self-punishment but also, in a dark twist on Hickey's program, as his only hope for peace.

Rosa Parritt, Harry's long-dead wife Bessie, and Hickey's newly deceased wife Evelyn—news that he reveals to everyone's shock—loom as the absent women behind the failed lives of the play's three primary male characters. Like the other men venturing out of the barroom to take up their old lives, Harry has succumbed to Hickey's relentless cajoling, what Larry sardonically calls "the Revolution starting on all sides of you" with "the great Nihilist, Hickey" leading a final "movement that will blow up the world!" (CP3: 622). When Hickey goads him into doing what he insists Bessie would have wished, Harry departs warily into the streets of his old New York ward, but his adventure ends abruptly with an automobile, or so Harry claims, nearly killing him as he crossed the street, a confrontation with modernity that sends him scurrying back for the safety of his back room and its illusions. One by one the others do likewise, forcing Hickey to confront the ultimate failure of his local revolution: "Don't you know you're free now to be yourselves, without having to feel remorse or guilt, or lie to yourselves about reforming tomorrow? Can't you see there is no tomorrow now? You're rid of it forever!" (CP3: 689). Hickey's perverse pursuit of freedom has meant avoiding the burden of reforming himself into the sober and faithful husband that his wife, Evelyn, hoped he could be. In his crucial monologue, Hickey justifies his murder of Evelyn by claiming a desire to free her of the burden of loving him.

As Larry and the others, briefly, come to realize, the only real freedom from the burdens of living is not reform or revolution, in fact, but death. Or rather, the only true freedom resides in the choice of evading the fact of death or confronting it. After Hickey is led out by the policemen he himself has summoned, the others manage to recover their drunken good humor, each singing his own signature tune in the final scene as Hugo's "Carmagnole" from the French Revolutionary era rises above the others. Larry, however, *"stares in front of him, oblivious to their racket"* (CP3: 711), isolated on stage and alone with his realization that neither Hickey's act of murder nor Don Parritt's suicide brings freedom, that bearing the consciousness of death is the only real freedom. The decision by director Eddie Dowling in the 1946 production to have Larry leave the stage before the curtain (Vena 1988: 164–65), as if escaping the weight of this discovery, seems false to O'Neill's vision of Larry as the audience's surrogate on stage who conveys to them the playwright's own sense of the liberating value of a tragic consciousness.

O'Neill defines modern American tragedy in this play not so much as the loss of American idealism, or a nostalgic past crushed by progress, but in terms of consciousness in conflict with action, thus striking at the heart of can-do, pragmatic American modernity—their instruments forever suspect, in Emerson's terms. O'Neill's tragic vision leaves no proper escape from its implications except perhaps through consciousness *as* action, that is, through the medium of theatre itself as a means of confronting the fact of death without dying. Winifred L. Frazer not only discerns the presence of Emma Goldman in the figure of Rosa Parritt, but sees a parallel to Goldman's work as an ideological agitator in O'Neill's work in drama. "In examining the anarchist culture in *Iceman*," writes Frazer, "O'Neill was also examining his life in the artistic culture—both unacceptable to the masses they were trying to elevate politically and artistically" (1974: 95). If Goldman explored new ways to live one's life according to new standards of freedom, O'Neill was sounding the limits of that freedom and some fundamental— to him, intransigent—features of American sensibility. Hickey's extended confession in Act Four, certainly one of O'Neill's great achievements as a playwright, exposes the darkness of an agenda pursued for others in the name of freedom that stems in fact from the need to expiate a crushing personal guilt. Good feelings are restored after Hickey's arrest and removal, but the "*weird cacophony*" of everyone's singing in the finale suggests that a provisional heterotopic discord, not the promise of a sustainable utopia, is their true element.

Set in the year just before as a young man O'Neill resolved to become a writer, with its premiere coming shortly after he could no longer write, *Iceman* seems a reflection on his long and productive if uneven career. Even before connecting with the Provincetown Players he had set out to revolutionize the American theatre, and largely succeeded, but not without numerous misfires and, more poignantly, a sense in his final years that he and his work had fallen into obscurity, eclipsed by newer playwrights and the triumphal modernity he had tried to resist as an artist. In his discussion of leftist criticism of O'Neill's drama in the 1930s, Joel Pfister astutely notes that such critics "risked shrinking the concept of the political, so that only 'radical' theatre would be seen as performing political work" (1995: 166). By insisting on the fully legitimate reality of theatrical experience, O'Neill affirmed the American theatre as a heterotopian counter-site where one can more powerfully imagine other lives and the otherness of one's own life.

CHAPTER 4
NEW WOMEN, MALE DESTINIES: THE "WOMAN PLAYS"

An important cultural revolution in the early decades of the 1900s in which O'Neill found himself a detached but inevitable participant was the emergence of women from the home into the public sphere. The New Woman, freed from various moral, political, and economic constraints of Victorian-era gender roles, became an iconic image of progressive America as women agitated for suffrage, sought access to professions, and embraced more overt and diverse sexualities. However, the "persistence, even the consolidation, of men's privileges within an egalitarian framework would prove a defining feature of twentieth-century American society," according to Christine Stansell, resulting in "the fundamental paradox of a sexual modernism that was also a patriarchal modernization" (2000: 227). Similarly, Lois Rudnick observes that the ideal of the New Woman often obscures "a much more conflicted figure," as women actually felt "a great deal of tension between their stated ideals about women's freedom and the pull of traditional loyalties and beliefs" (1991: 73, 77). This tension was evident in the drama of the period and in its seeming attacks on the ingrained beliefs of audiences and reviewers.

George Bernard Shaw summarized this tension in his take on Nora Helmer's departure from her home at the end of *A Doll's House*: "Woman has thus two enemies to deal with: the old-fashioned one who wants to keep the door locked, and the new-fashioned one who wants to thrust her into the street before she is ready to go" (1913: 112). Nora, he implied, was leaving of her own free will, but the world outside the Helmer household seems unready to receive her or for her to write her own destiny. The domestic ideal of what Shaw called the "self-sacrificing" or "womanly woman" (1913: 36) was firmly rooted in the traditional culture of the nineteenth century and, moreover, essential to the thematic core of the melodramatic stage practices that Ibsen, Strindberg, and Shaw himself confronted in their works. This ideal also served as a point of departure for American women playwrights in the early twentieth century such as Rachel Crothers, Alice Gerstenberg, and Susan Glaspell. The Greenwich Village that Eugene O'Neill encountered in the 1910s was reaching its peak as an important center of social activism by and for women in America, featuring such stalwart leaders as Emma Goldman and birth-control advocate Margaret Sanger, but also as a mecca for those seeking artistic freedom and self-expression. The Provincetown Players served as a laboratory for experimenting with new modes of gender roles and consciousness, and was a model of cultural enfranchisement for women. The Provincetown staged plays by Djuna Barnes, Edna St. Vincent Millay, Rita Wellman, Neith Boyce, and Glaspell, as well as creating opportunities for women to direct, design, produce, and perform on stage and manage its business operations. "The women of Provincetown," Cheryl Black argues, "were pursuing a formidable objective: to revolutionize all human relationships—to create a new world," including "their personal relationships—as lovers, wives, mothers" (2002: 31). Nonetheless, however much the men of the Provincetown, especially Jig Cook and Hutchins Hapgood, supported this egalitarian agenda in principle, in actuality, as Brenda Murphy points out, they did not easily let go of the traditional gender roles that shaped their own identities and "never overcame a deep psychological resistance to the perceived threat of the new, emancipated woman" (2005: 38).

Women in O'Neill's plays reflect the social upheaval of their times while suggesting the playwright's own ambivalence toward their new freedom, especially sexual and professional, as an indicator of human progress. In many respects extending rather than breaking from the melodramatic theatre that made his father's fortune, O'Neill took as a given its sentimental "Angel in the House" ideal and its dichotomy of good women portrayed as pure maidens, faithful wives, and nurturing mothers, on one side, with bad women overtly sexualized as prostitutes or otherwise "fallen," on the other. Several critics and scholars have noted that his women characters tend to combine these traits, erasing the Victorian dichotomy in some respects but still oriented primarily toward supporting the destinies of the men in their lives. In terms of contemporary psychological theory, O'Neill once claimed a preference for Jungian over Freudian models of the psyche (SL 386), perhaps from an affinity for Jung's theory of archetypes and especially the concept of a feminine *anima* that inhabits masculinity as a repressed complement. O'Neill's women characters may indeed be seen in terms of masculine anxiety in the early decades of the twentieth century that Marianne DeKoven sees as "accompanied by its dialectical twin: a fascination and strong identification with the empowered feminine," thus creating "an irresolvable ambivalence toward powerful femininity that itself forged many of Modernism's most characteristic formal innovations" (1999: 174). O'Neill's own brand of modernism "exposed many of the flaws in the patriarchal universe both within and outside his plays," writes Judith Barlow, and yet "he was, not surprisingly, also deeply invested in that universe. His female characters, including some of the modern stage's most memorable women, grow out of that ambivalence" (1998: 175). These roles have been portrayed on stage by many of the leading artists of the day, including Lynn Fontanne, Alla Nazimova, Ingrid Bergman, Glenda Jackson, Vanessa Redgrave, Cherry Jones, Jessica Lange, and, perhaps most definitively, Colleen Dewhurst; and big-screen adaptations of his works have featured such stars as Greta Garbo, Sophia Loren, and Katharine Hepburn. O'Neill's most challenging roles for women can exemplify Rita Felski's formulation that "gender is continually in process, an identity that is performed and actualized over time within given social constraints" (1995: 21), especially when those constraints are those of the performative tradition itself.

Several of O'Neill's early plays, however bold, are also beholden to traditional theatrical gender roles. In *The Web* Rose Thomas is both a prostitute and the mother of a baby girl. In her hopeless struggle to escape the cycle of exploitation, poverty, and disease, she becomes the object of struggle between two men: a cruel pimp and a sympathetic criminal fugitive. Despite O'Neill's seeming social realism, Rose's helplessness in a violent, male-dominated world is rooted in the traditional melodramatic conflict between a male hero and a male villain. Likewise, the two early plays that O'Neill set on lifeboats offer divergent female images that are framed primarily in terms of male conflict. In *Thirst* the Dancer offers herself sexually to the two men with her on the lifeboat, and after she dies, her body becomes the object of their mutually fatal conflict. Conversely, the silent Polish mother of *Fog* (discovered later to be dead) clutches her dead child with a mystical maternal devotion that appears to save the two men in the lifeboat with her. The disgraced young stenographer of *Abortion*, Nellie, dies unseen before the action of the play, leaving her brother Joe and the college sports hero Jack Townsend to hash out the moral burden of her death. In two of the four *Glencairn* plays—*The Moon of the Caribbees* and *The Long Voyage Home*—the arrival of female prostitutes is instrumental to showing the male sailors' inescapable bond to the sea. In *Before Breakfast* the man silent and mostly unseen offstage earns the audience's empathy instead of the one character, Mrs. Rowland, who is seen and heard. Only in '*Ile*, the other significant sea play of this early period, does O'Neill focus, along with *The Web* primarily on a woman's predicament, though mostly as a spectacle of despair.

Early portraits: *Now I Ask You* and *The Straw*

Attempting to craft a "moneymaker" (CC 381), O'Neill satirized the bohemian version of the New Woman while clearly affirming traditional gender roles. Rarely produced, *Now I Ask You*, the "Three-Act Farce-Comedy" he wrote in 1916 in Provincetown, portrays three modern female types, adapted from conventional drawing-room comedy. Lucy Ashleigh is a fledgling anarchist smitten by modernist plays and poetry, while her wise suburban mother, Mrs. Ashleigh, patiently guides her toward conventional happiness and respectability. Lucy's friend Leonora Barnes, the acerbic Greenwich Village poetess, provides Nietzsche-inflected commentary and maintains a cool distance from American bourgeois values. The willful Lucy insists that her good-natured businessman fiancé, Tom, sign a prenuptial compact that guarantees her individual freedom: "My highest duty is toward myself," she declares, "and my ego demands freedom, wide horizons to develope [*sic*] in . . . Castles in the air, not homes for human beings!" (CP1: 416). Meanwhile, Mrs. Ashleigh conspires with Tom to test the limits of Lucy's emancipation. Tom feigns an affair with Leonora, who likens him to "the Great Blond Beast" imagined by Nietzsche as the master of a new post-moral society. In pointed contrast to Lucy's straitlaced father, who fumes at their daughter's nonconformity, Mrs. Ashleigh understands that Lucy represents "the old, ever young, wild spirit of youth which tramples rudely on the grave-mound of the Past to see more clearly to the future dream" that is ultimately "tempered to a fine, sane, progressive ideal which is of infinite help to the race" (CP1: 411–12). The teasing action of the Prologue in which Lucy, overcome by Tom's seeming infidelity, appears to shoot herself à la *Hedda Gabler* (a play she passionately admires) is revealed in the Epilogue to be only the sound of a car tire that blows out just as she was raising the gun to her temple, upon which she faints. This is the only mildly inventive aspect of the play; indeed, an automobile's intrusion as a plot device and Mrs. Ashleigh's affirmation of the "progressive ideal" in her daughter seem a lighthearted triumph of simple modernity over aesthetic modernism. Lucy recovers from her shock, and having dodged the perils of actual radicalism, she will presumably realize the joys of a normal, healthy American womanhood in a marriage to a strong, empathetic, and prosperous young American man.

Lucy anticipates O'Neill's treatment of youthful bohemian rebellion in *Ah, Wilderness!*, but this kind of farcical satire was never his strong suit. By the time he began work on *The Straw* in 1918 he had turned, as in *Exorcism*, toward a more autobiographical mode. Not produced until 1921, *The Straw* pays "a debt to the ghost of Kitty McKay" (Bogard, *Contour* 1988: 114), the young tubercular patient whom O'Neill befriended during his stint at Gaylord Sanatorium in 1912–13 as he also began to see playwriting as his calling. Kitty is recreated as the eighteen-year-old Eileen Carmody, his most fully realized woman character of this early period. The motherless Eileen is burdened with a stingy, intemperate Irish father and with the raising of four younger siblings, stressful circumstances directly blamed for her advanced, incurable condition. In the fledgling story writer, Stephen Murray, O'Neill's counterpart in the play, she finds the empathy lacking in both her father and her fiancé, the rigidly bourgeois Fred Nicholls, the son of a factory owner who is drawn to Eileen's spirited beauty but terrified of her illness. Though O'Neill grants Eileen a measure of genuine tragic pathos, her primary role dramatically is to act as Stephen's doomed, selfless muse.

The modern routine of a sanatorium confirms Eileen's inexorable fate. A large Fairbanks scale is wheeled in for the ritual weighing that measures the patients' progress toward healthy "gaining" or ominous "losing"; in a crucial scene, Stephen discovers that his increase of three pounds is exactly equal to Eileen's loss, as if their fates diverge inversely. Looking ahead to Stephen's cure, Eileen encourages him to give up his joyless work as a reporter so he can pursue his true calling as a fiction writer. She even types his manuscripts at the sanatorium and otherwise devotes herself to his success. (In fact, this is the kind of spousal support O'Neill envisioned for himself as a writer, realizing it finally, if not without emotional cost, in his third marriage.) Several months after his discharge, Stephen returns from his new life as a writer in New York to visit Eileen at the sanatorium, downplaying his professional accomplishments and his new life in the city. Driven seemingly as much by his fear of professional failure as by his genuine affection for her, he offers to marry Eileen in her declining state: "I don't know how to live without you," Stephen pleads sincerely, though without true romantic feeling (CP1: 792).

In the final scene the wise sanatorium administrator, Miss Gilpin, tries to prod the two not-quite lovers toward seeing "some promise of fulfillment,— somehow—somewhere—in the spirit of hope itself" (CP1: 794). In her "*motherly, self-forgetting solicitude*," Eileen embodies hope in a pointedly gendered way that supersedes "the verdicts of all the doctors," as Stephen believes (CP1: 794)—inspiring, by implication, the work of young male writers as O'Neill himself was inspired by the real-life Kitty McKay. In contrast to the stoic Eileen, Stephen bears a larger share of the play's sentimentalism. Judith Barlow has noted that many of O'Neill's male characters show traits culturally marked as feminine and are often "emotional and verbal hemophiliacs looking for a sympathetic (usually female) ear" (1995: 117). Stephen's self-pity only amplifies Eileen's courage and selflessness in the face of death, and one wonders if Stephen will ever write again. The male theatre critic for *Billboard* issued an unfavorable judgment of *The Straw* in 1920 but acknowledged the jolt felt by the audience "like the touch of a live electric wire" when Stephen realizes Eileen's doom and her unrequited love for him, leaving the reviewer himself, in an apt gender-role twist, crying "like a man" (1921: CR 234).

Women and marriage in three plays of the early 1920s

By contrast, in three plays from the early 1920s, this sustaining female empathy is qualified or absent. All three plays were commercial failures but thematically revealing in their treatments of gender and marriage within the context of changing societal norms. In *Diff'rent* (1920) a young Emma Crosby condemns the earnest sea captain Caleb Williams, her presumptive fiancé, upon discovering his dalliance with a woman while on a voyage many years before. Though she was "a brown, heathen woman that ain't no better'n a nigger," as Emma's brother puts it in his casually racist manner (CP2: 13), Emma sees Caleb as no longer "diff'rent" from other men and refuses to marry him. In Act Two, thirty years later, Emma is having an affair of her own with a beau much younger and much less virtuous than Caleb. O'Neill stresses the visible consequences of Emma's moral discord in the "*grotesque aspect of old age*" in her dress and makeup, "*turned flighty and masquerading as the most empty-headed youth*," along with "*an obstreperous newness*" in the trendy modern décor of her once-staid New England parlor, including the raucous jazz playing on the Victrola (CP2: 27). Emma's unseemly modern turn, along with her self-abasing sexual freedom, drives the still-unmarried Caleb to despair and suicide. As he goes off to hang himself in her barn, he utters a scathing rebuke: "You used to say you was diff'rent from the rest o' folks. By God, if you are, it's just you're a mite madder'n they be!"

(CP2: 49). A kind of ironic New Woman caricature, for Emma the lure of modernity has the same corrupting influence as the primitive sexuality that she had unfairly accused Caleb of succumbing to on his sea voyages.

In the two plays that feature realized marriages, the collaborative if secondary roles that the wives play in their husbands' careers reach a point of crisis. In *The First Man* (1921), Martha Jayson faithfully supports her anthropologist husband, Curtis, in his quest across various far-flung, exotic locales for "the very origin of Man himself" (CP2: 84)—a scientific pursuit that also implies his high level of professional self-absorption. Now two years since the death of their young child, Martha feels unfulfilled because she is not a mother. "I wish I could tell you what I feel," she tells him, "make you feel with me the longing for a child. If you had just the tiniest bit of feminine in you—(*forcing a smile*) But you're so utterly masculine, dear!" (CP2: 85). Martha sees motherhood and his profession as complementary, imploring him "to reciprocate—to love the creator in me," and in a remarkable monologue, she reveals the epiphany she experienced when they were studying the natives of southern China: "And all at once the picture came of a tribeswoman who stood looking at us in a little mountain village as we rode by. She was nursing her child. Her eyes were so curiously sure of herself" (CP2: 86). Martha thus turns their scientific expedition, presumably to discover new insights into the human condition, into an affirmation of traditional, nurturing motherhood, and takes this image home with her as a model of female creativity.

Martha later does become pregnant, but dies giving birth. Jayson reads this misfortune as a sign that he should carry on with his work and leaves his infant son in an aunt's care. "What good would I be for him—or anyone—if I stayed?" he declares, seeing his parental duty only in terms of his professional ambition in spite of Martha's clear desire that he settle down to raise a family. With "*the light of an ideal beginning to shine in his eyes*," Jayson vows to return one day to his son and to "teach him to know and love a big, free life" (CP2: 116), imagining that this would (or perhaps should) have been Martha's actual wish. As the voice of womanly tradition, Curtis's aunt acknowledges disliking his unconventional late wife but avows that Martha "died like a true woman in the performance of her duty," and likewise blesses Curtis's choice to leave on the principle that "a man must do faithfully the work ordained for him" (CP2: 115–16). Along with this maudlin finale and a generally weak script, the play misfired in its 1921 premiere because the director, Augustin Duncan (brother of dancer Isadora Duncan), forced it into a naturalistic straitjacket instead of playing up its potentially engaging melodramatic "excess" (Wainscott 1988: 106). It closed after just twenty-seven performances.

O'Neill had even less success with *Welded* in 1924, which closed after just twenty-four performances. The first O'Neill play produced by his new theatrical partnership, Experimental Theatre, Inc. (also known as "The Triumvirate"), this chamber drama was justly panned by critics. O'Neill's use of follow spotlights—called "*auras of egoism*" in the first-act stage directions (CP2: 235)—on playwright Michael Cape and his actress-wife Eleanor seems a remnant of the expressionism of *The Hairy Ape* and *The Emperor Jones*. In fact, as coproducer Kenneth Macgowan acknowledged, its staging was in fact too naturalistic, "too close to Ibsen" and the "paraphernalia of everyday life" to convey fully its intended Strindbergian force (1924: CR 347)—what O'Neill himself called his "attempt at the last word in intensity in the truth about love and marriage" (SL 177). Just as O'Neill's attempts at innovative staging are sometimes undermined by a lingering dependence on conventional realism, his seemingly daring attempts to explore gender roles and conflicts often leave traditional gender boundaries intact.

In Act One, the Capes hash out the most interesting theme of the play in battling over which of them—husband-playwright or actress-wife—is the one who really "creates" the women in his plays. Calling them "wooden," Eleanor insists, "You ought to thank me for breathing life into them!" (CP2: 249). When she reveals her affair with their friend, John, the wounded Michael proceeds directly to the room of a prostitute whom O'Neill too symbolically names "Woman." She soon realizes that Michael is not seeking sex but emotional revenge on his wife. Finally, husband and wife reconcile at home, seemingly resolving their artists' dispute as Michael gallantly declares to Eleanor that she makes him "a whole, a truth," their bodies momentarily forming a cross followed by a kiss at the final curtain (CP2: 275–76). The metatheatrical potential of an actress who chides her playwright husband for writing unpersuasive female characters that she herself performs is blunted by an unpersuasive, and in this context tradition-affirming, theatrical image of their "welded" spirits.

Her own boss: *Anna Christie*

The prostitute of *Welded* is more plot device than character, and she certainly lacks the key supporting role O'Neill created for Cybel, the savvy, life-giving "earth mother" prostitute in *The Great God Brown* (discussed in the next chapter). From *The Web* to *Long Day's Journey*, O'Neill was obsessed by the mother-whore dichotomy; the shameful brothel story written into the suppressed *Exorcism* was clearly one of the most painful episodes of O'Neill's life, exploiting a prostitute solely to secure his divorce from Kathleen Jenkins, the mother of his child. O'Neill pushed this dichotomy to the fore in revising his 1919 script of *Chris Christophersen* as *Anna Christie* in 1920; he changed the female lead from a prim stenographer raised in England to a prostitute brought up in Minnesota, making her working-girl nickname his new title. In making this change O'Neill also took on the well-established "fallen woman" genre that included *Camille*, the durable stage adaptation of the novel by Alexandre Dumas *fils*, and Shaw's *Mrs. Warren's Profession*. In America, Eugene Walter's *The Easiest Way* was perhaps the genre's most prominent example to date. Theatre critic Alan Dale noted "the rush of women" in 1909 going to see Walter's play about a pragmatic young lady of flexible virtue, and speculated, "Perhaps women are tired of seeing themselves set forth as angels or devils. . . . Woman, in her heart of hearts, probably laughs at man's conception of her, colored as it is by impulse and decorated for his own delectation" (1909: 678). O'Neill was clearly mindful of a shift in audience sensibility from the moral sentimentalism of *Camille* to Shaw's Ibsenite social critique, along with the photographic realism of Walter's play that featured producer Belasco's elaborate reconstruction of an actual New York boardinghouse. Unlike Walter, however, O'Neill allows his heroine a moral transformation to a possible future as a daughter and wife. One of O'Neill's most commercially successful plays after it opened in November 1921, *Anna Christie* won him a second Pulitzer Prize and generated two feature-length movies. Yet O'Neill believed that audiences and most critics willfully mistook the play's final ominous tone as a more or less conventional happy ending and judged *Anna Christie* an artistic failure.

Though theatrically compelling, O'Neill's first portrait of an assertive, sympathetic central female character strikes an uncertain balance between its quasi-progressivist story of a reformed prostitute and the dark undercurrent the playwright strongly hints at, mainly through the repeated admonitions of old Chris, her mariner father, concerning the heavy price that the "old davil, sea" demands of those who live by it. He has sent his daughter as a young child to be raised on a farm by relatives, presumably kept safe from the sea's moral and physical dangers. Arriving in New York from a long train journey, Anna enters the "family" back room of Johnny-the-Priest's saloon (an early version of Harry Hope's bar in *Iceman*), where she encounters Marthy, Chris's salty paramour who lives with him on the barge he operates. Marthy had already learned that Anna was coming and agreed to move off the barge, boasting to Chris, "There's plenty of other guys on other barges waitin' for me. Always was, I always found" (CP1: 966). Marthy quickly realizes that the young newcomer now drinking whiskey with her in the family room and *"plainly showing all the outward evidences of belonging to the world's oldest profession"* is in fact Chris's supposedly pure country daughter. After *"the two women size each other up with frank stares"* (CP1: 968), Anna tells her, "You're me forty years from now" (CP1: 970)— the kind of sordid fate her father had tried to prevent by sending her away to the farm many years before.

The dual nature of the sea as both destructive and life-giving is also made deliberately ambiguous, as if O'Neill were projecting onto it the mother-whore duality without clarifying which would prevail. In her first taste of life at sea, Anna experiences a mystical sense of moral rejuvenation even in the harbor aboard her father's humble barge. "It's like I'd come home after a long visit away some place," she tells Chris. "It all seems like I'd been here before lots of times—on boats—in this same fog" (CP1: 982). Almost immediately after this declaration, Chris hears noises of distress from the water and pulls the shipwrecked Irish stoker Mat Burke onto the barge. Ominously, as O'Neill would have it, Mat soon falls in love with Anna, yet the happy prospect of Anna, Mat, and Chris living together in settled domestic harmony still seems haunted by Anna's own grim prediction of her own life becoming like Marthy's in forty years, a warning sign disregarded by the audience and most critics.

In some of O'Neill's most openly critical dialogue on gender and power, Anna lays out her case against the exploitation of women in terms that reflect a progressive social reformism. Confiding her life story to Marthy over whiskey early in the play, she identifies the villains in her personal story: "It was all men's fault—the whole business. It was men on the farm ordering and beating me—and giving me the wrong start. . . . Gawd, I hate 'em all, every mother's son of 'em!" (CP1: 972–73). In the next act, her father's barge now anchored near Provincetown, Anna appears strikingly "healthy, transformed" by her brief contact with life at sea and tells her father, "Gee, I'd yust love to work on it, honest I would, if I was a man" (CP1: 980). The rugged Irish stoker Mat offers her a vicarious entry to the seagoing life she now craves; however, as Mat and Chris squabble over their respective claims on her as lover and father, Anna herself is driven to reveal her true history to them, not as a nurse, as they believe, but as a working girl "in that kind of house—the kind sailors like you and Mat goes to in port" (CP1: 1009). Revitalized by her encounter with the sea, she can now reconstrue her identity as a sex worker not as a form of enslavement to men but as a means of independence from them: "Gawd, you'd think I was a piece of furniture! . . . But nobody owns me, see?—'cepting myself. I'll do what I please and no man, I don't give a hoot who he is, can tell me what to do! I ain't asking either of you for a living. I can make it myself—one way or other. I'm my own boss" (CP1: 1007).

Mat and Chris, reflecting the sensibility of O'Neill's 1920 stage audience, soon realize that a woman's self-ownership is precisely what they fear most: female sexuality asserting itself outside the traditional roles of wife and daughter. The resolution hinges on Mat, after much internal struggle, accepting Anna's past but only insofar as he can take credit for her transformation, and in terms directly related to the homosocial, heterotopic world of a ship at sea: "For I've a power of strength in me to lead men the way I want, and women, too, maybe, and I'm thinking I'd change you to a new woman entirely, so I'd never know, or you either, what kind of woman you'd been in the past at all" (CP1: 1023). This desire to erase Anna's past seems improbable as a practical matter and intrinsically nontragic; in any case, leaving off her cursing of men, Anna now attributes her moral rebirth to a man rather than to the spiritual rejuvenation of the sea as in Act Two before Mat appears. When Anna realizes that Mat and Chris, unknown to each other, have signed on for an ocean voyage on the same ship, she promises, "I'll get a little house somewhere and I'll make a regular place for you two to come back to—wait and see" (CP1: 1026). Any note of tragedy is thus offset by the ambiguous, vaguely comic fatalism that requires an audience's belief in this future prospect of conventional domestic bliss even as the two men ship out together on their lengthy sea voyage. "While Anna is destined to wait alone on shore," Katie N. Johnson notes wryly, "it appears as if the two men will have a honeymoon" (2006: 192). The distinct possibility remains, though unacknowledged, that like the inescapable dangers of the sea that may yet claim Mat or Chris, Anna's past as her "own boss" may prove harder to erase than Mat wants to believe.

In a letter to George Jean Nathan, who had read the pre-production script and criticized its ending, O'Neill admitted, "The devil of it is, I don't see my way out. From the middle of the third act I feel the play ought to be dominated by the woman's psychology," but that "with dumb people of her sort, unable to voice strange, strong feelings," this psychology could only be conventional and melodramatic: "In real life I felt she would unconsciously be compelled, through sheer inarticulateness, to the usual 'big scene,' and wait hopefully for her happy ending" (SL 148). O'Neill seems here to blame the artistic muddle in the final act on Anna herself—and on the dramatic tradition she embodies—rather than his own incapacity as a dramatist to sustain a convincing image of her "woman's psychology" in the finale to match her forceful entry in Act One. However, O'Neill also recognized that because Anna "is the only one of the three who knows exactly what she wants, she would get it" (SL 148).

O'Neill's "woman play"

He soon began developing this idea in a more fully realized "woman play," as he called the idea that would become *Strange Interlude*, sketched out initially in a 1923 scenario titled "Godfather," with a much more articulate heroine than Anna (Floyd 1985: 336). Over the next several years he drafted a two-evening-long script that he would cut to a one-evening, nine-act work with the unusual start time of 5:15 p.m., a ninety-minute dinner break at 7:40, and a final curtain at 11:00 (LFA 340). *Strange Interlude*, his greatest commercial success, is also O'Neill's most elaborate and forthright treatment of gender, psychology, and modernity. Directed by Philip Moeller, the Theatre Guild production opened in early 1928 and ran an impressive 426 performances. It won O'Neill his third Pulitzer, while spawning two touring companies, a best-selling print edition, and a major (if largely botched) Hollywood movie. *Strange Interlude* incorporates such timely themes as war, business, art, marriage, social class, sexual freedom, scientific progress, psychoanalysis, eugenics, birth control, and even intercollegiate sports, within a broad conceptual framework of historical progress, individual destiny, and cosmic fate. As O'Neill wrote to Alexander Berkman the year before it premiered, *Strange Interlude* "attempt[s] to do in a play all that can be done in a novel" (SL 238). During the run of *Beyond the Horizon* in 1920 he had acknowledged the goal of "wedding the theme for a novel to the play form in a way that would still leave the play master of the house" ("A Letter" 1920: sec. 6:2). *Anna Christie* had also emerged from his attempt to write a novelistic play in *Chris Christophersen*, which had nonetheless featured no distinct method for conveying novelistic exposition on stage.

O'Neill was very likely influenced by the stream-of-consciousness method in *Ulysses*, which he read just before he began drafting his play. Unlike the tight temporal framework of Joyce's novel, set in a single day in Dublin, 1904, O'Neill required breadth in time and space to achieve his novelistic effect on stage. The play's defining feature in which characters soliloquize to the audience as if unheard by the other characters on stage—usually called "thought-asides"—was introduced in a draft script in 1926 accompanied by a much more prominent role for the novelist character, the sexually ambiguous Charles Marsden. Some reviewers of *Strange Interlude* noted an American forerunner of spoken-thought drama in Alice Gerstenberg's 1913 experimental one-acter *Overtones* that featured two pairs of women characters on stage, one pair representing their polite, "cultured" selves and the other their "primitive" selves speaking their hidden thoughts and feelings. Perhaps also inspired by this experiment in dramatic point of view, O'Neill was clearly testing the expository limits of the traditional theatrical device of characters speaking their thoughts aloud to the audience, as he also pushed the audience's traditional assumptions about sexuality and gender in creating his main character, Nina Leeds as daughter, lover, wife, and mother, and exploring her relations with each of the play's other characters.

Strange Interlude spans twenty-five years—from 1919 to 1944—and thus coincides historically, if speculatively for most of that interval, with much of the modernist era in art and literature as well as the two world wars. In making Nina Leeds its focal character, O'Neill emphasizes the predicament of women as central to American modernity while also containing her within the gendered layering of the play's expository technique. In Nina, a modern woman seeking fulfillment beyond the dictates of patriarchy, he presents the feminine dimension of the psyche that Jung called *anima*, while in the novelist Marsden O'Neill projects the artistic challenge he has set for himself as playwright. He expressed a personal fondness for Marsden but considered most novelists, including those far braver than Marsden is shown to be in the play, "mere timid recorders of life, dodging the responsibility of that ruthless selection and deletion and concentration on the essential which is the test of an artist—the forcing of significant form upon experience" (SL 247). No play more fully conveys O'Neill's ambition as a modernist in its relentless imposition of form on experience, and thus reveals his inescapable involvement with the American modernity that he generally sought to critique, as well as his obsession with the feminine *anima* that he persistently sought both to reveal and to contain.

The play's signature device starts immediately in the opening scene when Marsden enters the office of Nina's father and his old mentor, Professor Leeds, a classics scholar at an unnamed New England college. With "*nothing apparent in either appearance or act*," Marsden has an "*indefinable feminine quality*" (CP2: 633); thus, the play's special novelistic technique is marked as feminine from the outset, in the ambiguous masculinity of the novelist. The *"cosy, cultured retreat"* of Professor Leeds's office (CP2: 633) with its timeless archive of classical wisdom is contrasted pointedly with the just-ended catastrophe of the Great War, modernity's greatest crisis to date, during the final days of which Nina's fiancé, Gordon Shaw, died in an airplane accident.

Nina, then twenty-four, soon appears onstage and quickly becomes the play's dominant character. Despite her nervous collapse following this event, Nina declares her quest for self-realization: "No, I'm not myself yet. That's just it. Not all myself. But I've been becoming myself. And I must finish!" (CP2: 647). Becoming herself means coming to terms with the death of the heroic Gordon, idealized throughout the play as an archetype of modern American manhood but also emblematic of Nina's frustrated destiny. Having failed to consummate her love with Gordon before his departure to Europe, Nina compensates after the war by working as a nurse and having sex with wounded soldiers. She soon marries Sam Evans, a boyish, diffident man whom she considers a good bet to father the child she comes to see as crucial to her quest for self-realization. However, after Sam's mother discloses to her the hereditary curse of insanity in the Evans family, Nina aborts her pregnancy by him and later conspires with Sam's friend, the physician-scientist Ned Darrell, to conceive a child through whom she can reincarnate the heroic ideal of Gordon Shaw. Still bitter toward her father for preventing her marriage to Gordon before his departure, Nina now rejects the entire societal and indeed metaphysical basis of patriarchy in renouncing her belief in "God the Father"; instead she identifies with a creative maternal deity inspiring her own act of creation while speaking in the mystical idiom of *Strange Interlude* that both thrilled and amused audiences: "Not Ned's child! . . . not Sam's child! . . . mine! . . . there! . . . again! . . . I feel my child live . . . moving in my life . . . my life moving in my child . . . breathing in the tide I dream and breathe my dream back into the tide . . . God is a Mother . . ." (CP2: 732).

The play's three major male characters are subsumed in Nina's quest for realization within this new cosmic matriarchy. "My three men!" she exults in a thought aside. ". . . I feel their desires converge in me! . . . to form one complete beautiful male desire which I absorb . . . and am whole . . ." (CP2: 756). Each is presented in terms of a key aspect of a flawed patriarchal modernity. Darrell gives voice to modern scientific rationalism, yet ironically this makes him vulnerable to romantic passion. Urging him to conceive a child with her, Nina appeals to his duty as a scientist: "I need the courage of someone who can stand outside and reason it out as if Sam and I were no more than guinea pigs" (CP2: 709). Darrell rationalizes his passion for Nina in terms of professional obligation, as if performing his "duty as an experimental searcher after truth" (CP2: 711). Sam comes to personify the naïve, unreflecting confidence of American commercialism; the hereditary insanity that hovers over him like a melodramatic cliché suggests O'Neill's view of American materialism as deluded and unsustainable. For his part, Marsden seems to reflect a modern Prufrockian crisis of self-knowledge and agency, prefiguring Larry Slade in *Iceman* in certain respects. His desire for Nina is not so much physical or romantic but instead a kind of sexless emotional refuge, just as the genteel evasiveness of his fiction offers his readers a shield from reality. His evident bisexuality seems a reflection of the duality of O'Neill's narrative medium, at once dramatic and novelistic, the two modes always in uncertain tension with each other.

This modern male trinity, convergent in their desire for Nina, occupies much of the play, but in Act Three Nina also finds common purpose with another woman, Sam's mother. In an exchange that shocked audiences, Mrs. Evans counsels Nina to abort her pregnancy with Sam and seek "a healthy male to breed by" for her own sake. "Being happy," says Mrs. Evans, keenly disappointed in her own life, "that's the nearest we can ever come to knowing what's good! Being happy, that's good! The rest is just talk!" (CP2: 690). Their solidarity is expressed in terms of motherhood, seeking their freedom within the dominant framework of male destiny. Later in the play, however, Nina encounters the next generation of American womanhood as represented by the young Madeline, who pursues Gordon Evans, Nina's son by Ned Darrell and in many ways the second coming of the heroic Gordon Shaw. Just as the new Gordon will likely achieve the glory that the doomed Gordon could not, the assertive Madeline, if not quite independent or feminist, seems inclined to take charge of her life in ways not available to women of previous generations such as Mrs. Evans or Nina herself.

The play's resolution in the ninth and final act finds Nina with sharply diminished options. Sam Evans is dead, having collapsed from a stroke in the previous act just as young Gordon leads the Yale crew to victory. Darrell departs for his biological research work after a half-hearted proposal of marriage. "I leave you to Charlie," he tells Nina. "You'd better marry him, Nina—if you want peace" (CP2: 814). It is now 1944 and Gordon, untainted genetically by the Evans family curse, flies off with Madeline into the glorious future that his symbolic father, Gordon Shaw, would never realize. Nina, however, declares her motherhood "a failure" when this Gordon like his namesake also leaves her behind as the new modern patriarchy asserts itself: "They pass through the mother," she observes of sons generally and fatalistically, "to become their father again. The Sons of the Father have all been failures" (CP2: 817). Nina seemingly renounces her faith in a Mother God by invoking an image that affirms both patriarchy and modernity: "Yes, our lives are merely strange dark interludes in the electrical display of God the Father!" (CP2: 817). Retreating from modernity's "electrical display" Nina acquiesces to marriage with Marsden, to linger on quietly in the timeless, tomblike house of her father, the dead professor of classics. In Marsden's ultimate victory O'Neill seems to assert the success of his own novelistic method, his marrying of "the theme for a novel to the play form" in its final image of Nina, the once dynamic, sexually assertive New Woman of the 1920s, resting in the novelist's arms. Concluding the play in the year 1944, sixteen years into the future beyond its 1928 stage premiere, while he was himself in the middle of a bitter divorce from his second wife, Agnes, O'Neill conceives the future in an image of female pacification and containment.

Dynamo and the modern goddess

"The electrical display of God the father" is recast in female terms in O'Neill's next play, also directed by Moeller and produced by the Theatre Guild in 1929. *Dynamo* did not come close to replicating the great success of *Strange Interlude*, but extended O'Neill's obsession with gender and fate as expressed in modern electrical technology. In a letter to Nathan, O'Neill described *Dynamo* as "a good symbolical and factual biography of what is happening in a large section of American (and not only American) soul right now":

> It is really the first play of a trilogy that will dig at the roots of the sickness of today as I feel it—the death of an old God and the failure of Science and Materialism to give any satisfying new One for the surviving primitive religious instinct to find a meaning for life in, and to comfort its fears of death with. (SL 311)

He took his inspiration for its central image from "The Dynamo and the Virgin," a chapter of the 1907 memoir *The Education of Henry Adams*, in which, according to one reviewer of *Dynamo* who noted O'Neill's source, Adams contemplates modern humanity's passage "from unity to multiplicity; from order to chaos; from love to power" (Wyatt 1929: CR 684). *Dynamo* also gives concrete scenic form to Nina's vision of a Mother God. O'Neill's eponymous machine is *"huge and black, with something of a massive female idol about it"* (CP2: 871), and Lee Simonson's set design, especially his four-level rendering of the electric power plant, was praised by reviewers as "imaginative and accurate, modern and beautiful, clean and gleaming" (Wainscott 1988: 252). In *Dynamo* O'Neill also partially reprises the thought-aside method of *Interlude*; however, with no strong central female character like Nina Leeds, he relies more heavily on his feminized stage image of modern technological power, seemingly a projection of male anxiety about technology rather than an affirmation of modern womanhood.

The young protagonist Reuben Light is seventeen and yearning for love, a true sense of vocation, and a new postreligious faith. His father, a fundamentalist Christian minister, staunchly bans all electric appliances from their home as playthings of the devil and insists that Reuben follow him and his forbears in becoming the next Reverend Light. Like his mother, who opposes this plan and blames being a minister's wife for "the poverty and humiliation" she has personally endured (CP2: 825), Reuben is a victim of his father's physical and emotional abuse. Both parents oppose his interest in the girl next door, Ada Fife, whom the possessive Mrs. Light condemns as shamelessly modern, a "painted flapper with her skirts hitched up over her knees!" (CP2: 827). Ada's modern, free-thinking father manages the local electric power plant, plays jazz on his Victrola, and is a strident atheist. Annoyed by the Lights' religiosity, Fife plays a trick on Reuben with Ada's help; humiliated, Reuben renounces his parents' beliefs—"There is no God! No God but Electricity!" (CP2: 852)—then departs on a fifteen-month exile working in jobs variously connected to electrical power as if to prove his devotion to the new technological deity.

Upon returning home Reuben discovers his mother has died. Ada gets her father to give Reuben a job at the power plant, and he becomes increasingly obsessed with its complex and powerful machinery, seeking in it the Mother God that Nina invokes in *Strange Interlude*. In the climactic third act, Reuben tries to get Ada to submit to his desperate devotion to the power of "Dynamo" and, in one of O'Neill's most maniacal, hyper-Nietzschean monologues, envisions himself a new messiah for the modern world:

Driving through space, round and round, just like the electrons in the atom! But there must be a center around which all this moves, mustn't there? There is in everything else! And that center must be the Great Mother of Eternal Life, Electricity, and Dynamo is her Divine Image on earth! Her power houses are the new churches! . . . She wants some one man to love her purely and when she finds him worthy she will love him and give him the secret of truth and he will become the new saviour who will bring happiness and peace to men! And I'm going to be that saviour. . . . (CP2: 874)

When Ada fails to share his obsession, Reuben kills her with a pistol. In a stunning stage effect suggesting a perverse Jungian return to the womb, he then flings himself into the dynamo, dying by electrocution in bright, sustained flashes created on stage with a spark-gap device on top of the dynamo structure and colored lighting mounted inside it (Wainscott 1988: 253). Oddly, not Ada herself but Ada's mother is portrayed as Reuben's true female counterpart in her own dreamy fascination with the dynamo, *"as if she had given herself up completely to the spell of its hypnotic, metallic purr"* (CP2: 882). The play ends as Mrs. Fife *"pounds the steel body of the generator in a fit of childish anger,"* scolding it, "You hateful old thing, you!" (CP2: 885). Ultimately all three women in the play are, like Reuben, victims of the new technological order that has displaced, and superseded, the more primal feminine life force that O'Neill sees, like Henry Adams, as the animating spirit of the premodern world.

Dynamo earned harsh reviews and ran for only fifty performances. However, two years later O'Neill would produce one of his most significant and critically hailed works, and bolstered by its success he would go on to win the Nobel Prize for Literature in 1936. *Mourning Becomes Electra*, the trilogy set immediately following the American Civil War, features Lavinia Mannon and her mother, Christine (discussed in Chapter 6), among his most important women characters. Lavinia's decisive, solitary retreat into the family mansion in the final scene of *Mourning* offered a far more assertive theatrical gesture than Nina's retreat from the world into a resigned and passionless marriage with Marsden.

A Moon for the Misbegotten: The limits of female representation

In his final completed work, he glanced back to 1923, the year his older brother Jim died, leaving O'Neill himself the only surviving member of his family. *A Moon for the Misbegotten*, written in 1943 and first staged in 1947, is set on a tenant farm in coastal Connecticut, a mostly barren enclave situated well outside, though connected to, the lively urban world of Broadway, real estate deals, barrooms, downtown hotels, trains, and American corporate power. The play's dominant presence, Josie Hogan, is twenty-eight and the daughter of Irish immigrants. "*The map of Ireland is stamped on her face*," according to the stage directions, but her body is "*so oversize for a woman that she is almost a freak*" and "*more powerful than any but an exceptionally strong man*"; nonetheless, O'Neill wants an audience also to see that "*there is no mannish quality about her. She is all woman*" (CP3: 857). Josie is a culmination and, in certain respects, a counterpoint to O'Neill's most significant female characters, his final attempt to stage archetypal American womanhood, this time without experimental devices but outside the standards of stage femininity. Josie's widower father, Phil Hogan, seems at first a theatrical cliché, a feisty, feckless stage Irishman, but ultimately he lets down his mask to reveal a more complex and humane spirit. Self-conscious about her appearance, Josie would have everyone else believe she's "a terrible wanton woman," as her father puts it (CP3: 866), an object of male desire who also dominates the men around her, but finally comes to terms with the fact of her virginity and embraces her unconventional fate to remain unmarried. Her most promising beau, the dissipated Jim Tyrone (the older brother in the recently completed script of *Long Day's Journey*), shows the ravages of unrelenting indulgence and in particular the depredations of a failed life as an actor in commercial American theatre, the legacy of his (and thus the playwright's) famous actor father.

In creating this exceptionally large woman, O'Neill defied the casting practices of Broadway. Lawrence Langner, producer of the ill-fated 1947 staging of *Misbegotten* for the Theatre Guild, reflects the practical bias of the industry in describing this challenge in his 1951 memoir: "In addition to the physical requirements of the actress, she must be tremendously experienced in the theatre and must have exactly the kind of emotional acting experience that it would be difficult for a girl of her stature to obtain" (403). As Laura Shea notes, this problem of casting led to the necessary practice in performance of stressing "the emotional amplitude of the character over a misplaced preoccupation with size" (2008: 38). In fact, O'Neill selected someone of relatively average size, Mary Welch, on the strength of her pure Irish descent and her willingness to gain weight for the part, but primarily, according to Welch herself, because he believed she understood "how Josie feels" (qtd. SA 593).

This disjunction between Josie's appearance in the printed stage directions and her inner life in performance seems to affirm the resistance to representing the feminine within a patriarchal symbolic order, as theorized by Julia Kristeva and Luce Irigaray among others. Judith Barlow argues that for Josie "the only roles she can even *imagine*—wife, prostitute, mother—are those that most reflect male desire" and that however critical he might be toward the standards of the commercial theatre, "O'Neill created patriarchal worlds into which women could fit only by assuming the narrow roles in which the male characters sought to cast them" (1998: 174). Even her pose as a shameless harlot "has been created," as Gloria Cahill points out, "not by Josie, but by the men of the town who fear ridicule if they are rejected by the woman *they* have cast in the role of town slut. Josie merely exploits the image, using it as a defense mechanism which enables her to wield power over them" (1992: 21). Within this mix of shame, pride, desire, and deception, Josie's power remains confined to the range O'Neill allows even his strongest women characters such as Anna Christopherson and Nina Leeds. The path from Eileen Carmody in *The Straw* a quarter-century earlier to Josie Hogan in *Misbegotten* demonstrates an obvious growth of vision and craft in O'Neill's representation of women, though in this final play it is Josie's "mannish quality" as an oversized and intimidating figure that must be overcome in performance to prove that she is "all woman."

Like Eileen, Josie is the maternal figure in the Hogan home, such as it is, her mother long dead. Her main duty to her three younger brothers has been to help them escape one by one from the farm and their father. Phil acknowledges that "there's no controlling" Josie, and she asserts her independence early in the first act: "I do my work and I earn my keep and I've a right to be free" (CP3: 866). Josie is nonetheless closely bound to her impish, hard-drinking father, who humors her harlot's pose, proud of being father to "the damnedest daughter in Connecticut" (CP3: 864). When they learn that Jim Tyrone, their landlord, will be along soon to collect the rent, Josie and Phil playfully envision her seducing him—"every woman's scheme since the world was created," Phil quips (CP3: 870)—as a way to force him to accept their below-market bid for the farm. Jim arrives looking drained of life but his rapport with Phil and Josie is still lively. He hides inside their house to watch as Phil and Josie rout their hapless millionaire neighbor T. Stedman Harder with ridicule and intimidation when he unwisely confronts them about their pigs invading the ice pond on his property. This comic interlude provides some early fun, but also prompts Harder's lucrative offer to Jim to buy the farm so he can be rid of his noisome neighbors. However, what Jim needs at this final, exhausted stage of life is not more entertainment or money. Though Josie considers herself "an ugly overgrown lump of a woman" (CP3: 870), in self-conscious contrast to Jim's Broadway ladies, she supplies the maternal empathy Jim needs to shed the "*Mephistophelean quality*" (CP3: 875) he wears on his face.

Eventually Jim confesses his drunken, extended dalliance with a prostitute on the train carrying his mother's body from California back east for burial. "The blonde—she didn't matter," Jim tells Josie. "She was only something that belonged in the plot" (CP3: 932). He is trapped in this guilty narrative cycle: "There is no present or future—only the past happening over and over again" (CP3: 920). Although she can't help Jim escape this memory as readily as she has aided her brothers in escaping the farm, Josie's maternal role is one she well understands and embraces. Late in Act Two, Josie offers obligingly to "be as different as you please," to play any role that pleases him, but Jim responds, "Thanks, Josie. Just be yourself" (CP3: 910). The authentic self that Jim wants Josie to assume here is perhaps yet another kind of male-sanctioned role for her to play, but in his way Jim also supports Josie in encouraging her to drop the defensive, self-degrading compulsion to play the slut.

Act Three concludes with the most memorable image in the play, modeled on the traditional Christian pietà of Mary cradling the dead body of Jesus in her arms, with Josie singing to the exhausted, self-loathing Jim "*in a tender crooning tone like a lullaby*" (CP3: 933). Far more persuasively than the mawkish cross image that concludes *Welded*, O'Neill refashions this traditional sacred image to suggest a new, separate destiny for Josie, who does not ultimately marry, wait for, die for, or sexually comfort Jim. Her act of forgiving him as if channeling the spirit of Jim's mother seems yet another traditional and limiting female role, but it serves to liberate her from her unseemly harlot's mask and bring her back to herself. After Jim departs the stage toward imminent death, Josie assures her father, "I'm all right—and I'm well content here with you" (CP3: 945)—by no means a triumphal feminist ending but one that affirms Josie's self-agency beyond the need of validation by a husband or lover. Along with Mary Tyrone in *Long Day's Journey*, she is O'Neill's most fully realized female character. O'Neill neither locks the door on Josie, to use Shaw's phrasing, nor does he "thrust her into the street"; Josie herself chooses to stay.

In letting down his guise as the ambitious modernist playwright in his later plays, O'Neill returns to the traditions of the medium, broadened and informed by the experiments of the previous half-century. He hadn't fully lost his power to shock, at least in the midwestern United States, as *Moon* was shut down during its pre-Broadway tryout tour by a police censor in Detroit who considered Josie's licentious talk a "slander on American motherhood" and insisted that words like "whore" be excised from the acting script (qtd. SA 595). However, its demands on the stagecraft of longtime collaborator Robert Edmond Jones were limited to the removable exterior wall revealing the living room interior in Act Two, replaced by the start of Act Three for the exterior action of the rest of the play. As in *Iceman* and *Long Day's Journey*, he returned in *Moon* to something closer to an Aristotelian unity of time, place, and action. Just as O'Neill acknowledges via Edmund Tyrone in *Long Day's Journey* his own limitations as a poet for the theatre, in *Moon* he seems to acknowledge his inability to fully represent women on stage. From Rose Thomas in *The Web* through Anna Christopherson, Nina Leeds, Lavinia Mannon, and finally Mary Tyrone and Josie Hogan, O'Neill creates a powerful if distorting lens into the lives of women in modern America, rooted equally in O'Neill's personal emotional mythology and the gender typology of an American theatre tradition that he could never completely experiment beyond.

CHAPTER 5
"SOULS UNDER SKINS": MASKS, RACE, AND THE DIVIDED AMERICAN SELF

In late 1932 O'Neill began publishing some reflections on the use of masks in theatre, including this aphorism with the heading "Dogma for the new masked drama": "One's outer life passes in a solitude haunted by the masks of others; one's inner life passes in a solitude hounded by the masks of oneself" (UO 407). In three short pieces in *The American Spectator* known collectively as the "Memoranda on Masks," O'Neill described the new psychology of Freud, Jung, and others as "a study in masks, an exercise in unmasking":

> Whether we think the attempted unmasking has been successful, or has only created for itself new masks, is of no importance here. What is valid, what is unquestionable, is that this insight has uncovered the mask, has impressed the idea of mask as a symbol of inner reality upon all intelligent people of today. (UO 406)

O'Neill had just rejected masks for *Mourning Becomes Electra* and was then drafting *Days Without End*, which included some use of masks but relied more heavily on the technique of two actors jointly playing the protagonist's divided self. So even as he was celebrating their use, O'Neill was moving away from actual masks in his plays. Indeed, his mix of literal and figurative meanings of "mask" in the "Memoranda" reveals the fluidity of their meaning for him, anticipating his move toward a more metaphorical, less physical conception.

The mask enjoyed a privileged status in modern stage theory through the influence of Yeats and Gordon Craig, who argued that for the theatre artist a mask should be "the visible creation of the mind—and must be a creation, not a copy" (1919: 108). O'Neill first used masks in *The Hairy Ape*, but *The Ancient Mariner*, his unsuccessful 1924 stage adaptation of Coleridge's poem, attempted to integrate them more extensively into the stage design in order "to cover the human face not only so as to accentuate movement but to reveal part of what lay hidden beneath the face" (Wainscott 1988: 142). The ritualized use of masks that Kenneth Macgowan called "an attempt to formalize the stage almost to the point of the Japanese No drama" did not work to the playwright's strengths in this staging (qtd. Wainscott 1988: 143). For O'Neill the psychological was inextricable from the ethnographic, and his representations of race and ethnicity, however detailed or seemingly critical of modern conditions, were most eff ective as depictions of the consciousness of his characters within specific historical and cultural circumstances. Masks served O'Neill's purposes well when evoking the otherness of non-Western cultures within or against mainstream American culture while also representing a character's state of internal alienation. O'Neill's experiments with masks in the 1920s gave way to a new, more realist phase in his dramaturgy in the 1930s, but they lingered as an implicit element, a "symbol of inner reality," in his representation of a self that is shaped by a tension between external identity and internal trauma.

Modernity as double consciousness

O'Neill's interest in masks reflects a convergence of the human sciences that were gaining currency at the turn of the twentieth century. In particular, the rise of psychoanalysis coincided with the development of cultural anthropology in the work of James Frazer, Franz Boas, and others. O'Neill was drawn to both of these emerging modes of human science and especially their shared interest in the primitive human psyche as a locus of truth. In the only work of Freud's that O'Neill himself had read by 1920, *Totem and Taboo* (LFA 223), Freud writes that "primitive man" is "still our contemporary: there are people whom we still consider more closely related to primitive man than to ourselves . . . their psychic life assumes a peculiar interest for us, for we can recognize in their psychic life a well-preserved, early stage of our own development" (1918: 1).[1] Certainly, Yank Smith in *The Hairy Ape* connects to audiences in this way, and the implied premise of Curtis Jayson's professional quest in *The First Man* is to uncover some primal mode of human culture, the "missing link" to a preconscious animal existence. O'Neill's avowed affinity for Jungian over Freudian psychology may be attributed in large part to Jung's own conception of the self,[2] as expressed in Jung's 1916 essay "The Structure of the Unconscious," as "nothing but a mask for the collective psyche: a mask which simulates individuality, pretending to others and to itself that it is individual, while it simply plays a part in which the collective psyche speaks" (1956: 289).

Following this logic, modernity itself, like individualism, may be seen as a kind of mask dependent on its necessary "other," a timeless premodern, to emerge as a new and distinct reality. Emerson lamented the "double consciousness" of modern existence as "the two lives, of the understanding and of the soul" that "really show very little relation to each other, never meet and measure each other: one prevails now, all buzz and din; and the other prevails then, all infinitude and paradise; and, with the progress of life, the two discover no greater disposition to reconcile themselves" (1983: 205–06). In the early twentieth century W. E. B. Du Bois refashioned this Emersonian doubleness in conceiving African American selfhood as an internalized otherness shaped externally by the gaze of the dominant Anglo-European culture. "It is a peculiar sensation, this double-consciousness," he wrote in *The Souls of Black Folk*, "this sense of always looking at one's self through the eyes of others, of measuring one's soul by the tape of a world that looks on in amused contempt and pity" (1903: 3).

Du Bois's project "to merge his double self into a better and truer self " (1903: 4) was taken up by black leaders and intellectuals in the 1920s. Alain Locke, recognizing that the African American's "shadow, so to speak, has been more real to him than his personality," declared the emergence of a "New Negro" who "now becomes a conscious contributor and lays aside the status of a beneficiary and ward for that of a collaborator and participant in American civilization" (1968: 3, 15). The Great Migration of the early twentieth century, when the descendants of slaves resettled in large numbers from the rural American south to the industrial north, created the conditions of this new syncretic cultural collaboration, most notably in what became known as the Harlem Renaissance in New York. These new city dwellers mingled with immigrants from Europe who had struggled in their own way to gain social and cultural enfranchisement. America was "where all the races of Europe are melting and re-forming," according to the hero of Israel Zangwill's popular 1908 play, *The Melting-Pot*, whose finale also includes "black and yellow" peoples in a broadening vision of "the glory of America, where all races and nations come to labour and look forward" (1909: 199). However, social critic Randolph Bourne declared in a 1916 essay the failure of the melting-pot ideal insofar as the so-called "Americanizing" of immigrants really meant "Anglo-Saxonizing" them and, echoing Du Bois, called instead for a radical cultural pluralism that sustained the distinct cultures of "minority peoples" (1916: 90).[3] Many immigrant groups had, for example, established ethnic theatres in their adopted cities as a way to maintain a sense of identity and community.

O'Neill's father, James, and the millions who emigrated from Ireland to America in the 1800s and early 1900s faced their own brand of social exclusion that, if rooted in very different conditions of migration, nonetheless shared a burden of prejudice with African Americans. "O'Neill knew, of course," writes Edward Shaughnessy, "from background and experience, that both black and Irish-Americans had been hated and alienated, even if he saw differences in the nature of their estrangements" (1998: 149). Not surprisingly, O'Neill's black characters tend to be more radically alienated from their own racial identity, as if forever trapped in a Du Boisian double consciousness. His Irish characters, by contrast, tend to embrace their Irishness as an inescapable if often, as with Con Melody in *A Touch of the Poet*, deeply conflicted condition of their being. The peculiar masking of minstrel blackface performance was an appropriation of identity to an extent not suffered by other groups represented by ethnic stage stereotypes, though the "stage Irishman" character fed the popular prejudice against that group.[4] O'Neill did not plumb the depths of Irish identity by deploying ancient Hibernian archetypes; indeed, he did not attempt to represent Irishness or its history farther back than the nineteenth century. Instead, it was African American history and African masks as images of its premodern primitivism that would serve O'Neill as the definitive American otherness in the first half of his career; his obsession with Irish identity would emerge more strongly in his later works.

The O'Neillian double consciousness is a process of masking and unmasking. Extending the path theorized for the modern theatre by Gordon Craig and championed by Macgowan, his producing partner in the Experimental Theatre, Inc.,[5] O'Neill regarded the mask as a supremely versatile stage device that sprang from diverse and ancient traditions, but his reflections in the "Memoranda" even more strongly convey his sense of a modern selfhood alienated by modernity. His dual interest in masking and ethnicity is evident in such early works as *Thirst*, produced in Provincetown in 1916, in which he played the mulatto West Indian sailor himself, probably in blackface.[6] The sailor functions in this very rudimentary allegory as a scourge of the two white characters' self-involved vanities and reflects the ineffectual anxiety of so-called civilized culture in confronting exotic otherness. The 1917 one-act *The Moon of the Caribbees* establishes its moody primitive ambience with the "*melancholy negro chant, faint and far-off*" that "*drifts, crooning, over the water*," according to the opening stage directions

(CP1: 527). The cannibalism averted climactically at the end of *Thirst* is here downplayed as the sailors try to tame their fears of primitive savagery into a more comfortable, familiar racism: "There ain't no cannibals here," says one. "They're only common niggers" (CP1: 529). The ship is a zone of cultural encounter where the elemental forces hidden "behind life" (SL 87) clash with the modern world represented by the steamer and its global commercial voyages. Indeed, the play blurs the line between the savage and civilized by portraying the white sailors as the drunken, lustful primitives and the island women as calculating entrepreneurs.

Up from blackface: *The Dreamy Kid*

The setting and music-induced mood of *The Moon of the Caribbees* provided an exotic thrill such that white actors in blackface (as the Caribbean women) at the Provincetown Playhouse could pull off O'Neill's intended effect, but the realistic urban setting of his next play with black characters required that black actors be cast for all four roles. Produced at the Provincetown in 1919, the one-act *The Dreamy Kid* featured black urban stage dialect not far from vaudeville minstrelsy, a kind of verbal blackface imposed on its African American cast. Because of the dialect's stagey artifice, the Provincetown's white audience could feel drawn into the title character's urgent predicament while remaining distanced from its underlying social reality.

"Dreamy" must choose between flight from the law after murdering (in self-defense, he claims) a white man, or risking capture by going to the bedside of his dying grandmother, Mammy, where the police will know to find him. Late in the play his tough gangster persona is revealed through Mammy's fading memory as an urban mask that conceals a more spiritual self from his boyhood in the South, prior to the family's migration to New York City: "An' yo' was always—a-lookin'—an' a-thinkin' ter yo'se'f—an' yo' big eyes jest a-dreamin' an' a-dreamin'—an' dat's w'en I gives yo' dat nickname—Dreamy" (CP1: 690). Even more powerful than the threat of arrest and the only thing that really seems to scare him is Mammy's curse if he breaks his promise to her. "If yo' leave me now," she warns him, "yo' ain't gwine git no bit er luck s'long's yo' live, I tells yo' dat!" (CP1: 688). As the police close in, Dreamy vows never to be taken alive—"Lawd Jesus, no suh!" (CP1: 691)—yet Mammy takes this as his prayer for her as both of them prepare to die. *The Dreamy Kid* offers a concise stage version of a narrative established by such black writers as James Weldon Johnson and

Jean Toomer "of the hapless southern negro migrating to the northern cities where, seduced by city life, they free-fall into depravity," Dowling observes (CC: 133), with no evident solution to the problem. O'Neill himself was less interested in any social solution to black urban problems than in how his predominantly white audience would feel the emotional impact of this representation, however stereotyped and sensationalized, of lives uprooted from the traditions that once gave them identity and meaning.

A nation's alienated history: *The Emperor Jones*

In 1920 O'Neill took this dynamic of a racial past divorced from the present in a far more innovative direction with *The Emperor Jones*. Its expressionist style brought experimental theatre to commercial venues and immersed mainstream white audiences more fully and vicariously in an experience of racial otherness, as Katie N. Johnson's essay in this volume makes clear. Determined to realize his grand vision for the play on the tiny Provincetown stage in Greenwich Village, director Jig Cook emptied the group's meager coffers to create a quarter-sphere cyclorama, his plaster dome inspired by Max Reinhardt's innovative use of the traditional *Kuppelhorizont*, that with its "combination of vertical and horizontal curvatures can achieve an illusion of greater depth than a cyclorama hung flat" (Sarlós 1982: 126). As demand for tickets grew well beyond the capacity of the Provincetown's 200-seat house, the production moved uptown after seven weeks to the much larger Selwyn Theater; it ran a total of 490 New York performances followed by a national tour and a production in London. Controversial for its apparent propagation of black stereotypes and for dialogue (like that of *The Dreamy Kid*) that seemed more stage minstrel idiom than actual black speech, *The Emperor Jones* was O'Neill's most aggressive critique of American social modernity of his early career.

Charles Gilpin, the African American actor who created the role of Brutus Jones in the 1920 production, was for O'Neill the performer who most completely realized one of his characters on stage. Eventually the two fell out as Gilpin started taking liberties with the script, toning down its racist slurs and performing drunk. Gilpin reportedly claimed after being turned down for the London production, "I created the role of the Emperor. That role belongs to me. That Irishman, he just wrote the play" (qtd. SA 37). In fact O'Neill seemed less intent on portraying the African American experience than in fashioning a racialized dramatic mask that when removed layer by layer, scene by scene, reveals a guilty national history. Notwithstanding Bertolt Brecht's judgment that the play turns an audience into "an auditorium full of Emperor Joneses" (1964: 87), the stylized portrait of racial difference functions performatively as a kind of mask that distances an audience from full identification with Brutus Jones even if fascinated by watching him being stripped methodically of the trappings of modernity.

In the opening scene, the *"cowardly and dangerous"* white English trader, Henry Smithers (CP1: 1031), is a kind of tutelary figure whom his black protégé has far outpaced in the art of graft. Modeled partly on the short reign in 1915 of Haitian president Guillaume Sam, who like Jones wielded a silver bullet as a charm to ward off would-be assassins, the régime of Brutus Jones is built on cunning and showmanship, including his shiny white palace with its throne *"painted a dazzling, eye-smiting scarlet"* (CP1: 1031) and a gaudy outfit derived from aristocratic European military garb if more directly from the uniform worn by Marcus Garvey, the black nationalist leader. An imposing figure, Jones *"has a way of carrying it off"* (CP1: 1033) with the self-assurance of a man in full control of his destiny and identity. He considers his persona as "emperor" a useful temporary mask, part of "de big circus show" he uses to beguile the islanders while seizing their wealth through graft and taxation: "I gives it to 'em an' I gits de money" (CP1: 1035). From his years as a Pullman train car porter he has learned from "listenin' to de white quality talk" that the bolder the theft the greater the thief's impunity: "For de big stealin' dey makes you Emperor and puts you in de Hall o' Fame when you croaks" (CP1: 1035).

In fact, holding himself above laws of his own making leaves him too dependent on his emperor's mask, a trap that becomes clear as he flees the palace into the forest along a carefully planned escape route. His unease begins precisely with the first sounds of a tom-tom *"at a rate exactly corresponding to normal pulse beat—72 to the minute,"* which *"continues at a gradually accelerating rate from this point uninterruptedly to the very end of the play"* (CP1: 1041); this ritual appropriation of temporality by the exploited natives—the "time of the other," in Elin Diamond's suggestive phrase (2001: 7)—is a theatrical device that first syncs with an audience's "normal" human heartbeat, then accelerates to create a sense of the increasing desperation of Jones's journey and the natives' evident takeover of time itself.

This seizure of time indicated by the drumbeat begins Jones's ruthless psychological delamination in the forest, pushing him back to reliving certain experiences in his personal life and beyond into places and times that Jones could not have experienced personally. The forest appears as *"a wall of darkness dividing the world,"* separating the seemingly controllable half from the realm of trauma that is unleashed as Jones tries to escape (CP1: 1044). These scenes correspond to tales of personal violence that he had claimed were invented to frighten the islanders; in expressionistic terms they play out Jones's personal guilt while drawing him, and an audience with him, into a much larger, even guiltier history of slavery and oppression. He falls victim to the very tokens of control that he had used to exploit the natives' fears, and now must struggle to maintain his last remaining shreds of modern selfhood: "Is you civilized, or is you like dese ign'rent black niggers heah? Sho'! Dat was all in yo' own head" (CP1: 1049). Even so, Jones sheds his "frippety Emperor's trappin's" as a burden to his escape (CP1: 1049), exposing his body and thus affirming O'Neill's insistence on casting an African American who could confront an audience with an elemental, theatrically exoticized presence.

The "Little Formless Fears" introduced in scene two are succeeded by more distinctly threatening forms as the play proceeds. Jones fires his gun at each in a futile attempt to erase them as the tom-tom pace increases. Eventually, in a kind of reverse-sequence Atlantic "middle passage" he finds himself the subject of a slave auction and then a captive on a slave ship as he joins the wailing of his fellow captives "*as if under some uncanny compulsion*" (CP1: 1056). In his final confrontations in the forest, first with a Congo witch-doctor and then the crocodile god to whom he is to be sacrificed, Jones enacts both parts of the spiritual/secular dichotomy we see at the end of *The Dreamy Kid*, when he abjectly cries out, "Lawd, save me! Lawd Jesus, heah my prayer!" but then defiantly proclaiming, "De silver bullet! You don't git me yit!" as he desperately fires his revolver at the crocodile's glowing green eyes (CP1: 1059). The final scene reverts to the play's initial realism when Jones's dead body is brought onstage by the now-liberated islanders led by Lem, "*a heavy-set, ape-faced old savage of the extreme African type*" (CP1: 1060), his primitive appearance seemingly an index of his authenticity. Combining technical skills and primitive superstition, Lem and his followers have appropriated Jones's magic and crafted their own silver bullet to kill him. Smithers delivers the play's final lines in his broad stage Cockney, "Gawd blimey, but yer died in the 'eighth 'o style, any 'ow!" (CP1: 1061), without himself having witnessed the spectacle of Jones's panic and dissolution in the woods.[7]

The realistically staged opening and closing scenes prompt the question of whose reality and whose trauma is foregrounded in the play's expressionist scenes. Audiences for the 1920 premiere must have noticed that Lem was played in blackface by white actor Charles Ellis, especially in contrast to Gilpin's conspicuous blackness. Various white leftists and black intellectuals assailed it for what they saw as its racist caricature; as Joel Pfister has noted, "the black people whom O'Neill thought of himself as uplifting through drama were, at times, white theatrical, psychological, and commercial stereotypes of black people. This was, for some, the real tragedy of *The Emperor Jones*" (1995: 135). It is doubtful that O'Neill thought of his play in terms of racial uplift, and the reviewer for *The Negro World* cautioned those who "with commendable racial pride, but unfortunate misunderstanding, object that the play 'does not elevate the Negro,'" praising both O'Neill and Gilpin for "a great play acted by a great actor in a noble manner" (1921: CR 134). Du Bois himself likewise praised its tom-tom device as a true rendering of the spirit of African music, calling it "low, sombre, fateful, tremendous; full of deep expression and infinite meaning" (1925: 186), perhaps overlooking its more expedient purpose as a stage effect, while Montgomery Gregory predicted in *The New Negro* that the play would "tower as a beacon-light of inspiration" for the further development of "the serious play of Negro life" (1968: 157). More recently, Michael Hinden has argued that *The Emperor Jones* "explores not racial psychology—if by that term one means 'black psychology' as opposed to 'white'—but the nature of the American past" (1980). Shannon Steen sees Brutus Jones's experience as "sufficiently different from the experience of the white spectator-subject to suggest a sense of distance from and control over the experience of that figure" (2000: 347). Both readings imply that the African American experience as portrayed in *The Emperor Jones* serves primarily as a theatrical mask of white experience and Euro-American national history. Lem and his followers decide Jones's fate offstage, while Smithers as the on-stage surrogate of a predominantly white audience has the last word on the presumed spectacle of Jones's moment of death, which, like the audience, he does not directly witness. The "style" Smithers attributes to Jones's death is therefore his own projection, the mask he chooses to see.

All God's Chillun Got Wings: Race and American modernity

Following the success of *The Emperor Jones*, O'Neill brought out another major play with an African American protagonist, *All God's Chillun Got Wings*. O'Neill dismissed any suggestion that challenging American racism as such was his central dramatic concern, or that he was deliberately trying to shock audiences with the troubled marriage of his two main characters, the black Jim Harris and the Irish-American Ella Downey. "Of course, the struggle between them is primarily the result of the difference in their racial heritage," he remarked in a 1924 interview. "It is their characters, the gap between them and their struggle to bridge it which interests me as a dramatist, nothing else" (Kantor 1924: CEO 46). That "racial heritage" included racial bigotry strong enough to move the district attorney of Manhattan to revoke the permit for children to appear on stage in the play's opening act featuring Jim and Ella as children from adjoining city neighborhoods. This action was an obvious attempt to shut down the play entirely and prevent the staging of its most controversial scene, when as adults Ella kisses Jim's hand in a fervent gesture of devotion. Mixed-race marriages were still illegal in much of the country; inevitably, the Ku Klux Klan proffered various threats, including one to blow up the Provincetown Playhouse and one against the life of O'Neill's young son, Shane, to which the playwright replied succinctly by return mail, "Go fuck yourself!" (qtd. LFA 281). The production went forward, with the first act read aloud in front of the curtain by director James Light. Critics reviewing the play's opening in May 1924 noted the controversy while praising the work of Paul Robeson as Jim Harris, fresh from succeeding Charles Gilpin in *The Emperor Jones*, though many reviews dismissed the play itself as one of O'Neill's lesser works to date—"a vehement exposition," according to one grumpy critic, "of a marriage between a stupid negro and a stupid white woman" (Hammond 1924: CR 371).

In moving from an island forest to the urban streets of *All God's Chillun*, O'Neill also shifts the ground of his expressionistic use of blackness from Jones's solitary, archetypal journey to an interpersonal, interracial clash that mixes realistic and expressionist modes more freely. O'Neill stresses the racial divide of New York City "*at the edge of a colored district*" by playing up essentialized attributes of whites and blacks. "*Negroes*" in the opening set directions are "*frankly participants in the spirit of Spring*," with "*the whites laughing constrainedly, awkward in natural emotion*"; this contrast, we are told, signifies "*the difference in race*" (CP2: 279). Meanwhile, "*the clattering roar of the Elevated, the puff of its locomotives, the ruminative lazy sound of a horse-car, the hooves of its team clacking on the cobbles*" all evoke a recent bygone era that corresponds to something like the nostalgic youth of urban modernity (CP2: 279). As children Jim Harris and Ella Downey play together across the city's color line, each expressing a desire to be a member of the other's race, Jim even admitting to drinking "chalk 'n' water" three times daily to make himself "whiter." The other neighborhood children, acting out the boundary separating black and white neighborhoods, impose masks that

Jim and Ella must wear: Jim is "Jim Crow," the blackface minstrel figure who became synonymous with post-slavery segregation laws in the American south, and Ella is "Painty Face," an inverted-blackface nickname inspired by her "*rose and white*" complexion and the notion that her empathy for Jim makes her whiteness fake (CP2: 279–81).

As the characters grow up the city itself becomes "*more rhythmically mechanical, electricity having taken the place of horse and steam*" (CP2: 283), and its color line hardens. Jim, on his way to graduate from high school as a step toward professional success in the white world, now endures Ella's openly racist hostility and a rebuke from his black friend Joe for aspiring beyond his racially determined place: "Is you a nigger, Nigger?" (CP2: 288). Jim presses on, determined to realize his two dreams of becoming a lawyer (the career Robeson himself pursued initially) and winning the love of Ella. However, Ella is claimed by the tough white boxer Mickey, who threatens Jim with a beating and accuses him of "tryin' to buy yerself white—graduatin' and law, for Christ sake!" (CP2: 286). Five years later, having lost her baby by Mickey and stuck in a hopeless factory job, Ella turns back to her old friend Jim, who pledges with a self-debasing devotion to be her "black slave that adores [her] as sacred!" (CP2: 294). He also plods on in law school, but in a revealing confession to Ella he describes an anxiety in which Du Bois would see the psychopathology of racial double consciousness, even amid the racially tolerant:

> I stand up—all the white faces looking at me—and I can feel their eyes—I hear my own voice sounding funny, trembling—and all of a sudden it's all gone in my head—there's nothing remembered—and I hear myself stuttering—and give up—sit down—They don't laugh, hardly ever. . . . They're considerate, damn them! But I feel branded! (CP2: 292–93)

Jim promises Ella that they will marry and move to Europe, where people are more enlightened and "wise to see the soul under skins" (CP2: 294).

Yet Ella feels isolated in Europe as the white American wife of an African American man, and upon their return to New York she becomes obsessed with the loss of her own racial identity. Her own anxiety is only increased by the wedding gift from Jim's younger sister Hattie that becomes the key stage property in the play's latter half, set in the apartment of Jim's prosperous family. The "*Negro primitive mask from the Congo,*" described as "*beautifully done, conceived in a true religious spirit,*" but also within the mundane furnishings *"dominates by a diabolical quality that contrast imposes upon it"* (CP2: 297). For Hattie the mask embodies the Africanist pride that, as a progressive New Negro, she tries to inspire in Jim. "Our race needs men like you to come to the front and help," she tells him (CP2: 301). However, Ella is just as determined that Jim will fail because his success threatens the sense of white superiority that is crucial to her sanity. Caught between these two positions, Jim seems to voice the playwright's own position: "You with your fool talk of the black race and the white race! Where does the human race get a chance to come in?" (CP2: 309). The play takes a shocking but seemingly inevitable turn when Ella, now completely deranged, stabs the Congo mask apparently in a final desperate attempt to expunge the threat of Jim's blackness, an act that drives him with equal desperation to denounce her as a "devil white woman!" (CP2: 313). However, Jim soon repents his anger and takes up his burden of loving someone who denies him full adult status. "Be my little boy, Jim," Ella asks him in the final moments, in a significant reversal of their old nicknames: "Pretend you're Painty Face and I'm Jim Crow" (CP2: 315). Jim declares his undying devotion, but this finale suggests that a mature mutual acceptance is ultimately impossible.

In the "Memoranda" O'Neill would stress "the Expressionistic background" of *All God's Chillun*, "a world at first indifferent, then cruelly hostile, against which the tragedy of Jim Harris is outlined" (UO 408). In the final two scenes O'Neill uses an effect he had also used in the stokehole scenes in *The Hairy Ape*, with the interior space shrinking so that by the final scene *"the ceiling now seems barely to clear the people's heads, the furniture and the characters seem enormously magnified"* (CP2: 311) as their lives close in on them. That the two main characters bear the names of O'Neill's own parents, James and Ella, suggests that the racial conflict that dooms the marriage at the center of this play is perhaps itself a kind of mask that covers the more personal history of conflict and trauma of the playwright's own youth. The expressionism-with-realism approach supports his stage aesthetic in a way that straight realism or naturalism could not, at least not at this point of his journey as an artist. "The dramatist does not present life, but interprets it within the limitations of his vision," O'Neill asserted in an interview just before the play opened. "Else he's no better than a camera, plus a dictograph . . . you can say practically nothing at all of our lives since 1914 through that form" (Kantor 1924: 47–48). Unlike Brutus Jones, whose demise in the expressionist forest is triggered by his own misdeeds and brings closure to his story, Jim Harris must find a way to live on under near-impossible circumstances. Especially in this play, race is for O'Neill not a documentary subject but an expressionistic means for conveying and interpreting "our lives"—that is, the struggles of individuals and their personal relationships caught in the larger web of American modernity, including his own.

The Fountain and Marco Millions as mirrors of modernity

Probing the ideological roots of modern America, O'Neill wrote two historical plays in the early 1920s that did not conform strictly to realism, each exploring the links between race and conquest. *The Fountain*, written in 1922 but not produced until late in 1925, portrays the beginnings of Europe's global sea voyages to the New World as simultaneously a quest for power and a search for beauty. As in *The Emperor Jones* its expressionist method, if less pervasive, creates moments that force the protagonist to confront the values he embodies. Juan Ponce de Leon, the legendary Spanish explorer who sailed with Columbus to the Caribbean islands in 1493, gained near-mythic status for his search for Fountain of Youth in the land he claimed as Florida for the Spanish. O'Neill presents Juan as a *"romantic dreamer governed by the ambitious thinker in him"* (CP2: 169), tendencies that might aptly describe O'Neill himself in his drive to be the leading American playwright and to create a theatre as a font of poetry and truth. Audiences and critics were, however, not persuaded that O'Neill had achieved his truly poetic theatre in *The Fountain*, and the Greenwich Village production by the Experimental Theatre, Inc., closed after just two weeks.

Having read James Frazer's anthropological classic *The Golden Bough* while researching the play for its "atmosphere, mood, method, or myth" (Bryer 1982: 19, 21), O'Neill creates as the central myth of his play an Edenic refuge, "a sacred grove where all things live in the old harmony they knew before man came" (CP2: 177). Like Columbus, Juan initially makes the long journey west across the ocean believing that the riches of China await him there. His bigger challenge in the world he actually finds, however, is navigating the religious clashes, political intrigues, hostile natives, and, not least, the demands of his own heart following a fateful love affair in Spain and an even greater emotional jolt later in the New World when he encounters Beatriz, his Spanish paramour's daughter. In the play's climactic, visionary scene the Indians ambush Juan, shooting him with arrows as he drinks from a forest spring he believes to be the elusive fountain. Delirious from his wounds, he sees an image of Beatriz, *"the personified spirit of the fountain*" (CP2: 223), followed by various figures including representatives of four different religious traditions, culminating in the appearance of "*an old Indian woman*" who, unmasked, also becomes Beatriz, "*grown tall, majestic, vibrant with power*" (CP2: 225). The unrelentingly rapture of the scene is meant to depict Juan's ecstatic realization that his search is not for a Fountain of Youth but rather the "Fountain of Eternity"—that is, not a fountain at all but a cycle, like the rain, comprising the eternal recurrence of life and beauty through death, as he declares in verse: "Ever returning / To kiss the earth that the flower may live" (CP2: 231).

In Ponce de Leon's quest O'Neill does not reprise the atavistic journey of *The Emperor Jones* as the spectacle of a racialized other; instead, he wants an audience to share the hero's vision as its own. Yet in his self-alienation Brutus Jones generates a dramatic tension lacking in *The Fountain*. Robert Baker-White judges that the play "collapses into an abyss of non-differentiation between the human and the non-human" (2015: 153). This judgment echoes the generally low regard of critics and scholars for *The Fountain*, typified by Alexander Woollcott's comment in his 1925 review likening Juan's vision scene to "a pageant organized by the Miami Ladies Auxillary [*sic*]" (CR 453). O'Neill himself came to reject it, grouping *The Fountain* with *The First Man*, *Welded*, and *Gold* as "too painfully bungled in their present form to be worth producing at all" (UO 408). Yet as his first attempt at historical drama and only significant dramatic portrayal of Native Americans, this work does reveal certain key aspects of O'Neill's assessment that America was founded not in the spirit of reason or religious freedom but rather by using those seeming virtues to mask bigotry, avarice, and genocide. Both Juan and Beatriz oppose the killing and exploitation of the natives advocated in the play by Columbus and others. O'Neill himself does not avoid the romantic cultural trope of the Noble Savage who voices the conquerors' guilt: Nano, the captive Indian elder who eventually leads Juan to the ambush in the forest, observes of the Spaniards, "They see only things, not the spirit behind things" (CP2: 214), perhaps also voicing O'Neill's opinion of modern theatre audiences.

Nano's judgment of the Europeans in *The Fountain* even more aptly describes the hero of *Marco Millions*, O'Neill's other early 1920s foray into historical drama. A satire of American mercenary greed, O'Neill dresses up his critique in the form of the Venetian merchant Marco Polo and his adventures in China, or Cathay, as Europeans called it in the thirteenth century, chronicled in his widely read *Travels*. Originally optioned for a lavish production by the maestro of Broadway spectacle, David Belasco, its premiere was delayed until early 1928 when it became the first O'Neill play to be mounted by the Theatre Guild, the company that emerged in 1918 from the demise of the Washington Square Players. Not quite a comedy, *Marco* was both bitingly satirical and mystically poetic, a Janus-faced critique of what O'Neill saw as the conflicted, spiritually impoverished materialism of the West versus an enlightened "Oriental" wisdom. "O'Neill vacillates" in *Marco Millions*, James A. Robinson writes, "between a Western acceptance of a tragically dualistic universe, and an Eastern suspicion that those dualities are part of a larger monistic rhythm" (1982: 30). O'Neill's Marco, however, a young exemplar of Western values, seems altogether blind to any such tragic dualism in his naïve pragmatism, and is philosophical only as an alternately fascinating and appalling object of study for Kublai, the Great Kaan, the philosophical emperor of Cathay.

Marco's journey begins with his early efforts at writing love poetry, followed by an apprenticeship in the family business. The papal legate Tedaldo, soon to become Pope Gregory X, assures Marco he "will be happier as a Polo than as a poet" (CP2: 397), a clash of commerce and art evident in many of O'Neill's plays. Upon arriving in Cathay, Marco's father and uncle become valuable commercial instruments to Kublai, but fail to bring with them the "hundred wise men of the West" that Kublai has requested "to argue with his Buddhists and Taoists and Confucians which religion in the world is best" (CP2: 395). Upon meeting the cocky young Marco, Kublai aims to find out whether he—and by implication the Christian West—truly has the spirituality it claims. Marco wields a heavy hand when put in charge of one of the Kaan's cities, stifling its once-thriving traditional culture. "He has not even a mortal soul," Kublai realizes, "he has only an acquisitive instinct" (CP2: 420). Marco only briefly drops his officious, naively ruthless manner when Kukachin, the daughter of Kublai who secretly loves Marco, elicits a brief moment of true selfless passion from him. But just as *"their lips seem about to meet in a kiss,"* Marco recovers his truer instincts upon hearing the triumphant cry of his uncle counting gold: "One million!" (CP2: 445–46).

As with *The Fountain*, the climax of *Marco Millions* turns on a distinctly nonrealistic scene that reverses the play's dominant perspective of Westerners peering into the mysterious East. Kublai conjures a vision using a magic crystal, and along with the theatre audience, witnesses the lavish banquet in honor of Marco and his betrothed Donata following Marco's return to Venice (CP2: 457). Reviewer Benjamin De Casseres likened much of Lee Simonson's set design in the play to the commercial stage with its "Follies costuming and setting," but he praised this scene as "perfect" in rendering

107

the material excess and conspicuous consumption of western culture and Kublai's disapproving view of it (1928: CR 548). The banquet scene plays out upstage in front of Kublai and his Taoist mentor Chu-Yin, who are "*seen dimly, behind and above, like beings on another plane*" as they watch the Venetians gorging themselves on rich food and gaze awestruck by the Polo family's opulent display of gold and jewels (CP2: 456). Marco is shown "*in the grand Chamber of Commerce style*" addressing his countrymen on the huge money-making potential in bringing to Venice the silk production of Cathay, clearly thrilled by the prospect of the free labor supplied by "millions upon millions upon millions of millions of worms!" (CP2: 460–61). In disgust at this display of materialist excess, Kublai smashes the crystal and the scene before him fades to darkness. Renouncing the theology he had learned from the Christian missionaries, Kublai declares, "Now all is flesh! And can their flesh become the Word again?" (CP2: 461).

Though cut from the original Theatre Guild production,[8] an epilogue to the published text serves as O'Neill's answer to Kublai's question. Seated in the audience, Marco looks about him at the other playgoers "*without self-consciousness, very much one of them,*" as his "*face begins to clear of all disturbing memories of what had happened on the stage.*" Indulging both metatheatrical anachronism and unstageability, O'Neill has his hero disappear finally into "*a luxurious limousine*" and concludes, "*Marco Polo, with a satisfied sigh at the sheer comfort of it all, resumes his life*" (CP2: 467). O'Neill clearly wants modern readers and playgoers to see themselves in Marco's crass materialism, yet this device undercuts itself theatrically by emphasizing his costumed otherness even while trying to demonstrate his relevance to modern America.

The play of masks in *The Great God Brown*

Marco is incapable, as O'Neill had once described American culture, of seeing "the true valuation of all our triumphant brass band materialism" (Mollan 1922: CEO 16). In *The Great God Brown*, O'Neill takes this theme and builds it directly into the play's central dilemma. He also offers his first explicitly masked hero, not stripped bare to his soul like Brutus Jones or crushed by modernity like Yank Smith in *The Hairy Ape*, but one who enacts the intransigent divide between modernity and one's soul that O'Neill discerned as the source of American tragedy. "Studying *The Great God Brown*," writes Stephen A. Black, echoing the reaction of many critics during its premiere run in 1926, "is rather like analyzing a very complex Cubist painting" (1999: 326). In no other play, except perhaps *Strange Interlude* with its relentless thought-asides, does O'Neill push a nonrealistic method of stage exposition so thoroughly from beginning to end.

Baffled yet fascinated audiences sustained a run of 283 performances despite the play's occasionally convoluted themes and its complicated use of masks to suggest its characters' various internal and external conflicts. O'Neill himself felt compelled not only to make printed copies of the play available to critics ahead of the premiere at the Greenwich Village Theatre, but also to publish an explanation of his aims in the New York newspapers. His title character, the prosperous but ungifted architect William Brown, should be seen as "the visionless demi-god of our new materialistic myth—a Success—building his life of exterior things, inwardly empty and resourceless," O'Neill wrote, while his friend and rival Dion Anthony, much to Brown's envy, combines the creative energy of the Greek god Dionysus with the soulful asceticism of the martyred St. Anthony. O'Neill links Margaret, Dion's devoted wife who is coveted by Brown, to Goethe's Marguerite from *Faust*, modern Americanized as "the eternal girl-woman with a virtuous simplicity of instinct, properly oblivious to everything but the means to her end of maintaining the race." The prostitute Cybel he calls "the pagan Earth Mother" who, by contrast, affirms life as an end in itself beyond profit or family. O'Neill concluded his public statement by asserting his overriding goal in *The Great God Brown* to achieve not clarity of meaning but to convey "the mystery any man or woman can feel but not understand" ("The Playwright Explains" 1926: sec. 8:2), as if acknowledging that his play could not really be explained.

Most reviewers had no difficulty discerning how the masks distinguished the creative soul in Dion Anthony from William Brown's philistinism, or how the dramatic device of masks in general can denote an outward self that shields an alienated inner life. Likewise, the difference was clear between Margaret's desire to keep her husband Dion masked within a conventional, materially secure family life, and Cybel's role of providing him a free and maskless sensual refuge from that life. It was the break between the second and third acts, when Dion dies and Brown assumes Dion's mask and thereby his identity, including his internal torment, that critics declared baffling. "The exchange of masks," John Mason Brown complained, "and the manner in which [Dion and Brown] merge and separate and merge again, brings on a confusion which overtakes all of the other characters" (1926: CR 505). For a playwright inspired by such works as Strindberg's *A Dream Play* whose characters "split, double, multiply, evaporate, condense, disperse, assemble" even as "one consciousness rules over them all" ("Author's Note" 2007: 95), this effect may have seemed to O'Neill fairly straightforward by comparison. A more perceptive criticism of O'Neill's challenge was offered by Gilbert W. Gabriel, who saw the "poet and the technician in him come to grips and fight it out," concluding, "It is the fate of O'Neill in so many of his plays, to imprison himself in some technical scheme," with the masks in this play "always a thorn in your imagination" (1926: CR 482–83). Here as elsewhere, O'Neill's struggle with his chosen method can frequently be the focus of dramatic interest rather than his intended or implicit themes or actions.

If not quite a self-portrait of the artist, *The Great God Brown* presents the clash between American theatrical modernism and American modernity in terms that mirror the life choices an artist must make, and the psychic and cultural sense of otherness that are, in O'Neill's aesthetic, an artist's burden. Beginning with the prologue set on Brown's and Anthony's graduation from high school, the latter's face and mask are established as distinct: "*The mask is a fixed forcing of his own face—dark, spiritual, poetic, passionately supersensitive, helplessly unprotected in its childlike, religious faith in life—into the expression of a mocking, reckless, defiant, gayly* [sic] *scoffing and sensual young Pan*" (CP2: 475). The play's title sardonically echoes "the great god Pan," a Victorian-era phrase for the Greek god associated with a lost pagan vitality and oneness with nature. Billy Brown, on the other hand, has no mask at first, apparently no need of one with his "*likeable smile and a frank good-humored face*" and "*the easy self-assurance of a normal intelligence*" (CP2: 473). Dion dubs Billy "the great god Brown," an avatar of happy American modernity in contrast to the premodern spirit of Pan. Margaret also wears a mask but it is "*an exact, almost transparent reproduction of her own features,*" with the intended effect of "*giving her the abstract quality of a Girl instead of the individual, Margaret*" (CP2: 477). Like many women in O'Neill's plays she is primarily an agent of male destiny, though with her own agenda to create a family and transform Dion into a conventional husband and father. Moved by Margaret's love and vision, Dion declares his submission to the modern order and conventional morality: "Wake up! Time to get up! Time to exist! Time for school! Time to learn! Learn to pretend! Cover your nakedness! Learn to lie! Learn to keep step! Join the procession! Great Pan is dead! Be ashamed!" (CP2: 482).

The prologue summarizes the themes and methods that audiences could readily grasp, but from there O'Neill offers a more complicated, often unwieldy mix of realism and symbolic expressionism primarily through the variable meanings he applies to the characters' masks, especially the mask of Dion that Brown assumes after Dion's death. In becoming Dion, or rather, setting himself in conflict with his new Dion persona, Brown also appropriates Dion's role in his architectural firm along with his subversive modernist aesthetic. In the first act when a client's review committee finds Brown's concept for a city government building too blandly classicist he hires Dion to fix it. "The Committee want it made a little more American," Brown tells Margaret when she comes seeking a job for her struggling husband. "They want an original touch of modern novelty stuck in to liven it up and make it look different from other town halls" (CP2: 489). This becomes Dion's role in the firm: in Nietzschean terms, adding touches of Dionysian vitality to the staid Apollonian order of Brown's aesthetic, fundamentally cynical arrangement that ultimately kills Dion's creative spirit. Dion's resulting design for a cathedral includes features so perverse that, in his own description, "It's one vivid blasphemy from sidewalk to the tips of its spires!—but so concealed that the fools will never know" (CP2: 509). Again, one sees a touch of O'Neill's own assessment of modern theatre audiences in this remark, and perhaps in his masking scheme of *Brown* he also tried deliberately to conceal his meanings from them, notwithstanding his very public explanations.

Following Dion's death and Brown's appropriation of Dion's mask, work, and persona, along with his wife, family, and tortured creative psyche, Brown's life becomes a relentless alternating of masks. His struggle to keep up a dual appearance for others as both Dion Anthony and William Brown can seem forced and even a bit farcical at times, but clearly reflects the otherness that now dominates his inner self. Dion's posthumous spirit so fully infiltrates him that Brown's own design for a new state capitol building, like Dion's cathedral plan, secretly lampoons the very institution it houses: "Only to me," Brown scoffs in the final act, wearing Dion's mask while keeping the fact of his death a secret, "will that pompous façade reveal itself as the wearily ironic grin of Pan as, his ears drowsy with the crumbling hum of past and future civilizations, he half-listens to the laws passed by his fleas to enslave him!" (CP2: 524). As Brown expects, the review committee is delighted with the design—"Exactly what we suggested!" (CP2: 527)—but wearing his Brown mask, he declares that the building that is "a terrible, blasphemous insult" to their core beliefs as he rips up the plans before their disbelieving eyes (CP2: 528). Switching back quickly to Dion's mask, he pronounces the death of "Mr. William Brown" and exits. Meanwhile the committee members discover what they believe is Brown's dead body in an adjacent room, really just his mask, and take it up *"as if they were carrying a body by the legs and shoulders"* (CP2: 529). The action concludes at Brown's home when, in the mask of Dion, he is shot as his own murderer by the police, who also seem confused by the identities of the victim and the perpetrator; finally, in a mood of spiritual exultation he dies in Cybel's arms.

At the end of the play's epilogue, set four years later, Margaret bestows *"a timeless kiss"* on the mask of her late husband (CP2: 535). However, given Margaret's blindness to Dion's face beneath the mask, this act of devotion seems primarily sentimental, a reversion to an illusion rather than a moment of epiphany, recognition, or resolution. Not unlike the epilogue of *Marco Millions*, this one offers the perspective of an audience oblivious to the meaning of the preceding action. W. B. Worthen has argued that *The Great God Brown* highlights how O'Neill's use of masks creates a mutually shaping tension between audience and actor in which "'Character' in this drama never escapes its subjection to and falsification by the coercion of the spectator, by the spectators in the audience, those on the stage, and those haunting the theater of the self" (1992: 67–68). By this logic Cybel is the strongest, most self-knowing character in the play because she so readily understands and accepts this condition of her selfhood: "I gave them a Tart. They understood her and knew their parts and acted naturally. And on both sides we were able to keep our real virtue, if you get me" (CP2: 497). For O'Neill such "real virtue" is earned by those who, by acknowledging the inescapable presence of an audience, embrace and accept their masks as themselves.

Unmasking Irishness in *A Touch of the Poet*

O'Neill continued to use masks—most conspicuously in the biblical-historical pageantry of *Lazarus Laughed*—but also strove to integrate them and the complex subjectivity they convey in more conventionally realist modes. In *Days Without End* he applied a mask to his *doppelgänger* character, the cynical Loving, *"whose features reproduce exactly the features"* of the face of John, his alter ego (CP3: 113), simplifying the scheme of *The Great God Brown* but nonetheless conveying "the idea of mask as a symbol of inner reality" that he had just recently outlined in the "Memoranda" (UO 406). At this time O'Neill was also moving beyond the use of masks, preparing to explore the implications of his own ethnic identity as an Irish American, a theme he had treated only fitfully and not since 1920 in creating the brawny Irish sailor Mat Burke in *Anna Christie*. After the failure of *Days Without*

End in 1934, O'Neill turned away from the demands of production to begin writing his American history cycle with its multigenerational story of an Irish-immigrant family and its rise to power and wealth. In its one finished play, O'Neill treats Irishness as a mask to be worn or shed according to the identity one chooses to follow in America, alternately a source of shame and pride.

A Touch of the Poet portrays an immigrant family in New England in the context of an America in transition in 1828. Written initially in 1936, the play was completed in 1942 but not performed until its 1957 premiere in Stockholm, followed the next year by a well-received New York production. With the revival of *Iceman* in 1956 and the landmark American premiere of *Long Day's Journey* later that year fresh in their minds, most reviewers readily discerned in Con Melody the persistent O'Neillian theme that life without illusion is unsustainable, and that a coherent self is a kind of performative mask sustained by agreement with an audience of others. In his approving review of *A Touch of the Poet*, Gore Vidal frames this theme in larger national terms: "What is it in modern American life (1828 is as good a date as any to start the 'modern') which forces so many to prefer fantasy to reality? . . . It is all a game. Who shall I be? Who am I? And the person who drops the brick of truth is the only villain" (1958: CR 915). By presenting Irish ethnicity as a psychological mask within the bounds of traditional stage realism, O'Neill mounts his critique of American modernity without obtrusive trappings of theatrical modernism like actual masks, thought-asides, and expressionist set and lighting design. In this stripping down he conveys an even more harrowing image of modernity's alienating effects, especially as a relentless "brick of truth" that shatters the self-fashioned yet other-dependent masks of modern selfhood. His focus in the later 1930s and early 1940s on Irish-American identity expressed this conflict in more overtly historical as well as more autobiographical terms as he labored through his final productive months as a playwright.

An Irish immigrant's son who never himself visited Ireland, O'Neill embraced his identity as a "Black Irishman," as Croswell Bowen called him in a 1947 profile, the term denoting "an Irishman who has lost his Faith and who spends his life searching for the meaning of life." Bowen quotes O'Neill's claim that an Irish heritage "explains more than anything about me" and "is something that all the writers who have attempted to explain me and my work have overlooked" (1946: CEO 203–04). Irish or Irish-American characters in his earlier works are generally figures of romantic nostalgia or futility, including the ill-fated Eileen Carmody of *The Straw* and the brawny seaman Driscoll who keeps vigil over the dying Yank in *Bound East for Cardiff*; the aging Irish shipmate Paddy of *The Hairy Ape* rhapsodizes over the bygone days of wooden sailing ships, replaced by the steel in which Yank Smith exalts. In both *Long Day's Journey* and *A Moon for the Misbegotten*, O'Neill figures Irish selfhood not as a mask but as the more transparent "*map of Ireland*" on one's face, a phrase applied to both Jamie Tyrone and Josie Hogan (CP3: 761, 857). Neither quite fits Shaughnessy's two categories of O'Neill's Irish-American characters: those "who accept the logic of the American dream" as immigrants seeking a better life; or, the smaller "company of existential misfits who can never belong" and instead "look to a past, real or imagined, that cannot be recovered" (1998: 155). O'Neill himself clearly belongs to the latter group. Failing to recover a foundational American past in his history cycle, in his late Irish-American plays he turned instead to exploring the tenuous connection of the past to the present implied in his own ethnic identity.

The path from Brutus Jones in 1920 to Con Melody in the later 1930s traverses the common ground that O'Neill perceived between African and Irish-Americans. In a short tribute he wrote for Du Bois in 1924, soon after the publication of *All God's Chillun*, O'Neill acknowledged this connection: "Dr. Du Bois speaks somewhere of how gladly people should give their own souls to endow their children's souls with a great guiding, exalting ideal. As one whose own ancestors struggled against intolerance and prejudice, I believe I can feel the value of such an ideal."[9] Accordingly, writes Shannon Steen, "In order to dramatize the problem of whiteness, or at least Irishness, O'Neill turned to blackness to represent his own crisis of psychic and social alienation" (2000: 356). In his later plays, however, O'Neill reshaped the lively tradition of Irish stage stereotypes in popular nineteenth-century plays through the modernist idiom of Ibsen, Strindberg, and Synge, as Joel Pfister notes: "O'Neill's project in his late masterpieces (which he called his 'Irish plays') was to resignify the colonized, subjected Irish as aristocrats of subjectivity" with their own distinctive and complex sense of destiny (1995: 31), not unlike Du Bois's project for African Americans in *The Souls of Black Folk* and elsewhere.

The main characters of *A Touch of the Poet* are all distinguished by their way of managing their Irish-immigrant traits as distinct from the "Yankee" attributes of New Englanders descended from English colonial settlers. Con Melody—"*Major* Cornelius Melody, one time of His Majesty's Seventh Dragoons"—grandly recalls his exploits in Wellington's army and suppresses all outward traits of his Irishness (CP3: 217). Jamie Cregan, Con's distant cousin and old comrade-in-arms from the Napoleonic Wars, and Mickey Maloy, the young barkeep of the Melody tavern near Boston, are both *"obviously Irish"* in appearance (CP3: 183) and speak unashamedly in a lively immigrant brogue. The contrast between Con's wife Nora Melody and their twenty-year-old daughter Sara is especially striking. Nora's self-denying devotion to Con is crucial to supporting his self-image as a great gentleman of higher birth but has made her *"too worn out to take care of her appearance"* (CP3: 190) or to pretend to any higher station than cook and keeper of their under-patronized, debt-ridden establishment. Nora's accent marks her plainly as Irish peasant, whereas Sara, likewise compelled to work in the family business while her father drinks and plays his role as gentleman, like her father suppresses her own *"tendency to lapse into brogue"* as if caught between her two parents' different versions of Irishness (CP3: 188). Yet Sara shares her father's proud temperament and hopes to escape her family's current lowly socioeconomic rung by marrying the young intellectual Simon Harford, scion of a prominent local Yankee family, who lies abed unseen in an upper room while recovering from an illness. Con Melody, whose father had been a lowly rural "shebeen keeper" but grew wealthy as a landlord and moneylender, attended school in Dublin where he acquired the brogue-free idiom of the Irish upper class. He keeps a prize mare at ruinous cost while puffing himself up around his family and the bibulous Irish cronies who sponge drinks in his barroom. Con is stuck between two cultures: "The damned Yankee gentry won't let him come near them," says Cregan, "and he considers the few Irish around here to be scum beneath his notice" (CP3: 186). His preening manner is *"a role which has become more real than his real self"* (CP3: 197), and never more than when he dons his elaborate officer's uniform annually to celebrate his exploits in the great victory of fellow Irishman Wellington over Napoleon at the Battle of Talavera in 1809.

These barroom cronies are the audience Con bribes into believing in this grander self, but the ritual most important to sustaining his identity involves the mirror on the tavern's dining room wall, where he recites from Byron's masterpiece of heroic isolation, *Childe Harold's Pilgrimage*, *"as if it were an incantation by which he summons pride to justify his life to himself"*:

> I have not loved the World, nor the World me;
> I have not flattered its rank breath, nor bowed
> To its idolatries a patient knee,
> Nor coined my cheek to smiles—nor cried aloud

> In worship of an echo: in the crowd
> They could not deem me one of such—I stood
> Among them, but not of them . . .[10]

This self-regarding posture and its manifest "touch of the poet" defines Con just as the physical mask defines Dion Anthony, and then William Brown, in *The Great God Brown*: an internalized surrogate of "the Other" that, as Jacques Lacan suggests, is necessary for the subject "to constitute himself in his imaginary reality" (1978: 144). O'Neill was himself known to recite Byron's lines in his younger days;[11] from Con's mouth they have an elegiac tone as if to mark, and perhaps hinder, the passing of his more glorious youthful persona. Con's opposition to the populist Andrew Jackson, about to be elected president, derives not from any love of the Yankee incumbent John Quincy Adams but from this need to stand apart from his fellow Irish immigrants who support the man he calls "that idol of the riffraff" (CP3: 199).

Despite his nostalgia for past glory, Con also sees that the United States in 1828 is an economic world power in the making: "This country," he predicts, "with its immense territory cannot depend solely on creeping canal boats, as short-sighted fools would have us believe. We must have railroads. Then you will see how quickly America will become rich and great!" (CP3: 201). With Con's prediction of an emerging modern America O'Neill was clearly situating the play historically within the larger cycle, the fifth of the projected eleven plays; more immediately he was foreshadowing the transition from Con's downfall to the ascendancy of his daughter as Simon Harford's ambitious yet devoted wife, driving her family toward power and wealth in the upstart American empire.

The fourth act highlights this transition in simultaneous offstage events. Badly shaken earlier when Deborah Harford, Simon's mother, comes looking for her son and, encountering Con in his full uniformed glory, smells his alcoholic breath and sees through his pose, Con becomes incensed by the Harford family's assumption that Sara is unworthy to marry Simon and that Con is merely seeking a payoff to block it. As Cregan reports back at the tavern, he and Con have stormed the Harford mansion determined to give Simon's father a public thrashing, but are instead set upon by police and arrested. After his release Con returns to the tavern looking utterly defeated and dazed, his grand British uniform *"filthy and torn and pulled awry"* (CP3: 264), like the early stages of Brutus Jones's imperial uniform being stripped away in the forest. After departing briefly to shoot the mare that signifies his pretense to high station, he proclaims "the Major's passin' to his eternal rest." Speaking now in the broadest peasant brogue he pathetically recites his trademark passage from Byron—"Among thim, but not av thim"—and then declares his intent to "vote for Andy Jackson, the friend av the common men like me. God bless him!" (CP3: 277, 278). His physical, psychological, and social breakdown is complete. Meanwhile, Sara has been pursuing her own scheme against the Harfords by seducing Simon and coaxing from him a sincere if sudden proposal of marriage. Their love is genuine, but Sara is also wedding herself to the promise of America's industrial and economic future that her father describes. A contradictory mix of Nora's devotion and Con's pride, Sara grieves her father's defeat despite hating his pretensions. "May the hero of Talavera rest in peace!" she declares near the curtain, adding, "But why should I cry, Mother? Why do I mourn for him?" (CP3: 280–81).

In her way, Sara admires and identifies with her father's struggle to transcend his Irish identity. In the surviving draft of the cycle's next play, *More Stately Mansions*, spanning the years 1832 to 1842, Con is dead and Nora is bound for a convent while Sara takes charge as the matriarch of a burgeoning Harford mercantile empire. This portrait of Irish-American identity converging with American modernity and power is central to the unfinished cycle plays. However, in his three late masterpieces O'Neill offers a very different picture of the Irish in America. The Hogan family clings to its feisty if impoverished outsider status in *A Moon for the Misbegotten*, and the Tyrones of *Long Day's Journey* are burdened by the American dream of material success instead of enjoying its rewards. In *The Iceman Cometh*, Larry Slade, with his *"gaunt Irish face"* (CP3: 566), may be O'Neill's most irredeemably counter-modern character, rejecting all notions of human progress. If Sara Melody's face combines *"what are commonly considered aristocratic and peasant characteristics"* (CP3: 188), O'Neill asserts the "map of Ireland" on Josie Hogan's face as a marker of almost archetypal female power that can bully, chasten, and heal but never fully participate in the Yankee-dominated world represented by their wealthy neighbor, T. Stedman Harder.

O'Neill could not embrace a melting-pot ideal of American society any more than he could convincingly dramatize a resolution of the conflicting selves that he represented with masks on stage in such plays as *The Great God Brown* and *Days Without End*. His theatrical modernism was largely a quest to make theatre a medium of metaphysical rather than social truth, often by redefining reality in terms of theatre rather than making theatre conform, in the manner of conventional verisimilitude, to observed social reality. African, Asian, and Irish ethnicity interested him primarily as masks signifying the otherness that perpetually and irresolvably haunts the self, while modern psychology was useful to him insofar as he could translate its insights into characters "hounded by the masks of oneself" as he put it in the "Memoranda." However, O'Neill abandoned this "Dogma for the new masked drama" almost immediately upon formulating it. His modernist's faith in the power of the mask could not always be realized on stage, and he came to recognize that portraying his own family, only thinly veiled in its dialectic of unmasking and concealment, would offer him the ultimate theatrical challenge.

CHAPTER 6
TRANSIENCE AND TRADITION: O'NEILL'S MODERN FAMILIES

Nearing death at Boston's Shelton Hotel in 1953, O'Neill felt a bitter fulfillment: "I knew it I knew it! Born in a goddam hotel room and dying in a hotel room!" (qtd. SA 670). The son of a touring actor, he had entered life in a Broadway hotel and attended boarding schools for much of his youth. His only stable home while growing up was his family's summer cottage in New London, Connecticut, rendered with poignant precision decades later in *Long Day's Journey Into Night*. Voicing that play's key theme, Mary Tyrone reflects bitterly on no longer having a real home like the one she recalls nostalgically from her girlhood and, according to the prevailing national ideology, considers essential to true happiness. For O'Neill as for the Tyrones, the hotel room signifies the transience of modern life and the uprooting of the settled, traditional American family. *Long Day's Journey* is of course his most autobiographical work but also portrays a culture reckoning with threats to traditional family life. If plays such as *The Hairy Ape* and *The Iceman Cometh* explored the heterotopian bonds among steamship crews and barroom habitués, the utopian ideal of traditional American family life confounded by the forces of modernity offered O'Neill an even more compelling means of framing a vision of modernist tragedy.

O'Neill entered life late in the era of the idealized American home, neatly expressed in Tocqueville's observation decades earlier in 1832:

> When the American retires from the turmoil of public life to the bosom of his family, he finds in it the image of order and of peace. There his pleasures are simple and natural, his joys are innocent and calm; and as he finds that an orderly life is the surest path to happiness, he accustoms himself without difficulty to moderate his opinions as well as his tastes. Whilst the European endeavors to forget his domestic troubles by agitating society, the American derives from

his own home that love of order which he afterwards carries with him into public affairs. (1864: 389)

As the number of Americans living on farms declined, homes became less important as sites of education or economic production. In the increasingly specialized socioeconomic life outside the home they served as a family's moral and emotional haven. However, by the end of the 1800s the United States had the world's highest divorce rates and birth rates had dropped among the white, non-immigrant population. "[T]he American family was widely perceived to be in a state of crisis," writes Laura L. Lovett, noting that a progressive "nostalgic modernism" emerged that promoted a new agrarian family ideal not as reactionary but as "a powerful tool for early twentieth-century reformers" (2007: 7, 12). Notwithstanding Tocqueville's cozy image of the nineteenth-century American family, in the post-agrarian United States, the "democratic family" was shifting "from an institution in which all members were expected to contribute to an integral family economy to a unit in which individuals lived together for the sake of each other's emotional well-being and development" (Mintz and Kellogg 1988: 45) Bonds of sentiment thus became the family's most important principle, inevitably with new opportunities for emotional betrayal.

In European drama, Ibsen's *Ghosts* and *A Doll's House* and Strindberg's *Miss Julie*, *The Father*, and *The Dance of Death* had already marked a provocative shift from the formulaic, melodramatic affirmation of the traditional Victorian family to an exposé of its patriarchal oppression, sentimental hypocrisy, and legacies of guilt. Modeled on Ibsen, James Herne's *Margaret Fleming* (1890) in fact depicts a seemingly happy American marriage based on mutual love, reduced to dutiful cohabitation after the title character discovers that her husband has fathered a child by another woman. Margaret, made blind from the physical shock of these revelations, tells him, "The wife-heart has gone out of me" and directs him in the final scene to "take up your work again, as though this thing had never happened," declaring with an admirably stoic optimism, "The past is dead. We must now face the living future" (1957: 543–44).

Late in the nineteenth century and into the twentieth, Freudian psychology also revolutionized the concept of family by recasting the conflicting forces within the individual self as a psychodrama of primary relations. Personal neuroses emerged from deep, unresolved clashes with parents and siblings, and the complexes Freud named for classical Greek figures such as Oedipus and Electra suggested a link between ancient tragedy and modern emotional trauma. The modern bourgeois "private tragedy," in Raymond Williams's phrase, was obsessed with the inescapable and fundamentally destructive bonds of family, most notably in Strindberg. "Men and women seek to destroy each other," writes Williams, "in the act of loving and creating new life, and the new life is itself always guilty, not so much by inheritance as by the relationships it is inevitably born into" (1966: 108). O'Neill, he argues, takes this mode even further, beyond Freud or Strindberg into "the characteristic metaphysics of the isolate, for whom life in any form but the suffering of frustration and loss is impossible" and whose "characteristic resolution is neither Greek nor Freudian, but simply the achievement of death" (1966: 119). Even for these isolated characters, however, the inexorability of family bonds may be the most definitive mark of O'Neill's modernist tragedy, set starkly in contrast to the family ideals of affection, intimacy, filial respect, and material prosperity essential to both traditional and progressive American culture.

Beginning with such minor early efforts as *Warnings, Bread and Butter, The Personal Equation*, and *Now I Ask You*, followed by the more substantial works like *Beyond the Horizon* and *Desire Under the Elms*, and most grandly in the later 1930s with his outsized American history cycle, O'Neill showed a distinct preference for conventional realism in his representations of family. Some included experimental or partially expressionist elements, notably *Desire* and *Dynamo*, but he seemed to hold that the intrinsically haunted nature of family relations required less theatrical innovation to portray. For O'Neill, family life and the identity of family members, however psychically tortured, was bound up in the aesthetic of the realist stage. In 1956, right after the publication of *Long Day's Journey*, Arthur Miller observed of O'Neill that "so long as the family and family relations are at the center of his plays his form remains—indeed, it is held prisoner by—Realism. When, however, as for instance in *The Hairy Ape* and *The Emperor Jones*, he deals with men out in society, away from the family context, his forms become alien to Realism, more openly and self-consciously symbolic, poetic, and finally heroic" (1978: 73). Miller acknowledges that "Realism itself is a style, an invention quite as consciously created as Expressionism, Symbolism, or any of the other less familiar forms" (1978: 70). Miller's insights suggest that in his late plays O'Neill, if far less experimental, was also devising a critical style of realism that could represent the family on stage against the grain of theatrical convention and beyond his own earlier methods.

Filial strife in *The Rope* and *Exorcism*

The Rope, a one-act play O'Neill finished in March 1918, was his first family-centered play in the naturalistic mode that would also shape *Beyond the Horizon* and *Desire Under the Elms*. In this transitional work, O'Neill stressed a realism of character over plot as the key element in his approach to dramatizing the family. Shortly before the play opened at the Provincetown on 26 April, he wrote to director Nina Moise, "*Make them act!* Don't let them recite the lines. . . . I really just want raw character in this play. You see, I see the exposition as a perfectly logical outcropping of the mood the different characters are in" (SL 81–82). In the nonetheless detailed exposition we learn that five years earlier the rebellious son Luke fled the coastal New England farm of his old, greedy, now half-demented father, Abraham Bentley, having made off with one hundred dollars of the old man's money. A noose hangs in the barn, signifying the father's apparent wish that Luke hang himself if he ever returns. We also learn that old Bentley's first wife had died, according to Annie, his daughter by that marriage, from his unrelenting abuse. His next wife, Luke's mother, was a woman of loose morals whose ill temper Annie has escaped by marrying an Irish Catholic, Pat Sweeney.

Luke's sudden reappearance has forced the questions of who will inherit the farm and where Bentley's presumed stash of one thousand dollars in gold might be hidden. Sweeney and Luke make a pact: Sweeney and wife Annie get the land and Luke keeps the gold, once they find it. Old Bentley seems oddly ecstatic that his young son has returned home, yet points wildly at the noose as if encouraging Luke to hang himself. This moment marks the crisis of exposition in the play and the emergence of "raw character," in O'Neill's phrase, with the incapacitated old Bentley unable to speak at all as he gestures toward the rope in the barn. Luke and Sweeney show their cruel natures in hauling the old man away to torture him with a branding iron into revealing the whereabouts of the gold. Left alone in the barn, Mary, the Sweeneys' mentally impaired child, pulls on the noose, releasing a bag of gold coins; gleefully flinging them one by one into the sea, she unwittingly foils the adults' greedy plans.

In his letter to Moise, O'Neill stresses a certain brand of naturalism in noting that Luke's character is shaped not only by the hard labor that Bentley forced on him, but by "his sweet [immoral] mother's influence squirming in his heredity" (SL 81). Luke recounts his own prodigal adventures over the past five years in the broader world, and his time away from the farm in the larger world has made him more cynical than even his half-sister Annie and her husband, whom he derides as "country jays": "I was green as grass when I left here, but bummin' around the world, and bein' in cities, and meetin' all kinds, and keepin' your two eyes open—that's what'll learn yuh a cute trick or two" (CP1: 561–62). Luke's lust for money seems a trait derived from both parents but has been enhanced by his contact with the mercenary world beyond the farm, especially in contrast to the Sweeneys' more traditional if self-serving goal of making the family farm prosper. The finale of little Mary flinging the much-coveted coins into the sea seems ironic rather than tragic; however, *The Rope* does at least suggest the tragic potential of the American farm family undermined by rootless modernity, especially where no strong mother-figure is present to counter the family's moral decline.

The absent mother in the recently recovered one-act *Exorcism* is the most notable deviation from autobiography in this highly personal work. The young Ned Malloy rejects his family, first through attempted suicide and then, after he survives, by resolving to skip out on them. His father, a prosperous business owner, has come to persuade him to return to the family home, even though he kicked Ned out for quitting his job in the family business. The elder Malloy at first scolds his son for a desperate act "which amounts to a crime—without consideration for your family" (Ex 45) and speculates on the effect on Ned's "poor mother" were she still alive—another absent mother unavailable to heal this rift in her family. He then assures his son that his wife loves him "like a true woman" and has withdrawn her divorce petition (Ex 48). The play's conventional realism seems torn between a standard realistic approach to family-centered drama and some mode, as yet undetermined, that could better express the highly personal trauma from his own life on which O'Neill based the play, just as Ned himself is torn between family life and personal freedom. Ned's quest for undetermined destiny—"as long as it's new" (Ex 55)—parallels O'Neill's own drive to pursue the new, as he would do soon in such plays as *The Emperor Jones* and *The Hairy Ape*, while abandoning the one-act play for longer, often less-realist forms. As Arthur Miller notes, in most of these experimental works O'Neill's focus shifts from family relationships into personal trauma. As noted in Chapter 2, *Exorcism* was a crisis in dramatic form for O'Neill, ill-positioned as a full-length theme in a one-act play, but also trying to straddle the line Miller emphasizes in O'Neill between plays that emphasize the solitary hero such as Yank Smith or Dion Anthony and the more fully entangled interpersonal drama of family.

Remaking the dramatic family: *Beyond the Horizon*

The production of *Beyond the Horizon* in 1920 was O'Neill's first major achievement in the kind of family tragedy that would shape much of his subsequent work and that of many American playwrights to follow. It marked the first O'Neill play to receive a professional Broadway production, giving him one foot in the bold amateurism of the Players and the other in the more formulaic, risk-averse commercial stage. Despite their reservations about tacky backdrops and cumbersome scene changes alternating between interior and outdoor settings, reviewers of the 1920 production were impressed by the play's somber vitality, with "none of the deadening dullness of the merely literal and photographic," according to Heywood Broun (1920: CR 61). Both of O'Neill's parents lived to see what would also be his first Pulitzer Prize–winning work. The old-school romantic actor James was especially moved by the performance but also warned his son that "people come to the theater to forget their troubles, not to be reminded of them" and that he not "send them home to commit suicide" (qtd. SP 477). He had attended a few of his son's previous works in Greenwich Village, but the period of O'Neill's initial success on the commercial stage during his parents' final years was as close to a sense of filial harmony they would know in his adolescent or adult years, even if the family life he depicted in his plays was bleak.

O'Neill's description of the interior of the Mayo farmhouse in Act One is perhaps the clearest evocation in all his works of a traditional, harmonious family home: "*Everything in the room is clean, well-kept, and in its exact place, yet there is no suggestion of primness about the whole. Rather the atmosphere is one of the orderly comfort of a simple, hard-earned prosperity, enjoyed and maintained by the family as a unit*" (CP1: 584–85). Against this idealized picture one can see the subsequent dissolution and death of the younger Mayo son Robert, along with the degradation of his wife, Ruth, and older brother Andrew. In suppressing his natural wanderlust, Robert Mayo commits a kind of spiritual suicide in staying home on the farm, as the play inverts such traditional bulwarks as farm and family, showing them to be susceptible to the destructive pressures of modernity and therefore the very sources of the Mayos' tragedy. The romantic mythologies of American farming as a noble calling rooted in nature and the seagoing trade as an adventure for rugged souls and youthful dreamers are posited as conflicting sides of American aspiration. Because Robert stays on the farm to marry Ruth Atkins and make a life there, Andrew, whom their father calls "a born farmer" sure to make the Mayo farm "one of the slickest, best-payin' farms in the state" (CP1: 588), abruptly goes off to sea with their ship-captain uncle.

This conflict is expressed directly in an exchange early in the play as Robert tries to explain that "it's just Beauty that's calling me, the beauty of the far off and unknown, the mystery and spell of the East which lures me in the books I've read, the need of the freedom of great wide spaces, the joy of wandering on and on—in quest of the secret which is hidden over there, beyond the horizon" (CP1: 577). Andrew, however, sees primarily the business opportunities awaiting a shrewd young American in "some of those new countries that are just being opened up," yet also tries to reassure the poetical Robert that "we've got all you're looking for right on this farm" including a nearby beach and "plenty of horizon to look at" (CP1: 576, 577). However, Robert's love for Ruth, daughter of the neighboring family, disrupts their father's hope of merging the Mayo and Atkins farms under Andrew's capable management as Ruth's husband. Instead, Andrew takes the berth on their uncle's sailing ship that Robert has given up so he can stay home and marry Ruth. Robert has no aptitude or enthusiasm for farm work, whereas Andrew has no real inclination to experience any of the distinctive adventure of the foreign lands he touches on in his voyages. Robert's poetic spirit is ground down by the relentless demands of farming while Andrew is uprooted from the land that gives him strength. As in *The Rope* but far more effectively, character is fate in *Beyond the Horizon* because the full-length form gives O'Neill the scope to integrate character more fully into a tragic plot rather than presenting it "raw."

The play's form and scenic methods, though conventionally realistic in many respects, also show O'Neill striving to bring an experimental freedom uptown to the commercial stage. O'Neill had been free to realize his vision with one-acters in Greenwich Village and now on Broadway he "demanded that the stage adapt itself to him" (Wainscott 1988: 17), especially in terms of length. Despite cuts his final performance script was still long enough to inspire some grousing among critics at its matinee premiere who resented being detained "in the theatre until the witching hour of six o'clock" (Dale 1920: CR 74). Alexander Woollcott found the play "a bit unyielding both to the habits of the average audience and the physical limitations of the average playhouse" (CR 68), particularly the demands swapping exterior and interior scenery within each of its three acts. However, Ludwig Lewisohn, comparing *Beyond the Horizon* favorably to Moody's *The Great Divide*, praised the "unfolding" action in which "the tragic outcome must be the last link in that chain of causality of which the earliest words and gestures of the characters are the first" (CR 84–85). In an interview O'Neill himself explained that pairing outdoor scenes evoking "desire and dream" with those "indoors, the horizon gone," suggests "the alternation of longing and loss," an effect that he believed most of the audience perceives "unconsciously": "It is often easier," he observed, "to express an idea through such means than through words or mere copies of real actions" (CEO 35–36).

Reinforcing this effect, in contrast to the happy domesticity of the first interior scene, Act Two begins three years later in the same Mayo family sitting room replete with *"evidence of carelessness, of inefficiency, of an industry gone to seed . . . causing even inanimate objects to wear an aspect of despondent exhaustion"* (CP1: 602). Old Mayo has died, and with Andrew off to sea, Robert marries Ruth and takes up running the farm without enthusiasm or skill. Soon their household also includes a *"sickly and aenemic looking"* daughter named Mary (CP1: 606) and both of their widowed mothers. Ruth's mother, Mrs. Atkins, is especially hard on her seemingly feckless son-in-law. Even their farmhand Ben scorns them, announcing that the "mowin' machine's bust" as he departs to work for a more successful farmer nearby (CP1: 612–13). For her part, Ruth bemoans ever falling in love with a man whose poetic inclinations are so starkly in contrast to the healthy, capable manliness of his brother Andrew, and she soon claims that Andrew is the one she has always really loved.

However, in the exterior scene that follows, Andrew, having returned from his voyages, exhibits a hard, materialistic outlook contrary both to Robert's romantic vision of life at sea and to his own previous harmony with the land. He remains devoted to Robert, but as the two brothers converse on a hilltop with the sea in the background, Andrew debunks his younger brother's book-derived notions of life at sea and particularly his idealizing of "the East," which he decries as "filthy narrow streets with the tropic sun beating on it" that "would sicken you for life with the 'wonder and mystery' you used to dream of" (CP1: 620). Andrew's own dreams have become fixed on getting rich in Argentina, and he hopes to parlay his knowledge of farming into success in the grain markets of Buenos Aires. "It's a new country," he tells Robert, "where big things are opening up—and I want to get in on something big before I die" (CP1: 621). Each brother is thus trapped within a twisted version of the other's thwarted dream, their fates illustrating the sorry effect of deviating from one's true destiny.

Robert's decline into illness and death brings on a moment of rapture, a mingling of defeat and affirmation. Countering both the economic confidence and its agrarian nostalgia of the era, the Mayo brothers play out the limitations of the land as a source of spiritual and physical health, as well as the false lure of wealth. In the first scene of Act Three, the farm in ruins and his daughter now dead, Robert envisions starting a new life in the city "where people live instead of stagnating" and where he can pursue his vague dream to "write, or something of that sort" (CP1: 635). This half-hearted notion of fulfillment in the modern urban world is a sign of desperation rather than hope. While acknowledging his own failures, however, Robert condemns his brother's choices as even more self-destructive. When Andrew returns once more to the Mayo farm with tales of a new scheme, speculating in grain markets, Robert offers this judgment and prophesy:

> You—a farmer—to gamble in a wheat pit with scraps of paper. There's a spiritual significance in that picture, Andy. (*He smiles bitterly.*) I'm a failure, and Ruth's another—but we can both justly lay some of the blame for our stumbling on God. But you're the deepest-dyed failure of the three, Andy. You've spent eight years running away from yourself. . . . You used to be a creator when you loved the farm. You and life were in harmonious partnership . . . your gambling with the thing you used to love to create proves how far astray—So you'll be punished. (CP1: 646–47)

O'Neill here channels Emerson: "The glory of the farmer is that, in the division of labors, it is his part to create. All trade rests at last on this primitive activity. . . . The farmer times himself to Nature. . . . His entertainments, his liberties and his spending must be on a farmer's scale, and not on a merchant's" (1892: 133, 135). Thus, when Robert dies in the play's final scene, he envisions himself as "freed from the farm," his death "a free beginning— the start of my voyage!" (CP1: 652); his case is made to seem less tragic than the hopelessness that settles over Andrew and Ruth. Some critics in 1920 found this final scene gratuitous, but for O'Neill it was essential to a thematic resolution of the alternating inside/outside design of the play as Robert earns his "right of release—beyond the horizon" while Andrew and Ruth seem trapped within the confines of regret. Ned Malloy's decision at the end of *Exorcism* to seek renewal by working on a farm after his suicide attempt must have seemed to O'Neill a muddled and rushed resolution as he was simultaneously constructing a story of the American farm ideal gone horribly wrong in writing this first successful full-length play.

The Theatre of Eugene O'Neill

Removing the walls: *Desire Under the Elms*

A profile of O'Neill in *Theatre Magazine* during the 1920 run of *Beyond the Horizon* quotes the young playwright's credo—"Life is a tragedy—hurrah!"—while depicting him living out of what seems a sunny version of his own play: "In the winter he brings his wife and baby and typewriter to the Provincetown Inn. He no longer yearns for the life of cities and strange ports; his happiness is bound up in his home and his work" (Coleman 1920: 264, 302). In contrast to this cozy picture, audiences in 1924 would see an even fiercer counter-mythologizing of the American family farm in *Desire Under the Elms*. Likely spurred by the plot and setting of Sidney Howard's *They Knew What They Wanted*, which O'Neill had read shortly before drafting his own play, O'Neill reported to Kenneth Macgowan that "he had dreamed a play, one that he felt had great possibilities," presumably beyond the more genial tones of Howard's (SA 126). The Greek tragic drama had begun to loom large in O'Neill's mind as a model for his work. The play's lively mix of Dionysian lust and Puritan moralism, along with the innovative stage design and direction of Robert Edmond Jones, also intensified O'Neill's naturalistic technique. Like the stony ground of rural New England on which Ephraim Cabot has built the farm, the Greek tragic drama is the bedrock on which O'Neill situates the Cabot farmhouse. In Jones's unit-set design with its removable outer walls, the audience could simultaneously witness the tense conflicts and sexual energies within the house, along with the brooding elms, the changing colors of the sky, and the surrounding farmland outside the house, thus creating a more integrated version of the alternating interior and exterior scenes in *Beyond the Horizon*.

Set in the New England of 1850, *Desire Under the Elms* depicts the transition in American cultural history between a rooted agrarian life and the more restless, transient existence driven by industrial mechanization and enabled by new communication and transportation networks. The end of the Mexican War opened new Western territories to Americans, and the nation's "manifest destiny" to inhabit a transcontinental expanse was fueled by dreams of great wealth, most famously exemplified by the California gold rush beginning in 1848. O'Neill dramatizes this transition by contrasting the traditional Puritan ethos of hard work voiced by the patriarch Ephraim Cabot and the promise of quick riches pursued by his two older sons, Peter and Simeon, in the California gold rush. As John Patrick Diggins explains, the play also reflects the increasing contentiousness of property ownership as the stability of primogeniture laws that had long ruled the inheritance of land gave way to a notion of property as the reward of struggle (2007: 97). After Eben buys off his two half-brothers by giving them money for their passage by sea from New England to California, ownership of the Cabot farm comes down to three primary contenders: Eben, who sees its mystical connection to his mother, worked to death by his father; Ephraim, who claims a moral right for having redeemed the land from its rocky primeval state; and Abbie, Ephraim's new young wife, with her traumatic need for the stable home she has been denied through years of abuse as a child and by her previous husband. In a conventional melodrama the outcome of this struggle would eventually affirm the sentimental values of home and motherhood by purging the external threat to domesticity—some manner of "villain"—but O'Neill disrupts convention by opening the Cabot farmhouse visually and exposing supposedly sacred domesticity itself as a kind of mask for something primal and possessive. During the mid-1800s, the American house "became perceived as an island of stability in an increasingly restless society" (Clark 1986: 24); however, with its removable exterior walls the Cabot farmhouse is marked theatrically by this modern restlessness, far from a stable refuge with the traditional comforts of home and family.

O'Neill himself reflected in 1926 that in *Desire Under the Elms* "the farmhouse plays an actual part in the drama; the old elms too; they might almost be given in the list of characters" (Cowley 1926: CEO 80). As Wainscott observes, the collaboration of O'Neill and director-designer Robert Edmond Jones "combined poetic imagery with stark realism, innovative staging with familiar techniques, and sensitive subject matter with traditional classical tragedy," and in particular the design of the house grew from O'Neill's original sketches into "artistic expression and completion in the graceful eye of Jones" (1988: 160, 161), suggesting a close integration of scenic design and theme. While avoiding the set change delays that had hampered *Beyond the Horizon*, the design also intensified the domestic space as a dynamic theatre of the characters' internal and interpersonal conflicts rather than simply a squalid correlative of their moral state. O'Neill stated that his larger goal, inspired by the ancient Greeks, was "to develop a tragic expression in terms of transfigured modern values and symbols in the theatre which may to some degree bring home to members of a modern audience their ennobling identity with the tragic figures on the stage" (SL 195). For Robert Mayo, the decision to marry and settle on the farm means giving up his dream of adventure at sea; Eben Cabot's dream is to possess the farm as a means of reuniting spiritually with his mother, and he exploits the lure of California gold and the money to expedite his older brothers' departure by sea after selling him their claims to the family property. In reversing the regional perspective of *The Great Divide*, which moves from the violent mining territory of the West to the civilized, redeeming sentimentality back east, O'Neill locates the roots of this violence in the rocky soil of New England and identifies a key facet of American tragedy in the mix of self-serving puritanism and personal entitlement by which Americans justify their presumed national birthright of wealth and land.

Following the success of *The Emperor Jones* and *The Hairy Ape*, both laced with modern American slang and street dialect, O'Neill crafted a more distinctive regional American idiom in *Desire Under the Elms* than he had attempted in *Beyond the Horizon*. Such coarse New England locutions as "purty" and "hum" (for home) have always struck some playgoers and readers as mawkish, even cartoonish; the caustic reviewer Alexander Woollcott called the production, not unjustly, "an almost perfect illusion of a bad stock company giving a New England drama" (1924: CR 414). Late in the first act, for example, Eben Cabot declares his newly strengthened claim to the farm "*with queer excitement,*" according to O'Neill's stage directions,: "It's Maw's farm agen! It's my farm! Them's my cows! I'll milk my durn fingers off fur cows o' mine!" (CP2: 331). The basis for this dialect, as for Brutus Jones's, appears to be not a documentary ear for regional speech but the dialogue of rustic stock characters in folk drama, which for O'Neill constituted a kind of American cultural mythology that could effectively be adapted as a national tragic sensibility akin to the Greeks'. O'Neill himself claimed that he was not pursuing strict linguistic realism but "trying to write a synthetic dialogue which should be, in a way, the distilled essence of New England" (Cowley 1926: CEO 80). He perceived that in theatrical performance a rigorously "synthetic" idiom could have a more powerfully tragic effect—what Robert Baker-White calls in this play a "fusion of mythical and actual" (2015: 89)—in conjunction with desperate behavior and horrific actions that an audience would not have previously associated with such familiar stage conventions or national ideals of agrarian life.

The success of this fusion of styles and thematic registers depended on a convincing amalgam of this folk tradition with Old Testament allegory, American history, Freudian theory, Strindbergian naturalism, and classical Greek tragedy, all within the framework of an otherwise straightforward if lurid tale of a family fight over property. Ephraim Cabot, the patriarch whose name in *Genesis* means "fruitful," takes stubborn pride in transforming the stony New England landscape into a prosperous farm while showing a certain gullible confidence in his sexual powers at the advanced age of seventy-five. In comic terms, Cabot is a classical archetype, the *senex iratus* or irascible elder. He is duped by his new bride and cuckholded by his son while he himself sleeps with his cows in the barn. Yet Cabot is formidable, the embodiment of the Old Testament conception that, as he explains to Abbie, "God's hard, not easy! God's in the stones!" in a key monologue (CP2: 349), even as she and Eben act out their vibrant sexual attraction through the interior wall that separates them, a scene made visible with the outer wall of the farmhouse removed. Cabot disdains the lure of instant wealth in California and values even his prosperity as a farmer only as the fruits of struggle. He had followed the nation's westward movement as a young man and settled in the fertile plains "whar the soil was black an' rich as gold"—too easy, in other words, for his satisfaction. "God's in the stones!" he declares of the New England landscape. "I picked 'em up an' piled 'em into walls. Ye kin read the years o' my life in them walls, every day a heft ed stone, climbin' over the hills up and down, fencin' in the fields that was mine, whar I'd made thin's grow out o' nothin'—like the will o' God, like the servant o' His hand" (CP2: 349). This stands as Cabot's condemnation of modernity, the "easy God" that bestows wealth through facile advantage, mechanical efficiency, and ready opportunity rather than back-breaking labor, a moral stance that O'Neill himself would find admirable as a playwright disdainful of easy commercial formulas and in search of solidity amid modernity.

Set against old Cabot's severe and solitary egotism, the mutual lust of Eben and Abbie takes on its own palpable reality, transforming their equally fierce conflict over control of the farm into a mutual passion. Eben's claim rests on his conviction that the farm was stolen from his mother (whose parents had contested the deed), that Ephraim "murdered her with his hardness" (CP2: 354), and Abbie's equally fervent belief, born of her life of struggle and rootlessness but also based in strong American cultural norms, that a "woman's got t' hev a hum!" (CP2: 335). Their affair begins in the parlor where Eben's mother had been laid out after death. Abbie approaches him with "*a horribly frank mixture of lust and mother love*" (CP2: 354) and coaxes Eben's first declaration of love for her and ultimately his sexual assent. This Oedipal merging of Abbie with Eben's mother completes his symbolic possession of the farm. Strindberg's influence is evident along with Freud's, and the party that opens the play's third and final part, set in the following year, seems modeled in part on the servants' midsummer's eve celebration in Strindberg's *Miss Julie*—a late-spring party in honor of the new Cabot baby whom all the townspeople seem to know is really Eben's. The conditions for a quasi-classical tragic conclusion are set when Eben begins to suspect that Abbie has tricked him into giving her a child so she can solidify a separate claim on the farm via a male heir descended from Ephraim. To prove her absolute commitment to Eben she suffocates the baby in its crib. Modeled on the infanticide in Euripides' *Medea*, Abbie acts not from vengeance but as a desperate expression of love, as well as a willing sacrifice of her previously paramount need for a home. Moved by this sacrifice, Eben recognizes her devotion, declares his own, and acknowledges their mutual guilt as both are taken away to justice.

For his part, the humiliated Ephraim, having just set his cattle free and declared his intention to burn down the house and depart for California, heads offstage instead to round up his stock and resume his lonely existence, now with "*grudging admiration*" for Eben. "They's no peace in houses, they's no rest livin' with folks," as Ephraim had declared at the party, feeling the unease on the farm (CP2: 363). Likewise, just before they are led off by the sheriff Eben and Abbie stand together gazing at the farm "*raptly in attitudes strangely aloof and devout*" with a new understanding of the terrible beauty behind their deeds. The final lines go to the sheriff, however, as O'Neill ironically traverses the gap between the awful events just unfolded and the commercial norms of modernity: "It's a jim-dandy farm, no denyin'," the sheriff remarks. "Wished I owned it!" (CP2: 378). The ironic tone tips the play back toward comedy, as does the reconciliation of sorts between Eben and his father, and between the two lovers—almost the kind of "tragedy with a happy ending" that Howells had said Americans preferred. The lingering effect, however, is to bring the audience back to the contemporary world beyond the theatre, underscoring the hidden human cost of the lust for sex, property, and wealth that for O'Neill lies behind the traditional iconography of American family life.

Family as mask in *Mourning Becomes Electra*

Desire Under the Elms was O'Neill's first major play to adapt a classical sense of fate to an American setting. However, in a letter to *New York Times* critic Brooks Atkinson several months after the 1931 premiere of *Mourning Becomes Electra*, O'Neill took on the question of whether modern audiences could feel the spirit of Sophocles and Aeschylus in his own three-part play. "We are too far away, we are in a world of different values," he told Atkinson. His own challenge, he explained, was "to contrive an approximation of

Greek fate for my trilogy (without benefit of God or morals but taken from the Mannon family itself), that a modern intelligent audience, as well as the author, could believe in! A modern psychological fate—the faith of an unbeliever in anything but man himself" (SL 390). The absence of a sustaining metaphysical order outside the self and family had been implicit in many of his previous works, but in *Mourning Becomes Electra* O'Neill puts this premise to its fullest, most explicit test. Updating the vengeful Greek tale of the House of Atreus to the final days of the American Civil War, O'Neill focuses on the irreconcilable hatreds and inescapable bonds that determine the fate of each Mannon within the family's collective destiny.

O'Neill made two crucial decisions in the later stages of writing *Mourning Becomes Electra*. One was to eliminate the use of "stylized soliloquies," as he called them in his work diary, a kind of long-form variant on the thought-aside method of *Strange Interlude*. He came to see the writing of these soliloquies as necessary to his creative progress but ultimately felt the need "to stop doing things to these characters—let them reveal themselves—in spite of (or because of!) their long locked-up passions," and to do this "naturally in straight dialogue—as simple and direct and dynamic as possible" (qtd. Floyd 1981: 206). O'Neill also decided eventually not to use even half-masks on the Mannons' faces and instead to script the family's distinctive mask-like appearance in the actors' faces as "a dramatic, arresting, visual symbol of the separateness, the fated isolation of this family, the mark of their fate which makes them dramatically distinct from rest [*sic*] of world" (Floyd 1981: 206). O'Neill thus naturalizes these two key techniques that he had previously used as external artifice to fascinate audiences, relying instead on intensified if conventional dialogue performed by actors conveying the appearance of masks with their own faces. In fact, in the "Memoranda," published soon after the production of *Mourning*, O'Neill would imply a connection between his decision to drop its soliloquies along with the masks: only "great language" from the mouths of his characters, he believed, could keep such masks from seeming artificial, language he acknowledged was beyond his own literary powers. He never renounced experimentation but the writing of *Mourning Becomes Electra* marks a crucial step in O'Neill's career as he moves toward achieving his vision in a naturalistic mode, and especially in formulating a sense of family or collective destiny.

Remarkably self-critical, O'Neill recognized that inventing a new tragic language was beyond his power as a dramatist; his dialogue in fact often echoes a long tradition in American drama of such grandiloquently "serious," essentially melodramatic plays of the previous century as

Metamora, *The Octoroon*, and *Shenandoah*. In *Electra* he therefore hewed to an essentially naturalistic dialogue, intensified for emotional power and thus melodramatic in a way that audiences would find vivid and theatrical but sufficiently modernized with new psychological concepts and classicized with Greek-derived characters and themes. Even positive reviews remarked on the play's melodramatic force; most pointedly, Robert Benchley downplayed the playwright's evident literary ambitions and deemed his play "filled with good, old-fashioned, spine-curling melodrama" while imagining the ghost of James O'Neill in the wings, bewigged in full Monte Cristo splendor, declaring, "That's good, son! Give 'em the old Theatre!" (1931: CR 707, 706). To estrange the melodramatic diction, O'Neill and director Philip Moeller devised what Wainscott describes "an external approach to acting" in which the Mannon actors "kept their faces 'rigid and motionless,' while still revealing the characters' suffering and repressed passion"; the effect for one reviewer was that "you finally view the players as physical manifestations of ideas" (1988: 258–59). Director Moeller succeeded in realizing the playwright's vision by crafting a style of acting that could generate a mythologizing, pseudo-classical distance for modern audiences within the play's familiar melodramatic idiom.

In this sense, O'Neill had begun trusting his audiences to perceive the effects he had conveyed previously through more conspicuous stage devices. He recognized also that access to the published editions of his plays (*Strange Interlude* had been the first such bestseller) would complement and perhaps clarify one's experience in the theatre. As in *Desire Under the Elms*, in the *Electra* trilogy O'Neill positions the family home as the dominant thematic presence but this time without introducing non-realist stagecraft such as ceilings pressing down on the actors' heads, expressionist phantoms, or removable exterior walls. In the opening stage directions the "*resentful glare*" of the windows and the front "*temple portico*" of the Greek Revival home are "*like an incongruous white mask fixed on the house to hide its somber gray ugliness*," establishing the Mannon family physiognomy (CP2: 893). Whereas *The Great God Brown* had depicted a self-conscious, isolated subject concealed behind a personal mask, the Mannons' collective "mask" is conveyed by the actors' own faces and becomes a shared and conspicuous marker of family destiny, visible as such to the non-Mannon characters and (as written) to the audience. O'Neill makes this plain when, for example, Christine Mannon—analogue to the Greek matriarch Clytemnestra who murders her husband Agamemnon back from the Trojan War—is described in the stage directions early in the first part, titled "Homecoming," as having "*a wonderfully life-like pale mask*," which one of the townspeople dubs "the Mannon look" (CP2: 896). Similarly, her daughter Lavinia, O'Neill's Electra, has "*the same strange, life-like mask*" (CP2: 897) even though she cultivates a more austere appearance to differentiate herself from the voluptuous mother whom she simultaneously envies and hates. The Mannon men, patriarch Ezra (Agamemnon) and son Orin (Orestes), also have mask-like faces, projected visually back through ancestral generations via the family portraits that line the walls of the house. Adam Brant is a dashing sea captain who becomes, like Aegisthus, Christine's lover and a conspirator in Ezra's murder; fathered illegitimately by Ezra's brother, he also has the Mannon mask-face. Even the family's longtime gardener and handyman Seth Beckwith has acquired the Mannon look from his many years of close association.

The Mannon mask projects a family identity but serves to conceal the emotional and hereditary forces that drive them. Hazel and Peter Niles, the respectable, upright siblings whom Orin and Lavinia seem destined to marry can never really see behind the Mannon façade. The Mannons' motives and obsessions are largely determined by O'Neill's synthesis of his Greek sources and modern psychological discourse, notwithstanding his disavowals of the latter influence, and visible only to each other (SL 386). For example, when Lavinia discovers proof that her mother has murdered her father, Christine plainly declares Lavinia's Electra complex, *à la* Freud: "I've watched you ever since you were little, trying to do exactly what you're doing now! You've tried to become the wife of your father and the mother of Orin! You've always schemed to steal my place!" (CP2: 919). Lavinia desires Adam Brant because he is her mother's lover and seems a younger, more dashing version of her father; likewise, Orin's Oedipal bond to their mother Christine is clear when he and Lavinia secretly catch her plotting with Brant to run off to the islands of the south Pacific where Orin had dreamed he would go himself for refuge with his mother. These "blessed isles," derived from such sources as ancient Greek myth, Melville's 1846 sea romance *Typee* (as Orin acknowledges [CP2: 972]), and the journeys of Nietzsche's Zarathustra,[1] are for the Mannons a virtually pagan, idyllic paradise of peace and unashamed, prelapsarian sexual freedom, and most important an escape from a family history burdened by "men's dirty dreams of power and greed," for which the illegitimate Brant denounces the Mannons and their family commercial enterprises (CP2: 910). A traveler himself to these islands as a ship captain, Brant perpetuates this dream of an earthly paradise, which for both Christine and Lavinia is really their hope of escaping psychological entrapment in the Mannon family curse.

After murdering Brant for his part in their father's death and, in Orin's mind, his violation of their mother, Lavinia and Orin depart to spend a year in retreat together in those same islands. Upon their return in the third part, "The Haunted," Lavinia proclaims her sensual awakening among the free and uninhibited islanders while Orin is even more haunted by his deeds and his sense of doom. "Can't you see I'm now in Father's place and you're Mother?" Orin asks his sister. "That's the evil destiny out of the past I haven't dared predict!" (CP2: 1032). He refers to the tell-all Mannon family history he has been writing, detailing his own deeds with Lavinia and other transgressions two generations back—a "true history of all the family crimes," as he calls his unfinished project, that will "trace to its secret hiding place in the Mannon past the evil destiny behind our lives!" (CP2: 1029). He hopes it may reveal what lies in store for the remaining Mannons, while blackmailing Lavinia into breaking off her engagement to Peter Niles and thus keeping her bound forever to himself.

A kind of surrogate for the playwright, Orin's obsession with chronicling the Mannon past mirrors O'Neill's drive as a playwright to see the roots of American modernity in terms of family history. In a seemingly comic scene on the Boston waterfront in the middle of "The Hunted"—part two of the trilogy that climaxes with Orin's shooting of Brant—a drunken Chantyman laments the passing of "the old days" of sailing ships displaced by steamers: "Everything is dyin'! Abe Lincoln is dead. I used to ship on the Mannon packets an' I seed in the paper where Ezra Mannon was dead!" (CP2: 987). He goes on to condemn the working conditions on Mannon ships, implying that the family's wealth and position were built on the cruel and greedy exploitation of their ships' crews. Similarly, although Orin returns from the war a wounded hero celebrated for his heroic attack on the Confederate line, his own account of events is decidedly anti-heroic and stresses instead the insanity of warfare. "I had a queer feeling that war meant murdering the same man over and over," he tells Lavinia, "and that in the end I would discover the man was myself!" (CP2: 977). Overwhelmed by guilt for his part in their mother's death, Orin kills himself, and Lavinia resolves to live alone virtually entombed within the Mannon house among the family ghosts. In this she is emblematic of a modern America that remains "unreconciled with its own history," as John Patrick Diggins observes (2007: 213), undercutting some of the most revered tenets of American ideology such as the freedom earned through acts of war and happiness grounded in material prosperity. The most pointedly tragic aspect of Lavinia's final retreat behind the great mask that is the Mannon house is her utter rejection of her family's place in the new America that would emerge from the Civil War.

The happy modernism of *Ah, Wilderness!*

By the fall of 1932 O'Neill and wife Carlotta had moved to their own "blessed isle" on the coast of Georgia, the home they called Casa Genotta, a pseudo-Spanish blending of their names "Gene" and "Carlotta." His struggles while writing *Days Without End* there brought him to this realization: "Evidently my unconscious had been rebelling for a long time against creation in the medium of the modern, involved, complicated warped & self-poisoned psyche and demanded a counter-statement of simplicity and the peace that tragedy troubles but does not poison" (Commins 1986: 136). *Ah, Wilderness!* served as such a counter-statement. In both plays O'Neill was looking back to his own youthful anarchist self but framing it in *Days* as part of an individual spiritual journey estranged from a happy childhood, while in *Ah, Wilderness!* Richard's youthful rebellion is absorbed within the Miller family's healthy emotional bond.

In the 1920s O'Neill had praised Strindberg as the first to recognize the need for "some form of 'super-naturalism' that we may express in the theatre what we comprehend intuitively of that self-defeating, self-obsession which is the discount we moderns have to pay for the loan of life," while dismissing the conventional theatrical realism as "our Fathers' daring aspirations toward self-recognition by holding up the family kodak [*sic*] up to ill-nature" ("Strindberg" 1988: UO 387). If *Ah, Wilderness!* represents O'Neill's portrait of a decidedly good-natured American family in 1906, it also seems a deliberate attempt to extend and complement rather than escape from the tragic family mythology he had been developing at least since *The Rope* and most forcefully in *Beyond the Horizon, Desire Under the Elms*, and *Mourning Becomes Electra*. In the Miller family of *Ah, Wilderness!* O'Neill creates a normative image of American modernity, not the intensely "real" force he admired in Strindberg but nonetheless archetypal within contemporary national culture whose deeper roots he would soon attempt to probe in the American history cycle.

Most remarkable in terms of O'Neill's own persistent resistance to modernity is the inversion of modernism, represented by "those awful books Richard is reading," as Mrs. Miller denounces the works of Shaw, Wilde, Ibsen, and Nietzsche that inspire young Richard's nihilistic pose and pretentious self-dramatizing (CP3: 11). His racy literary overtures to his sweetheart Muriel outrage her father, David Macomber, the very type of the small-minded New England puritanism who stands as the play's greatest evil; by contrast, his own father, local newspaper editor Nat Miller, shows a humane wisdom that tames the dangerous conceits of Richard's modernist heroes. In the final act, not only has Nat taken the time to look into these scandalous volumes and conceded, "There's something to them" (CP3: 98), but even Essie Miller has come around to seeing her son's interests as proof of an "exceptional brain" and his future greatness (CP3: 99). The frank discussion of sex and venereal disease that Nat tries to have with his son after learning of Richard's date with a prostitute likewise keeps a potentially troubling topic safely awkward and deflected from any sordid truths. O'Neill's own intellectually and sexually promiscuous experiences as a young man, recalled through Richard, are thus recast as a healthy path toward happy maturity with his modernist heroes recast as tutelary spirits. *Ah, Wilderness!* thus offers a vision, however fleeting within his larger body of work, of modernist rebellion reconciled with progressive modernity and wrapped in the loving bonds of a traditional American home.

Homelessness in *Long Day's Journey Into Night*

Not long after the successful run of *Ah, Wilderness!* and failed production of *Days Without End*, however, O'Neill made notes in September 1934 for a very different Miller family play. This sequel, set after the Great War, would show the previously upbeat Richard now "maimed, embittered, idealism murdered" by the war, his father Nat "lost, bewildered in changed times," and his mother Essie dead from cancer caused by "worry over sons in war" (Floyd 1981: 241–42). In 1936 O'Neill turned briefly back to this idea while at work on the American history cycle, then abandoned it altogether. He probably realized that a tragic, postwar negation of the Miller family's life-affirming family mythos would serve no good artistic purpose that he was prepared just then to manage. But his impulse to write such a play would persist through the next several years as he tried to distill the full range of American cultural, economic, and moral history in his planned eleven-play chronicle.

As Dowling notes, "a play idea about his family that had been haunting him at least since 1927" forced itself into O'Neill's consciousness more strongly in the late 1930s as he followed the ominous events in Europe and felt the touch of mortality in his increasingly frail body (LFA 432). In a preliminary scheme written during the summer of 1939, O'Neill planned to set his "N. L. [New London] family" play in 1907, one year after the 1906 setting of *Ah, Wilderness!* (Floyd 1981: 284). He decided instead to move it to 1912, a pivotal year in his own family's life. It marked the onset of his tuberculosis and subsequent resolve to become a playwright, but also the year of James O'Neill's final stage performance as Edmund Dantes in his long-running vehicle *Monte Cristo*, and therefore a kind of transitional moment in American theatre history. Completed at Tao House in California and locked away in 1941, *Long Day's Journey Into Night* represents O'Neill's fullest reflection on his predicament as an artist in the form of a retrospective journey into the history of a family deliberately similar to his own.

In his astute (if ambivalent) review of the 1956 premiere in New York, Harold Clurman noted that the play evoked "a period when the American experience—no longer a fresh adventure, a healthy exercise in discovery, pluck and epic struggle—hung heavy on the citizens of our big cities and towns. . . . This was the later-day period of America's coming to consciousness and no one in the theatre ever expressed it nearly as well as O'Neill." However, Clurman continued, "there is less of this atmosphere in *Long Day's Journey*, which purports to be a forthright document, than in his dramatic inventions, which often range very far from home" (1956: CR 878). Clurman's remarks suggest that this story of a particular American family, presented within the traditional "unities" of time, place and action, seems less modern than his more overtly experimental plays. The Tyrone house is seemingly presented as a refuge from the tumult and transience of American modernity in 1912, but when it appeared in 1956 *Long Day's Journey* seemed as much an elegy for the demise of the modern American family and the modernity that shaped it as an autobiographical document for the stage.

Even more than Miller's *Death of a Salesman,* notes Steven F. Bloom, *Long Day's Journey* "is the quintessential American family drama" in its "demands that the audience consider multiple perspectives on the family" (2007: 159–60). The play's release by his widow Carlotta Monterey has a complex story of its own which scholars are still sorting out; in any case, O'Neill's directive to delay production until twenty-five years after his death (1978, had it been followed) suggests very strongly his own sense of a "drama of modernity" in which he, his body of work, and his family were participants. Instead of writing a multi-play family saga across three different centuries of American history, he focused on the life of a family on a single day, addressing some fundamental themes of American modernity while alternately confronting and concealing his own demons.

As Michael Manheim has persuasively shown, "O'Neill had been writing versions of *Long Day's Journey Into Night* throughout his entire career" (1982: 4), but Jean Chothia reminds us that "it takes art of a very high order to so recreate the private and the personal in the public medium which drama is ... that it achieves intensity without embarrassment and leaves no impression of special pleading" (1998: 193). A case in point, the early one-act *Exorcism* of 1919 is not a terrible play but O'Neill suppressed it probably because it retained too much of this special pleading in portraying his youthful divorce escapade and suicide attempt in 1912. He includes this incident many years later in the third act of *Long Day's Journey* but only briefly in an exchange between Edmund Tyrone and his father. The dead mother of *Exorcism* must likewise have seemed a dramatic evasion, more than redeemed perhaps in the fully realized, deeply moving presence of Mary Tyrone in the later play. Edmund Tyrone, though clearly a later correlative of Ned Malloy of *Exorcism*, seems a far more open book of O'Neill's own youth, yet neither supposedly confessional play acknowledges the son that O'Neill had fathered by his first wife Kathleen Jenkins in 1910. The "Tyrones" of *Long Day's Journey* are in fact a family that O'Neill has invented for the theatre and therefore subject to its representational limits as well as the playwright's own selective vision. In contrast to Clurman's 1956 review, Marc Robinson shrewdly discerns O'Neill's characteristic brand of modernism not in the earlier experimental plays but in his instinct for "measuring his distance from regions of private life that neither his nor any theater can make us see" (2009: 164). Though in dedicating the play to his wife Carlotta O'Neill declares the goal to "*face my dead at last*" (CP3: 714), he maintains a distance even here from the family members on whom he based the Tyrones and whose masks, in effect, they wear. The legacy of his previous work is that the self behind the mask, no matter how assiduous the theatrical means of self-revelation, remains an unseen, unknowable other. The Tyrones in their fog-enshrouded summer cottage represent O'Neill's consummate representation of an American family as both fully exposed and forever concealed, tragic in their confrontation with and retreat from American modernity.

As in *Ah, Wilderness!* the play opens on a sunny August morning, the Tyrones having just finished breakfast. The parents, James and Mary, are first to emerge from the dining room, full of affectionate, teasing good cheer. These opening moments establish a normative image of a genuinely loving marriage extending back several decades. Soon the sons appear, however, and hints of trouble emerge: Edmund's worrisome cough, Jamie's aimless cynicism, Tyrone's dread of poverty, and most ominously, Mary's recent lapse, as yet unspecified, from her "dear old self" (CP3: 721). Then Edmund relates the tale (as enacted by Phil and Josie Hogan in *A Moon for the Misbegotten*) of their tenant farmer Shaughnessy and his "great Irish victory" (CP3: 726) over the local millionaire whose neighboring ice pond Shaughnessy's pigs had invaded, and the four Tyrones enjoy a fleeting moment of cheer. Yet Tyrone feels the old pinch of class anxiety. As a once-impoverished immigrant who has risen in the world, he warns Edmund against any "damned Socialist anarchist sentiments" critical of his prosperity or status (CP3: 726).

What seems to be the establishing scene of a family comedy, seeming at first not far removed from *Ah, Wilderness!*, quickly changes as the Tyrones being to uncover each other's most debilitating flaws and move toward what seems a variant of the *anagnorisis*, or recognition, of classical tragedy that deflects the burden of individual guilt onto the other family members. Although Mary is featured on stage through much of the play, her frequent retreats to "the spare room" upstairs and growing detachment from the men as the effects of relapse to morphine addiction forces Edmund, Jamie, and Tyrone to confront the conflicts and failings that define their relationships and roles within the family. Each embodies a particular aspect of American modernity. The elder Tyrone touts success borne of hard work, having risen from the poverty he endured as a young immigrant working in a factory for almost no pay. With the same work ethic and "wild with ambition," he later "studied Shakespeare as you'd study the Bible" to make himself "one of the three or four young actors with the greatest artistic promise in America" (CP3: 809)—only to become trapped by material success, seduced by the easy money of a crowd-pleasing show, as he confesses to Edmund and to himself. "I had life where I wanted it!" Tyrone recalls. "And for a time after that I kept on upward with ambition high. Married your mother. . . . But a few years later my good bad luck made me find the big money-maker . . . and then life had me where it wanted me" (CP3: 809–10).

On the other hand, Edmund is a fledgling modernist who embraces the writers and thinkers most critical of his father's art and values. Their clash is established scenically in the two bookcases featured in the opening scene directions—one stocked with the writings of such iconoclasts as Nietzsche, Marx, Rossetti, and Strindberg, all favored by Edmund and some by Jamie; the other with more mainstream nineteenth-century *romanciers* like Alexandre Dumas and Victor Hugo as well as Tyrone's primary cultural touchstone, the works (indeed, three sets) of Shakespeare (CP3: 717). Though not readily visible to a theatre audience, these volumes participate in the drama nonetheless in the plentiful, often dueling literary quotations proffered by Tyrone and his sons. In one such exchange, Edmund's recitations from Baudelaire make clear the Dionysian bent in his outlook: "Be drunken, if you would not be martyred slaves of Time; be drunken continually! With wine, with poetry, or with virtue, as you will." Tyrone parries this by calling it "morbid nonsense" and declaring it already "nobly said in Shakespeare," though acknowledging Edmund's skill in recitation (CP3: 797). Even more pointedly, Edmund sees his brother Jamie, who is off carousing in a brothel, as the very type that Baudelaire had in mind in writing these lines from *Les Fleurs du Mal*:

> I love thee, infamous city! Harlots and
> Hunted have pleasures of their own to give,
> The vulgar herd can never understand. (CP3: 798)

Presenting Jamie as an exemplar of Baudelairean modernism with its contrarian ethos of decadent yet more refined tastes, Edmund's view of his brother conflicts directly with Tyrone's bitter, disappointed condemnation of Jamie late in the final act: "My first-born, who I hoped would bear my name in honor and dignity, who showed such brilliant promise! . . . A waste! A wreck, a drunken hulk, done with and finished!" (CP3: 822). His father sees in Jamie's squandered life the dead end of his own ambitions and thus the American dream gone awry. Even more poignantly, Jamie accepts his father's judgment. First quoting drunkenly from *Richard III* to insult his father, Jamie then quotes Rossetti to mock himself: "Look in my face. My name is Might-Have-Been; / I am also called No More, Too Late, Farewell" (CP3: 822).

In Edmund's own poetic "stammering," as he calls his monologue describing his mystical experiences at sea—"Original, not Baudelaire," he tells his father (CP3: 812, 811)—he seeks to create a register of literary meaning beyond the play's welter of quotations from authors living and dead, and thus a language of his own, however inarticulate. At sea, Edmund declares, "I belonged, without past or future, within peace and unity and a wild joy, within something greater than my own life, or the life of Man, to Life itself. To God, if you want to put it that way" (CP3: 812). Yet he also realizes that these moments in life are elusive and fleeting, and that he is one "who can never belong, who must always be a little in love with death" (CP3: 812). Yet Jamie reminds Edmund that there is no point of origin, even for Edmund's literary ambitions, outside the family. "And because I once wanted to write," Jamie tells him, "I planted it in your mind that someday you'd write. Hell, you're more than my brother. I made you! You're my Frankenstein!" (3:819). Jamie wants some part of himself to live beyond the wreckage of his own life as Edmund proceeds, according to the play's tenuous autobiographical logic, to realize his literary potential. Yet even that hope, best adumbrated in Edmund's poetic monologue, is undercut not only by his potentially fatal illness but by his recognition that he can never quite articulate what he hopes to say: "Stammering is the native eloquence of us fog people," he declares, with perhaps just a touch of his father's grandiloquence (CP3: 812–13).

Finally, Mary Tyrone's return to the stage at the end of Act Four pulls the motion of the play backward so fully into the past that the men's retrospective confessions lose any prospect of some future redemption. Her drug-induced regression becomes the most powerful image in all of O'Neill's plays of the failure of modernity with its faith in progress and in the capacity for the human will to overcome the past. Midway through Act One some affectionate praise from James brings out "*the girl she had once been, not a ghost of the dead, but still a living part of her*" (CP3: 728). By the end of play, however, her face has become more fixed and remote, "*a marble mask of girlish innocence*" (CP3: 823) as if signaling her final interment in a house she has never considered a true home. As Gerardine Meaney observes, "In removing herself from them and from the social, historical, literary and interpersonal processes that define them, she denies the male Tyrones a sense of relation to the processes of life and death which, as mother, she is culturally constructed to hold in reserve for them." In this way, Meaney explains, Mary "denies them their relation to origin" (1991: 211–12). Mary's own fatalism is explicit when she tells her sons in Act Two, "None of us can help the things life has done to us . . . until at last everything comes between you and what you'd like to be, and you've lost your true self forever" (CP3: 749). The death in early childhood of her second son, Eugene, represents just such a life blow for her; significantly, the playwright gives his own first name to this dead child and calls his own Tyrone counterpart Edmund, the name of the real-life O'Neill child who died in 1885 at just eighteen months old, three years before O'Neill's birth, as if in reconstructing his family's history the playwright identified more strongly with his dead brother than with the actuality of his own life.

The theatricalizing of the Tyrone home is perhaps the play's keenest irony. Rather than a stable refuge from the itinerant life of an actor and his family it becomes a site of dramatic conflict and spectacle. "The play is about actors," playwright Tony Kushner insists, "about the theatre, it is a theatrical manifesto as much as it is a gravestone or a resurrection or the definitive family drama or an indictment of the marketplace or a definitive drama of American immigrant life, or anything else" (2004: 256). This quality in the play is most obvious in Tyrone himself, the actor with the "*stamp of his profession*" and its "*unconscious habits of speech, movement and gesture*" (CP3: 718). Despite his contempt for the theatre Jamie has some of his father's bent for histrionics, and his confessional scene with Edmund in Act Four is nothing if not the bravura performance he is never motivated enough to give in the roles he plays on stage. Edmund is the least theatrical of the four, but even he has his big moments, such as his poetic recreation of his epiphany at sea and the two rebuking punches he deals Jamie in Act Four. Yet the most theatrical presence in the Tyrone family, despite her strongly expressed aversion to theatre and bitterness over its effects on her married life, is Mary. She hates being continually watched by the men for signs of morphine use, but by the time she appears for the final scene with wedding gown in hand and delivers her monologue on the past, she has moved into a theatre of her own beyond her family's reach. Mary is thus O'Neill's most moving image of theatricality in conflict with modernity. The idea of home itself has been displaced by the transient, illusory theatre life from which, in her mind, a true home should provide refuge. The play's most poignant victim of modernity, Mary is also its most potent critic and gives voice to the burden of time that informs the play and a principle that may be said to shape O'Neill's entire body of work. "The past is the present, isn't it? It's the future, too. We all try to lie out of that but life won't let us" (CP3: 765). Her final line, "I fell in love with James Tyrone and was so happy for a time" (CP3: 828) freezes a moment of hopeful futurity into the now hopeless, motionless tableau that the four Tyrones endure together at the curtain.

An American modernity predicated on movement and the continuous reinvention or outright erasure of the past is tragically arrested in this moment. To know this, and yet continue, is for O'Neill the essence of tragic consciousness, like Larry's long stare at the end of *Iceman*. From *The Rope* and *Exorcism* through *Beyond the Horizon*, *Desire Under the Elms*, and *Mourning Becomes Electra*, and culminating in *Long Day's Journey*, O'Neill has focused on the American family as the primary force resisting modernity and its ideal of a wholeness that can repair a divided modern self. Yet only in *Ah*,

Wilderness! did he fully embrace that ideal, and primarily by sentimentalizing the internal and intrafamilial conflict. The later plays, including *A Touch of the Poet* and *A Moon for the Misbegotten*, forego modernist experimentation; the thematic exploration of internal family dynamics supplies its own complexity. O'Neill had learned this lesson initially from Strindberg, but could embrace it only after trying out the various theatrical methods to express individual psychology. With a characteristically American ambition, he attempted to create in *Long Day's Journey* what is either the definitive modern play or a magnificent concession that it cannot be written. As he lay dying in the Shelton Hotel in 1953, he realized bitterly that his journey toward something like truth in theatre, rejecting and embracing its traditions, could not rescue him from the drama of modernity.

CHAPTER 7
CRITICAL PERSPECTIVES

O'NEILL: BIOGRAPHY, AUTOBIOGRAPHY, AND STANDING IN FOR EUGENE (G.) O'NEILL

William Davies King

The life story of Eugene O'Neill was fundamental to his work as a dramatist, and it is integral to the way his plays unfold to critical reading. There are critics who will suggest that this tendency in interpreting the plays is taken too far, that, after all, an audience member or reader might encounter and understand his plays without any biographical knowledge.[1] But O'Neill is an exceptional case among self-referential playwrights. His plays summon up an authorial figure so distinct that it makes sense to refer to an "O'Neill play" as a species even though his plays range widely in topic, mode, and degree of success. O'Neill put a stamp of self-conscious seriousness on every play he wrote, leaving an impression of the self-aware, self-attentive signifying mode he adopted as an artist. The self he featured was a constructed and performed self, a fiction of his own devising, complicated by the facts of his identity (class, gender, ethnicity, etc.) and the quotidian and tragically beset life he endured. This essay looks at the life both lived and created by O'Neill in conjunction with the multiple perspectives on that life revealed by biography.

O'Neill's existence began in trauma, developed in introspection, suffered in awakening, and healed in a series of dramatic re-creations, which gave him not just wealth and acclaim but also solace. The "O'Neill" he cultivated through his career was an idealized stand-in for the tormented existence he suffered as "Gene." His dramas were a variable synthesis of the two. They clash in some works, fuse in others, and usually operate in ambiguous relation, so the biographies and external depictions must always tangle with the autobiographical and performative O'Neill. The inquiry never resolves because the work troubles the life, just as the life troubles the work, within an inconsistent periphery of history (social, literary, theatrical, etc.). The more one reads of O'Neill and the more closely one reads any particular O'Neill work, the more one faces an O'Neillness that transcends any single play or any biographical depiction. Through the man one finds the plays (where the playwright seeks the man), and through the plays one finds the man (who was always in pursuit of the play), and the life story of O'Neill is caught in this endless traversal.

What O'Neill did spontaneously was what is now known as personal branding. This activity, which has flourished in the age of social media, refers to a calculated manipulation of how the world views "you," that is, your identity within the medium, for purposes of profit, fame, or self-advancement. The degree of calculation with which a personal brand is constructed is counterbalanced by serendipity or even dysfunction, but people these days often go to great lengths to contrive or calculate a personal brand. Drawing upon a network of followers and creative acts of self-definition in a widely recognized form, personal branding has come to be seen as an essential element in the performing and media arts where it amounts to a sort of folk auteurism. Within a system of cultural and economic relations (like the Hollywood studios), the personally branded artist both creates and is created (like the auteur). O'Neill worked within the theatrical and literary systems and within larger systems of race and gender to define and be defined by a brand known as "O'Neill."[2]

O'Neill's personal branding came from no outsider perspective. He had immersed himself in the arts from his earliest years, and as he was cultivating himself as an iconic artist he would have been vividly aware of such American precursors as Walt Whitman and Mark Twain, both of whom became recognizable, performed, suitably costumed and groomed public figures, as well as widely read writers. O'Neill's models in the dramatic world were not American. Henrik Ibsen, August Strindberg, and George Bernard Shaw crafted strong personal brands, but American playwrights such as Augustus Thomas, Augustin Daly, and Charles Hoyt were content with being playsmiths for the star actors who would brand a theatrical product, as O'Neill's father had done with *Monte Cristo*. O'Neill aimed for a stronger authorial role right from the start, featuring his bold self-determination both as subject and as object. He would play the role he crafted for himself, as heroic in its own way as his father's, with conviction and skill, costuming and grooming himself in a way not unlike his models, for his entire career. Thus, the first biography of O'Neill was written by O'Neill, and, influenced by the autobiographical writing of Strindberg and the self-focused writings of American romanticism, he never entirely abandoned the project in the conceptualizing of his plays or the presentation of himself in the public eye.

Early in 1913, while he was recuperating from tuberculosis in a sanatorium, O'Neill resolved to make the transition from writer to author—and his aim was to be more than just a professional playwright. He wanted to epitomize in the American theatre the kind of artistic aspiration that was being defined by the European writers mentioned above, and he wanted that sort of artistry to be associated with the name O'Neill.[3] Not yet twenty-five, he had published a little poetry in the local newspaper while living with his parents, but the poems demonstrate a talent more imitative than original, and it seemed clear even to him that he lacked the talent or instinct to be more than a mediocre poet. He had a vantage point on the commercial theatre from observing his father's career as a star actor, and even the best of what he saw there he disliked artistically, though he would never disdain the material advantages of success or the authority of a strong character well played. The earliest sign that O'Neill was conceiving himself as a playwright is an article that appeared in the *New London Telegraph* on August 20, 1913 (less than three months after his release from the sanatorium), announcing "his first venture into theater writing" after "much worthy verse." *A Wife for a Life* was referred to as a vaudeville sketch, but emphasis was laid on the fact that he had "received the copyright for the act from Washington" and expected imminent production. Whatever effort he made "to market it" came to nothing, but the terms in this small news item reflect an early sense of professional intention as an author (SP 258–59).

The market for new American plays was rich, as Broadway and its tributaries were building to the peak point of theatrical prominence, the mid-1920s, aiming to answer audience demand for new, homegrown drama, plays that would express a modern, suddenly world-dominant American society. Theatrical pundits such as Montrose J. Moses in *The American Dramatist* (1910) and Richard Burton in *The New American Drama* (1913) made the case for a specifically American play, one that would express the reality of a geographically and demographically diverse country and the ideals of freedom and self-determination on which it was founded. Little evidence can be found that O'Neill saw his American predecessors and contemporaries (such as Bronson Howard, William Vaughn Moody, and Edward Sheldon) as models.[4] Instead, O'Neill concentrated on the plays of Ibsen and the Irish Literary Revival, and he was alert to Strindberg's writing from the moment of its earliest translations into English in the 1910s. He might well have noted that Huntly Carter's *The New Spirit in*

Drama and Art (1913) considered artistic advances in cities such as Zurich and Budapest, as well as London, Berlin, and Moscow, but made virtually no mention of America. By the following year, he would have been aware of Hiram Moderwell's *The Theatre of To-Day* (1914), which reported on the advances in a rapidly developing theatre artistry in Europe and strove to relate the new stagecraft to some trends in American theatre, such as the scenic realism of David Belasco. What Moderwell found conspicuously absent was an American drama worthy of such experimentation. Only 3 pages out of 322 address American plays.[5] The point is, O'Neill's quest to define a new American drama was not a solitary endeavor, and the serious modern American play was not "born" with the arrival of Eugene O'Neill, as some have said. Instead, he was operating within—and aware of—an ongoing project to expand the vocabulary of the American stage to give it world stature. The pundits suggest that what was needed was a playwright with a distinctive vision and the singular authority to coordinate the multiple artists of the theatre in a unified creation. O'Neill saw that as an attainable goal.

O'Neill's earliest plays show him groping for a distinctive and potent mode of expression to match the declaration he made in a 1914 letter to George Pierce Baker of Harvard University, whom he sought out as a teacher of playwriting: "I want to be an artist or nothing." What he expressly did not wish was "to become a mediocre journey-man playwright" (SL 26). He signed the letter "Eugene G. O'Neill," and he maintained that middle initial in his authorial "brand" until at least 1922.[6] He was constituting a unique self for his writing, and the Latin word for "I," *ego*, served that purpose. In that very first play, *A Wife for a Life*, one can find elements of the autobiographical worked into the contrived storyline.[7] At the suggestion of the drama critic Clayton Hamilton, who summered nearby in New London and was a friend of his father, he used his two years of experience working occasionally at sea as the material for gritty one-acts, which had the ring of authenticity, unlike much theatrical "realism," because he could draw on his personal experience. Consequently, he came to be known as the writer who had that sort of unusual background for a playwright. On the strength of his conviction about those early plays, and with his father's financial backing, he published a collection with the unusual title *Thirst*. Though the plays are not especially good, the book declares the thirst of that E.G.O. for recognition on his own terms.

Months later, midway through his year of study with Professor Baker at Harvard, O'Neill posed for a photograph taken by a fellow lodger at his boarding house, and it is truly a "portrait of the artist as a young man," taken at a moment when he was probably reading James Joyce's novel of that title, then being serialized in a prominent journal called *The Egoist* (see Figure 1). The book jacket author photo was not yet an established phenomenon in publishing, but this picture seems to do exactly the work implied by Joyce's famous title. American magazines like *Vanity Fair* and *Theatre* were at that

Figure 1 Eugene O'Neill early in 1915 in Cambridge, Massachusetts. Photograph by Daniel Hiebert. (Louis Sheaffer-Eugene O'Neill Collection, Linda Lear Center for Special Collections and Archives, Connecticut College.)

time taking advantage of new and better technologies for reproducing photographs of celebrities, though actors were more often featured than authors. The photographer here captures O'Neill in a way that anticipates a long line of pictures of the hard-working (but dashing) author, "interrupted." His newly regrown mustache takes the place of a smile to suggest his serious intent, and the lamp overhead figures a difficult reach into the darkness.[8]

This was the first of many posed photographs taken over the next three decades of his career by such outstanding celebrity photographers as Nickolas Muray, Edward Steichen, Carl Van Vechten, Arnold Newman, and Horace Bristol, in which he scowls at the camera from behind that mask of deep seriousness. He managed similarly several published interviews and profiles during the early years of his career, in which he typically represented himself as an artist dwelling in solitude and plumbing the depths, thus erasing wife, children, theatrical associates, and anyone associated with the box office, including the audience. The result was similar to what he knew of Joyce's self-portrayal in that he portrayed himself as an iconoclast and outsider to conventional values, one who could mix joke and tragedy in the same sentence. But he had also absorbed some of Strindberg's exalted pride in madness and meanness, running rings around the moderate values and average talent of his contemporaries. American notions of rugged independence also figured into the mix. However you figure the ingredients, O'Neill managed to create an image of himself alone with his genius, a self-possessed, unapproachable master builder grappling with immortality.

By the late 1920s, he removed himself as far as possible from the gossip-mongering press, which was more interested in scandal than success, but he continued to pose before the lenses of the foremost portrait photographers. His second wife, Agnes Boulton, wrote of his habit of looking at himself in any mirror, "as if desiring to find a companion who could understand him," and his friend and collaborator George Cram Cook once commented, upon seeing O'Neill regarding himself in a mirror, "You're the most conceited man I've ever known," to which O'Neill replied, "I just want to be sure I'm here" (qtd. SP 240). One might associate this behavior with some sort of existential anxiety ("Life is for each man a solitary cell whose walls are mirrors," says the title character in *Lazarus Laughed* [CP2: 572]). Or one can understand that he needed periodically to check on his mask, without which he could not play the role of O'Neill-the-playwright-destined-for-greatness. In ancient art, actors were often depicted staring into the empty eyes of the mask of the character they were to enact, in search of the being who sees the world of the play through those eyes. Much of the art of acting—and knowing one's role in a larger sense—comes down to effecting a passage through the metaphor of those empty eyes. O'Neill's eyes were repeatedly described as "deep" and suggestive of inner currents. When on rare occasions he was photographed smiling, that dimension drops away. In a 1931 photograph, taken upon his return from Europe for the production of *Mourning Becomes Electra*, the grin fits awkwardly, artificially on his face, as if the left side would laugh while the right would rather not (see Figure 2).[9]

The main way O'Neill figured himself as a public icon was in the impression he gave of himself as a generator of the unpredictable, the original, and the far-reaching in his plays. He did not repeat his successes

Figure 2 Eugene O'Neill in 1931. Photographer unknown. (Louis Sheaffer-Eugene O'Neill Collection, Linda Lear Center for Special Collections and Archives, Connecticut College.)

merely because they had succeeded, and he did not eschew his failures merely because they had not. What defined his plays during the first two decades of his career was their quality of uncontainment. Once he came to be known as a writer who portrayed life at sea in his early plays, he entirely stopped writing plays of the sea. When he came to be seen as a writer who investigated modern American life, he then wrote about historical subjects, plays of myth and the Bible and China. When someone drew attention to his skill in constructing coherent dramatic structure, he turned to plays that aspired to the novel. When attention came to him for writing plays that address the experience of African Americans, he dropped that subject. He's recognized as an Irish-American playwright, most of whose plays do not have an Irish connection. His plays seem to center on male experience, and then he writes a nine-act drama about a woman. If you identify him as an American playwright who experimented with expressionism, you have to address the fact that he publicly stated his rejection of many of its principles and methods.[10] He rejects Catholicism, but then he writes a manifestly Catholic play. He's seen as a writer who addresses depth psychology in his characterization, but he denies the influence of Freud. He seems to be intent on resisting definition, defiant against inclusion in any larger trend or pattern. Even the term "American playwright" seems to fit poorly, given his frequent repudiation of the political and aesthetic values of his country, and yet calling him revolutionary seems equally inadequate.

This O'Neill *sui generis* reflects an urge to realize the Nietzschean *Übermensch* (superman), who will not be defined by the other. Of course, the plays had to be written by a human O'Neill, who would fail nearly as often as he succeeded in the *Übermensch* quest or just in gaining the praise of critics and a decent following among audiences. But the totality of that work over the first two decades constitutes a "life story" of the entity known as Eugene O'Neill, who would be the Nobel laureate of 1936. The presentation address by Per Hallström of the Swedish Academy reviews the wide range of O'Neill's work, noting its affiliations with one or another trend in modern literature, and then, not to conclude that the author is merely eclectic, adds: "Yet in essential matters, he himself has always been the same in the exuberant and unrestrainably lively play of his imagination, in his never-wearying delight in giving shape to the ideas, whether emanating from within or without, that have jostled one another in the depths of his contemplative nature, and, perhaps first and foremost, in his possession of a proudly and ruggedly independent character." Singularity of character thus gives a virtual unity of form and signification ("for him life as a whole quite early came to signify tragedy"), and that singularity takes shape in the work as O'Neill ("Award Ceremony Speech").

Having reached that landmark of recognition, O'Neill did the predictably unpredictable thing and removed himself almost entirely from the public eye. A few rumors would leak out about an inconceivably grandiose project on which he was working (the so-called cycle), and he was known to have removed himself as far from Broadway as possible in the United States, to a ranch in the California hill country. The displaced "life" story he was telling in this self-sequestering was in an ever-lengthening series of plays covering American social history and its shaping values, from 1754 to the present moment, but he bogged down in the project, perhaps because he kept discovering intimations of his personal and family history. Also during these same years, his health was breaking down, such that he could not be in Stockholm to receive the Nobel, and within a few years there were days when he could not even hold a pencil to write. Feeling old and in retreat from the world, which was just then going to world war, he turned directly inward to memory, or in a sense memoir, in constructing his final plays. The specific details and implicit characterizations of these plays confirm that the works are autobiographical, meaning that aspects of O'Neill the man, as filtered and reconstructed by O'Neill the author, must be discerned.

In these plays, especially *Long Day's Journey Into Night*, the consummate author attempted to reconcile with the failing man from the doomed family, of which union art was to be made. The earlier writings that have a discernibly autobiographical element (especially *Exorcism, All God's Chillun Got Wings, Welded,* and *The Great God Brown*) all seem cynical by comparison, as if the inclusion of his life story in the dramatic material was an inside joke meant only for himself. The later plays seem to drop the sarcastic attitude, offering instead in their self-portraits (Larry in *The Iceman Cometh*, Edmund in *Long Day's Journey*) and their family portrayals (Jamie in *Long Day's Journey* and Jim in *A Moon for the Misbegotten*) a more sincere and sympathetic response to characters whose cynicism is seen as a hindrance in their lives. In these plays O'Neill laid the grounds for a revisionary reading of the creation called O'Neill. The "life" he was reflecting in these works was not *Übermensch* but *Untermensch*, the O'Neill of failed attainment and lower depths. The *telos* of his autobiographical plot was to become the man who had "the faith in love that enabled [him] to face [his] dead at last and write this play [*Long Day's Journey*]—write it with deep pity and understanding and forgiveness for *all* the four haunted Tyrones" (CP3: 714). With that gesture he could at last put down his pen and play out the gruesome pathos of how his life would actually come to an end, in no way so decorously or saintly. The stage sometimes allows for a mythic final curtain, as when Henry Irving spoke his final words on a stage, moments before he expired in 1905—the words of Tennyson's *Becket*: "Through night to light, *into Thy Hands*, O Lord, *into Thy Hands!*"[11] Eugene O'Neill's father, a more-than-capable romantic actor, might have carried off such a noble line on a stage, but his son reported that James O'Neill's final words (in 1920) were: "Glad to go, boy, a better sort of life—another sort—somewhere. . . . This sort of life—froth!—rotten!—all of it—no good" (LFA 202). The final curtain—the *telos* effect of a life story—draws on a genre of moralizing about the purpose of life, which provides the frame of the biography. O'Neill indicated in his inscription of *Long Day's Journey* to his wife, Carlotta, that he intended for the frame of his life story to begin and end with his "Journey into Light—into love" (CP3: 714). So he would solemnly transmit his *Night* into the hands of biographers with no hint of cynicism.

O'Neill was profiled, and his life and career recounted, numerous times during his lifetime, notably in Barrett H. Clark's *Eugene O'Neill: The Man and His Plays*, which initially appeared in 1926 and then in several revised versions through 1947.[12] Clark's chronicle organizes the public record of the plays, the successes and failures with emphasis on the former, and integrates that heroic narrative of achievement with some culled material about the private life, and the image that he produces supports the O'Neill that O'Neill built for publicity purposes. On reading the proofs of Clark's book in 1926, O'Neill wrote him a letter, praising the biography as "a damned good piece of work," which, after all, as a constructor of his own self-image, for public consumption, might be taken as self-admiration, though of course, as a responsible craftsman, he had editorial suggestions. To the letter he added a telling paragraph:

And when all is said and done—and this is, naturally, no conceivable fault of yours—the result of this first part [meaning the early part of his life] is legend. It really isn't true. It isn't I. And the truth would make a much more interesting—and incredible!—legend. This is what makes me melancholy. But I see no hope for this except someday to shame the devil myself, if ever I can muster the requisite interest—and nerve—simultaneously! The trouble with anyone else writing even a sketch is that I don't believe there is anyone alive today who knew me as intimately in more than one phase of a life that has passed through many entirely distinct periods, with complete changes of environment, associates, etc. And I myself might not be so good at writing it; for when my memory brings back this picture or episode or that one, I simply cannot recognize that person in myself nor understand him nor his acts as mine (although objectively I can) although my reason tells me he was undeniably I. (SL 203)

This fascinating statement captures the challenge of writing biographically about O'Neill, a problem faced even by the author himself. Classical notions such as wholeness, coherence, resolution, and balance seem to hold poorly for the self of the modern world, perhaps especially for the artist who has played so long into a shifting marketplace. Literature was, during the modernist period, as war-torn a concept as national sovereignty. The offensive of the literary/theatrical establishment—the agencies of production and review—came in the form of a tremendous surge in interest in biography. The fragmentation might be countered by potent "life" writing, and O'Neill factored into this trend at an opportune moment by dying as a man (at the relatively young age of sixty-five) in 1953 after "dying" as an author in 1943 when he could no longer write a completed play. The memory of his heft as a cultural icon was still fresh enough to alert the world that the loft of his throw after a decade of silence could be immense, and *Long Day's Journey Into Night* came to be known on that trajectory. In some ways, the play continues that arc, operating as a postmodern deconstruction of authorship and self. The author is here an O'Neill who both writes and is written by the play (of signifiers); the scene of recognition of father and son in Act Four is ironically a scene of branding, in which the father is seared on the son and the son is seared on the father in a family (or a play) that is anything but a unity. Their matching confessions of artistic failure and exaltation ironically reflect each other, and the lesson is that the actor has failed his author (Shakespeare) and the writer has failed to become an author. Father and son look at each other—know each other—as if through the empty eyes of that mask, which is at once the mask of "O'Neill" and the mask of tragedy.

When *Long Day's Journey* came out in 1956, first in print and later on stage, just three years after O'Neill's death, everyone could see that there was far more to the O'Neill story than a prize winner who peaked early and then virtually disappeared. The first writer to shed light on the "story" was Agnes Boulton, who had been O'Neill's wife during the years when he was constantly in the public eye. She recognized that *Long Day's Journey* had shifted the playing field for self-reflective narration. O'Neill had developed a single day/night as a synecdoche for an epic journey (not unlike James Joyce's Ulyssean saga), and she responded with *Part of a Long Story* (1958), which replaced that trope with part/whole and short story/long story. O'Neill, through her literary lens, was Leopold Bloom, on his unsteady way, and she his Molly, awaiting rendezvous. She intended to follow that book with a second, which would be more concerned with her story, but "herstory" would have to wait for another era, when it would not be consumed by his. Nevertheless, her book is crucial to reveal the constructedness of his authorial mask—how it is wedded to (and divorced from) her own.[13]

In the late 1950s, several biographical projects were launched, all determined to investigate the previously secret dimension of his life, of which even close associates were unaware. These projects adhered to the concept that in the totality of facts about an author, with special attention to those facts previously lost or obscured, one might find the coherence of the self. Croswell Bowen, Louis Sheaffer, and Arthur and Barbara Gelb all brought the skills of an investigative newspaper reporter to get "the whole story," which *Long Day's Journey* showed to be centered on family secrets. Bowen was the only one of the first wave of biographers who had interviewed O'Neill, in 1946 when *The Iceman Cometh* was on the verge of opening, in preparation for an article called "The Black Irishman" (Bowen 1946). He later drew on a connection he had made with Shane O'Neill, the middle of O'Neill's three children, to develop a family-centered biography. Shane was damaged by his parents' divorce when he was not quite ten, and he never found a satisfactory way of making a living. By the time Bowen's book came out in 1959, Shane's older half-brother, Eugene Jr., had committed suicide, and his younger sister, Oona, at the age of eighteen had married Charlie Chaplin, who was nearly as old as her father. Shane had been struggling for over a decade with a heroin addiction, and so it followed that Bowen developed a theme, "the curse of the misbegotten," which he used as the title of his book, in that way enfolding the story of the O'Neills in the terminology of O'Neill's idea of tragedy. His is a novelistic biography, strong in conception but undocumented and faulty in execution.[14]

The Gelbs, too, developed their account of O'Neill's life from within O'Neill's memorial frame. *Long Day's Journey* becomes the historical document out of which they narrate his early years, and they largely trust his characterizations of the Tyrone family as an autobiographical testimony. The play provides a story too good not to tell and retell in ever more convinced versions, up through their co-authorship of the Ric Burns film *Eugene O'Neill: A Documentary Film* (2006), in which O'Neill's play becomes the encompassing historical document, the alpha and omega, as if it were both faithful documentary and supreme fiction. The Gelbs performed extraordinary feats of investigation in preparing their original biography, *O'Neill* (1962), interviewing hundreds of people, traveling to all the significant locations, and scanning miles of microfilm, and their book accomplishes that effect often sought by a life storyteller—making the subject "come alive." The man they characterize is the dual avatar summoned up by O'Neill himself, the *Übermensch* and the underdog. As such, it is sometimes brutally unfair to others. Their 1973 edition was little more than a fact-corrected version of the earlier volume, but through a steady stream of shorter publications they consistently sharpened their ideas about O'Neill as well as managed his legacy in the pages of the *New York Times* where Arthur held various editorial posts.[15]

Sheaffer was also a newspaper reporter by background and subsequently press agent for the American premiere of *Long Day's Journey*. He then devoted his entire energy to assembling the most massive compilation of facts and testimony for his two-volume biography (1968 and 1973). He virtually moved into the family by developing abiding friendships with O'Neill's relations. He devoted years to interviewing actors and directors, editors and publishers, chauffeurs and gardeners, anyone who might confirm a supposition or illuminate an episode with an anecdote. His books are impressive and readable (the second volume won a Pulitzer), but somewhat lumbered with detail.[16]

The main problem with the Sheaffer, Gelb, and Bowen biographies is that the skills of a reporter do not necessarily extend to an ability to read a play, and yet O'Neill's life is, in a sense, located in his plays. Thus, a work like Travis Bogard's *Contour in Time* (1972; revised in 1988), which reassembles O'Neill's life in a chronological analysis of his life's work, crucially augments the biographies. The premise of his book is stated in its opening lines:

> An autobiographer is an over-reacher. Much as wind and water leave traces of their passage on the surface of the land, an autobiographer seeks to shape a contour in time. He denies that his is like the lives of most men—a random sequence, jumbling instinctual action and chance into a drift of days. Disregarding the self-cancelling interplay of mastery and infirmity, he asserts that the course of his life is rational, and that, like the action of a drama, it moves toward a fulfillment in the complete understanding of its author-subject.
>
> Eugene O'Neill's work as a playwright was such an effort at self-understanding. (1988: xii)

Because of this aspect of O'Neill's writing, his life is often best found in the vast critical literature that unfolds the logic of self-representation in his plays. The critic should never lose sight of the fact that a play or poem is a fictional creation, but a fictional creation traces to a fictive act—a time, a circumstance—and in O'Neill's case the process of creation was often preoccupied by self-fashioning.

Especially alert to the challenges of reading such work was Doris Alexander, whose three volumes of biographical study of the plays (the last subtitled *Separating Art from Autobiography*) came out over five decades and encompass the complete works.[17] The rigor of her approach led her to be most resistant to the sense that we become familiar with O'Neill's plays by knowing his family history. Her meticulous research proves again and again that a play is a slippery sort of creation for autobiography. Yet she makes it clear that the more we know of his life, especially the context in which his imagination was formed, the more we can appreciate, precisely, the achievement of his work.

Stephen A. Black put the focus of his 1999 biography squarely on the life story, using the skills of a psychoanalyst to develop a narrative of O'Neill coming out of a troubled childhood and using the art of drama, much as a patient would use psychotherapy, to attain greater self-consciousness, also relief from some of the torments of conflicted emotions and repressed feeling. As indicated by his subtitle—*Beyond Mourning and Tragedy*—Black's analysis seeks to reconcile psychoanalytic and aesthetic perspectives, but the story he places in the foreground is of a man using his art to therapeutic ends.[18]

The saga of a tormented genius who defines an era yet is unable to overcome the limitations and failures of his own humanity has many examples in the modern era, and in O'Neill's case the tragically beset childhood, the suicidally addicted young manhood, three troubled marriages, children betrayed, body racked by incomprehensible disease, and homes postulated then abandoned, all offer lurid material for a biographer to narrate. O'Neill as a writer spoke to millions of audience members and readers, but as a man he was often tongue-tied and reserved to a degree that approached agoraphobia. He loved to read detective fiction, listen to popular songs, and hear a good joke, but as a cultural seer he was dedicated to the profound, the tragic, the morbid, and he came to detest the values and culture of his country. Even his one fully realized comedy, *Ah, Wilderness!*, deals with the missed opportunities and failed promise of the world past. These paradoxes and discolorations have made him an elusive character to portray on stage or screen.[19] An actor who stares into the empty eyes of the mask of O'Neill sees a man staring into empty eyes, who in turn sees a man staring into empty eyes. The mass of facts and impressions that a biographer might gather will never capture the profundity of the creation/vacancy that was O'Neill. However, since O'Neill is a construct that exists in drama, in a sense every actor who plays one of his roles stands in for O'Neill and reconstitutes his life. Though he generally misdoubted the work of his actors, seeing in their performance a trace of his father's emptiness (evanescence? vacuity? mortality?), he ultimately offered, in a sense, a lifeline to actors who might fall into such an abyss by selling their souls. They could, instead, take up the mask of O'Neill, which is to be seen, as it were, in a convex mirror, such that the face (or text), which obtrudes into the foreground, covers up the placement in a background (or context). Each of the biographies has featured on the cover one of the many dour photographic portraits, and they are compelling, but alien. Perhaps O'Neill constructed a mask too self-conscious for an actor to wear.

The most recent biography, as of this writing, is *Eugene O'Neill: A Life in Four Acts* by Robert M. Dowling, which features a 1933 portrait by Carl Van Vechten—a half-shadowed figure staring out from the darkness. Dowling, who comes from an academic background, offers an admirable biography, less exhaustive than Sheaffer's or the Gelbs' but thorough, engaging, and well-documented. His book works especially well when accompanied by his encyclopedic two-volume *Critical Companion to Eugene O'Neill* (2009), two-thirds of which Dowling wrote, including the historical/interpretive survey of all the plays and other writings, with supplementary and collateral articles contributed by various current scholars. The benefit of recent research makes these volumes the most well-developed compendium of thinking about O'Neill's life and work. Having done that sort of due diligence, Dowling could dwell in his biography on the cultural, social, and psychological circumstances of the author's life and career, purged of myth by a century of careful scholarship and rooted in a well-integrated legacy of critical study. He probes less insistently into the plays than do Alexander or Bogard, but he finds narrative coherence—or dramatic form, as the subtitle implies—in the project of self-creation initiated by a young man named Eugene G. O'Neill.

By the time this essay comes out, *By Women Possessed: A Life of Eugene O'Neill* will have arrived, the second part of the Gelbs's revision of their biography. It promises to draw more deeply from the primary material they collected in their interviewing of O'Neill associates, especially the hours of taped conversation with O'Neill's third wife, Carlotta Monterey O'Neill. She was unquestionably a skillful and devoted architect of his immortality (or endurance, anyway), and the Gelbs trade heavily on what they feature as their intimacy with her in the form of many hours of interviews, though by the time of their interview she had been showing many signs of mental instability. Their title, *By Women Possessed*, implies a displacement of self-possession or authority in the author, which is shocking given the widely shared belief that O'Neill was such a dominant figure in American theatre history and in the creation of his E.G.O.

Also in the works is a volume of reminiscences of those who met O'Neill and for one reason or another described the experience. They are the ones who looked into those dark, searching eyes that we can only stare down in photographs. Put together by Brenda Murphy and George Monteiro, *Eugene O'Neill Remembered* will, in a sense, approximate the mirror that looks back at O'Neill in the act of making sure he is here.

He is.

THE LITERARY O'NEILL

Alexander Pettit

Looking back on his career in 1962, the dramatist Elmer Rice lamented that much of the American drama he admired had survived only in print (1963: 201–02). Rice's regret about the scarcity of productions is easy for any lover of live theatre to appreciate. His deprecation of published drama is less so, written texts having ably preserved all manner of performed works since antiquity. The bias is familiar: printed plays are vain attempts to concretize evanescence, repositories of lines and stage directions once animate and animable again only when the stars (and financiers) align in a manner propitious to a revival. This prejudice is attractive but unreasonable, given that theatrical innovation depends on the persistent writing of scripts.

Eugene O'Neill would not have sympathized with his contemporary. Unlike Rice and other theatrical memoirists of the day, O'Neill passed his career fretfully in dialogue with the stage rather than dewily in its thrall. The actor James O'Neill's itinerant, shabby-genteel maturity had impressed upon his son the tenuousness of reputation allowed to those who labor in the service of popular culture. Intent on claiming a loftier position in the canons of literary history, O'Neill came to value the durability of text over the fugitivity of performance. His pursuit of literary reputation was inseparably an artistic triumph and a marketing strategy, a collaboration between a talented young writer and an ambitious young publisher, Horace Liveright, who in 1919 spurned precedent by publishing a still relatively unknown playwright (Gilmer 1970: 23; Dardis 1995: 59). O'Neill was not the only great writer on Boni & Liveright's list, but he was among the first whose ascent to that status coincided with his tenure there. He published with the firm until 1932, by which time he had become a best-selling author as well as America's preeminent dramatist (Gilmer 1970: 176).[20]

Boni & Liveright's December 1924 publication of O'Neill's two-volume *Complete Works* codified the playwright's literary aspirations. The edition provided the bibliographical basis of the august figure we know as O'Neill, positing in its physical form as in its contents a divide between serious American drama and material too often dismissed as crude and essentially anticipatory. It affirmed O'Neill as the author of highbrow dramatic works rather than a mere playwright, as more interested in the composition of plays than in their performance. It announced the "O'Neill" that O'Neill would spend the rest of his career becoming.

Both elements of the edition's title were marketing ploys. "Works" shielded highbrow readers from the taint of commerce inherent in "plays." The term's pretentiousness had been noted way back in 1616, when Ben Jonson was mocked for publishing a collection of plays as his *Workes* (Greetham 1994: 123). Later periods have used the term more cautiously. As late as the 1920s, O'Neill's revered Ibsen remained unique among moderns in having his plays collected in English as "works," an honor that decorously postdated the author's decease. "Complete," too, is generally reserved for dead writers, while "collected" is the consensus pick for publishers of living authors. And the "complete" set wasn't complete anyhow. O'Neill withheld five self-published plays, three unpublished but performed plays, one complete but unoptioned play, and at least five plays whose publication and performance he would never authorize. His nondramatic works vanished.[21] O'Neill's *oeuvre* thus assumed a coherency and stature to which no prior American dramatist could pretend, none having been afforded an equivalent opportunity for self-fashioning. Boni & Liveright rose to the occasion. The volumes were cleanly printed on pricey laid paper, encased in handsome bindings designed and, in conformity to current vogue, stamped attractively on their spines. Their dust jackets would have raised the odd eyebrow, these newish features being thought superfluous by the stodgier sort of bibliophile.[22] As the publisher had stipulated, O'Neill autographed the first volume of each of the 1250 numbered sets, "1200 for sale and 50 for review" (Egleston 2004: 169). The *Complete Works* would be the sort of big, fancy edition that traditionally asserts an author's canonicity while acknowledging his or her death. O'Neill was thirty-four years old and not yet five years past his Broadway debut, talented and well known to be sure, but no Ibsen, and no Jonson, either.

Serious theatre was easy to define for a generation embarrassed by popular forms and, as Robert M. Dowling notes, discouraged by the deadening effect of commerce on recent attempts "to produce a lasting American drama" (LFA 123). Travis Bogard observes that "tragedy or nothing was the cry" for O'Neill in the early 1920s (UO 148); David Savran broadens the point by demonstrating the assiduity of Europhiliac reviewers in promoting the "consecration" of an O'Neill who "mark[ed] a decisive break with the domestic and social drama, comedy of manners, and melodrama" (2009: 251). I agree with Savran that several like-minded critics and one talented playwright willed the new American tragedy into being; indeed, criticism from the period sometimes conveys the impression that O'Neill became America's pioneering tragedian because a suitable mass of cognoscenti felt the want of such a figure. As Savran recognizes, however, iconoclastic critics overemphasized O'Neill's distance from his predecessors and contemporaries because it suited them to do so (2009: 231). A party to this image-making enterprise, O'Neill formalized his own "tragic" persona in the *Complete Works* by withholding a number of plays that declared his interest in comic form. From 1914 to 1924, O'Neill completed forty-four plays in addition to a lost pantomime and a dramatization of Coleridge's *Rime of the Ancient Mariner*. Seventeen were comic or metacomic, to denominate plays that both invoke and subvert the comic convention of the sexually and economically coalescent ending. The comedies per se are absent from the *Complete Works*, leaving as residue the dark metacomedies *Anna Christie, The Straw, Welded, All God's Chillun Got Wings*, and, starkly, *Desire Under the Elms*, in which the young lovers reunite but are bound for jail.[23] Although defensible on artistic grounds, the omission of plays like the marriage-comedy *Servitude* and the drawing-room comedy *Now I Ask You* creates an irony: the *Complete Works* artificially circumscribed the canon of a playwright celebrated for his formal experimentalism and thus legitimated the prejudices of tastemakers intent on representing O'Neill as unprecedented. This is the O'Neill whose approach to form Liveright found "radical" and whom he "market[ed] as the one playwright whose work deserved a large audience" (Egleston 2004: 75; Dardis 1995: 60). And this is the O'Neill of Harold Bloom's credulous proclamation that "it is an inevitable oddity that the principal American dramatist to date should have no American precursors" (2007: 1). O'Neill and Liveright would have relished Bloom's misconception, which they had in effect provoked.

His early recognition of O'Neill's merit speaks to Liveright's good taste and commercial savvy. The publisher drew on both qualities in conceiving the edition. For example, Liveright's April 3, 1924, memorandum of agreement stipulated that the edition contain "one play that has not been heretofore printed in any form" (Egleston 2004: 169). Whether or not Liveright knew that O'Neill was at work on the edgy *Desire Under the Elms*, he would have been aware of the uproar generated by the recent magazine publication of the biracial *All God's Chillun Got Wings*.[24] Both Liveright and O'Neill recognized the value of controversy, and financial problems of which O'Neill had been complaining must have made him appreciate Liveright's decision to publish the follow-up to *All God's Chillun* in a $12.50 set.[25] Liveright structured the agreement in a manner sure to keep O'Neill on track. O'Neill would be paid in four bimonthly installments of $500, commencing on the date of publication. This assured him of $200 more than he would have realized for a sold-out printing at his usual 15 percent royalty, while encouraging timely completion of the task by guaranteeing prompter payment.[26] O'Neill read proofs expeditiously, beginning the task on October 4, 1924, the day after he received them, and finishing eight days later.[27] When he did mark sheets for revision, he generally limited his work to corrections and to the excision of short passages.[28] This too signals a desire for prompt completion: revision of this sort requires a minimum of effort from the author and promises a maximum of efficiency to the typesetter, given the ease of extracting type relative to resetting it.

From Liveright's initial memorandum to O'Neill's final read-through, the process exemplifies what Liveright's first biographer calls the two principals' "serious, friendly cooperation" (Gilmer 1970: 175). In spite of O'Neill's diligence, however, the edition did not appear in "the fall of 1924," the date that Liveright had set in April, probably mindful of Christmas and perhaps to coincide with *Desire*'s likely premiere.[29] One plausible explanation concerns the press's reconceptualization of the edition shortly before its publication on December 27—an odd date to release an expensive niche set.[30] Liveright originally had expressed interest in publishing O'Neill's "complete plays." O'Neill might not have been aware of this intention or, if he were, might not have given it much thought. The memorandum was signed by O'Neill's agent, Richard J. Madden, not O'Neill himself; in his *Work Diary*, O'Neill refers to the project as his "Collected Works edition" or his "Collected Works."[31] In any event, eight months after formalizing his interest in O'Neill's "complete plays," Liveright publicized the project in a manner consistent with O'Neill's habitual wording. On December 14, Boni & Liveright ran a grabby full-page advertisement in the *New York Times* that prominently plugged "The Collected Works of Eugene O'Neill" (see Figure 3). The innovative use of author photographs, "heavy black borders," and "very bold type" across the spread is consistent with Walker Gilmer's comments on the press's creative and aggressive practices of advertising and the "enormous" financial outlay they entailed (1970: 90). But the pallor of the advertised title contrasts to the overall vibrancy of the ad. Surely such a presentation would have been better complemented by the emphatic "complete" than the less precise if more accurate "collected," the very aptness of which points up its equivocal nature: "collected" by whom, and to what end? The acknowledgment of selectivity works against Liveright's create-a-canon mentality, evident in the advertisement's promotion of a new Boni & Liveright series of Provincetown plays ("real additions to literature . . . [published] in a beautiful uniform format") and in its spread on the publisher's Modern Library imprint, a gutsy venture designed to insinuate newcomers like Waldo Frank and Ben Hecht into a grander lineage that ran from Voltaire to Dostoyevsky to Henry James.[32] A brief flirtation with truth in advertisement seems to have knocked Liveright off his game.

He soon recovered. Sometime after Liveright submitted copy to the *Times*, the edition became *The Complete Works of Eugene O'Neill*. The new title telegraphs its opportunism by ascribing a final form to the canon of a prolific dramatist even then shopping a completed play (*The Fountain*)

Figure 3 Detail of a full-page Boni & Liveright advertisement in the *New York Times Book Review*, December 14, 1924.

and working on two new ones (*Marco Millions* and *The Great God Brown*). The aggrandizing do-over is one of Liveright's attempts to insist on a living author's venerability, a Modern Library moment, if you will. In the case of the *Complete Works*, the disadvantage of this gambit became evident when the following notice appeared on both title pages: "*'The Fountain' is withheld from publication by its author pending its forthcoming publication.*" Liveright's "complete" here collides with the hard fact of O'Neill's productivity. But even this concession becomes a promotional opportunity: the notice stimulates interest in a play for which O'Neill was having a hard time finding a producer and whose textual value was therefore limited.[33]

Bibliographic data suggest Liveright's attraction to marketing an O'Neill more nearly akin to Ibsen than to, say, O'Neill's fellow Provincetown Player Susan Glaspell, who had published her modestly titled *Plays* (1920) with Boston's ho-hum Small, Maynard & Co. Analysis of the published volumes demonstrates the likelihood that sometime around Christmas 1924, Boni & Liveright's agent Van Rees Composition reprinted the first signature (i.e., sixteen pages) of the first volume. In the published volume, that signature bears the words "The Complete Works of Eugene O'Neill" four times, most conspicuously on the half-title and title pages. This realized Liveright's presumed intentions but left the first signature at odds with the verso running heads that commence in the second signature. These read "Plays of O'Neill." The spines of both volumes, which would have been stamped with the title at the bindery after the bindings had been affixed to full stacks of gatherings, read "Collected Plays of O'Neill."[34] Granting that titles on spines and running heads are often truncations does not account for the fact that these two renderings correlate to each other but not to the wording of the advertised title ("Works") or the final one ("Complete"). The appearance of similar but "wrong" title-forms on the binding and running heads suggests that both Van Rees Bindery and Van Rees Composition—separate branches of the same company—initially worked from orders that specified a title-form without a clear equivalent elsewhere in the edition's history (Atkinson 1974: 160). Fully countermanding this order would have meant partly resetting and completely reprinting and rebinding two volumes—an obvious impossibility. Hence the attraction of limited reprinting.

This tells us two things. First, until very late in the game, Liveright was fussing about with the title. Second, his deliberations, or perhaps his instincts, led him to select the "high-literary" option—that is, the "Ibsen option," not the "Glaspell option." In sum, Liveright was an ally and an analogue of Savran's laudatory critics.

Liveright's marketing of O'Neill would prove congruent with O'Neill's interest in presenting himself as a writer first and a playwright incidentally. Perhaps coincidentally, the publisher had given expression to a central fact of his client's career: O'Neill meant to write dramatic works. Not plays, really. Works. For readers. Plays are what works would become or had already been, the unavoidable if vexing consequences of one's occupation, like turf toe for an athlete. Crucially, O'Neill was not a man of the theatre. He did not number other playwrights among the intimates of his maturity, and his closest relationship to a theatre worker—Robert Edmond Jones—never became a friendship of the sort he shared with his and Jones's colleague, the critic and producer Kenneth Macgowan. He thought poorly of actors. He avoided New York, more resolutely the greater his celebrity. Inevitably, then, he did not frequent the theatre after he had made his mark in it. One account suggests a flurry of seeing and reading plays "at school and college" and during his recovery from tuberculosis at the Gaylord Sanatorium in his mid-twenties (Chothia 1979: 199). But afterward O'Neill seems to have had no more interesting in reading plays than in seeing them. He had in him a hint of Benjamin Disraeli, who once remarked, "when I want to read a novel, I write one" (qtd. Buckle 1920: 636).

The *Complete Works* manifests O'Neill's attraction to an author-focused, text-centered drama. The set's inutility to theatre workers is obvious: like Jonson's *Workes* in David Greetham's account, the *Complete Works* "could not be used as play-text, for it was simply too big, heavy, and monumental to function as prompt-book or script" (1994: 292). Producers would continue to secure scripts from Madden's American Play Company; the *Collected Works* would reside among what one Jonsonian calls "the cherished tomes of the literati" (Murray 1983: 261). At issue in both cases is the apportioning of authority for the creation of the dramatic text. Both Jonson's and O'Neill's editions centralize authority by redirecting focus from the theatre to the printed page. Like Jonson's, O'Neill's trajectory tends away the sweaty crucible of production, but O'Neill's tends as well toward a sustained, productive acceptance of the advantages of the printed text as a medium for his art.

The transition would comprise his full career. O'Neill's debut book *Thirst and Other One Act Plays*, a vanity press collection, was funded by James O'Neill with the intent of facilitating his son's entree into the theatre (SP 273). *Thirst* is a solicitation in book form, a perceived means to a precise extratextual end. Thirty-two years later, O'Neill would make a will stipulating that *Long Day's Journey Into Night* never be subjected to the vagaries of performance (LFA 447–48). The first discernible indication of O'Neill's text-centrism took the form of a cautionary tale. During rehearsals for *Beyond the Horizon* in January 1920, O'Neill complained that the actors "will never—can never—be my Robert, Ruth, and Andy" (SL 107). The statement is remarkable, given the inescapably transmutative effect of theatrical performance. Furthermore, at the time of this utterance, O'Neill had to strain even to represent the script as his. One week earlier, he had acquiesced in its radical truncation at the insistence of producer John D. Williams and leading man Richard Bennett. The principal textual result was a diminution in the lines allotted to Ruth Mayo, once a pathetic character but a cipher in the revision, and the concomitant elevation of Robert Mayo's importance, thus the creation of a meatier role for Bennett.[35] The principal dramaturgical result was a comparatively brisk pace and an obvious "hero," appropriately a reliable box-office draw. Bennett's revision fared well on stage. Five weeks after *Beyond the Horizon* opened on February 3, Boni & Liveright published the play in its earlier form, the use of a superseded text justifiable by its readiness for print and the expense of having made it so.

O'Neill may have preferred the published version, a chronicle of "his" characters. In an April letter to the *New York Times*, he observed that while working on *Beyond the Horizon* he had "dreamed of wedding the theme for a novel to the play form in a way that would still leave the play master of the house" (qtd. LFA 309). His wistful addendum "I dream of it still" gestures at the staged play by being inapplicable to the published version, with its more democratic characterization, its relatively complex appeals to sympathy, and its subtler layering of "theme." The pre-Bennett *Beyond the Horizon*, a clotted and overburdened play, reads better than its successor and reads best when we decline to do what we generally do when we read plays: imagine them on stage. An old hand, Bennett engineered a successful play and a superior one, too, albeit one unusual in O'Neill's canon for its verbal economy and unique in its endorsement of the star system that O'Neill's solo version rejected. The work and the play, being different, functioned differently. Bennett's complaint about O'Neill's script—"terribly stretched out, and a lot of words with little active material" (Bennett and Kibbee 1970: 64)—prefigures a common criticism of O'Neill's later drama and suggests that the playwright would remain truer to the spirit of his own work as writing than to that of theatrical collaboration, as indeed he would.

O'Neill would soon attempt a workaround. When director Arthur Hopkins requested deep cuts in *Anna Christie* in 1921, O'Neill authorized him to do the revision himself (Wainscott 1988: 78–79).[36] O'Neill recognized that he could entrust stage-specific cuts to the seasoned Hopkins. He knew, too, that he need not incorporate these cuts into the copy that he would submit to Boni & Liveright. The arrangement produced another successful play, if in this instance one that O'Neill openly disliked. A third such effort failed. Disgusted with the theatre and fearing backlash from his pending divorce, O'Neill left the United States in 1928, accompanied by his wife-to-be, Carlotta Monterey. Amid good news about the successes of *Marco Millions* and *Strange Interlude*, he began work on *Dynamo*, completing in September a version he found suitable for submission to the Theatre Guild.[37] The Guild optioned the play, which went into rehearsal in January 1929, an ocean's width from its author. In O'Neill's absence, director Philip Moeller assumed the unenviable task of sculpting a script that O'Neill soon declared "not right."[38] Like Hopkins a respected professional, Moeller had fared well with *Strange Interlude*, and *Strange Interlude* had fared well with critics and audiences—and in print, thus augmenting O'Neill's already considerable earnings (Egleston 2004: 164, 172). But Moeller was neither a telepath nor a magician, and after fifty performances and mostly bad reviews, *Dynamo* closed. O'Neill revised the text extensively in March and April, and again in June. The second revision would be published in the United States in October 1929, with the first, counterintuitively, following one month later in England (Atkinson 1974: 219). *Dynamo* thus has the distinction of being O'Neill's only play published in two substantially different and proximate editions, neither one much like the performance text. O'Neill never saw the play on stage and may never have seen a promptbook or transcription of the staged version.[39]

Even before he undertook the second round of post-performance revisions, O'Neill remarked that "my interest in the productions steadily decreases as my interest in plays as written increases" (SL 338). His purely textual attentions to the script underscore the verity of the remark: O'Neill spent a whopping thirty days rewriting a script for an audience of readers, delaying publication of a play that had no chance of being revived and was fast losing whatever claim it had held on the public's attention.[40] His commitment to after-production burnishing recalls his briefer engagement with proofs of the *Complete Works*. Back in October 1924, O'Neill had surely recognized that more than a few of the plays represented in that edition would not again be staged, yet he tweaked them for the benefit of the readers that he and Liveright were courting. This is something different from the venerable practice of fine-tuning successful—restageable—scripts for their initial publication.

By taking control of the text of *Dynamo*, O'Neill repudiated the collaborative, theatre-centric method that he had grudgingly employed in the case of *Beyond the Horizon* and dodged in that of *Anna Christie*. It is a short step to the late plays, all of which had troubled relationships to the stage. O'Neill finished *The Iceman Cometh* in 1940 but delayed its performance and publication until 1946, concerned about the rigors of rehearsal and the prejudices of wartime audiences. Even as the Guild lobbied for prompt staging, O'Neill was confiding to a correspondent that writing was "the only thing that still interests me about my profession" (qtd. SA 503). *The Iceman Cometh* was published one day after its premiere, a propinquity that emphasizes O'Neill's lack of interest in his script's development during rehearsal. O'Neill canceled plans for staging *A Touch of the Poet* and *A Moon for the Misbegotten* while authorizing their publication, albeit for financial reasons in the case of the latter (SA 597, 642). The one-act *Hughie* was neither staged nor published in O'Neill's lifetime. *More Stately Mansions*, intended for destruction along with drafts of two other plays toward the mammoth cycle that occupied O'Neill from 1935 to 1942, survived in spite of its author's attempts to suppress it (SA 548). And, again, there is *Long Day's Journey Into Night*, which O'Neill envisioned only as a book.

Having lost the "production freedom" that characterized his tenure with the Provincetown Players (Wainscott 1988: 15), O'Neill found a text-bound, literary model of drama that allowed him to exercise the sort of control whose elusiveness all playwrights must to some degree lament. That the model was hostile to performance is regrettable only in an abstract sense, given O'Neill's enduring popularity on stage. O'Neill's publishers would continue to cooperate. From 1925 to 1955, Boni & Liveright and then Random House issued and reissued high-dollar, multi-volume collections of O'Neill's drama. In 1988, O'Neill became the first playwright to be honored by a comprehensive Library of America edition. This abundance is partly a tribute to Horace Liveright, who recognized the playwright as a candidate for a literary canonization previously unavailable to his breed. The *Complete Works* first made the literary O'Neill palpable, to invoke both the word's literal signification ("tangible") and its figurative one ("present"). When we hold this or any edition of O'Neill's works, we hold a record of his achievement, his pretentions, his temperament, and his stature, honoring him as Liveright did if, one hopes, less calculatingly.

O'NEILL'S *EMPEROR JONES*: RACING THE GREAT WHITE WAY

Katie N. Johnson

Much has been written about O'Neill's centrality in cultivating not only American drama, but also a modern (and, at times, modernist) theatre. Such accounts inevitably focus on O'Neill's artistic production in Greenwich Village and his rise within and among the Provincetown Players. These narratives, like the annals of Broadway itself, focus on a trajectory of success that points toward the Great White Way.

But this is only part of the story.

What has been given surprisingly little attention is how O'Neill's work— and the artists who performed it—wove in and out of diverse theatrical spaces, as well as rich racial geometries, to use Shannon Steen's formation (2010), as well as a larger pattern of interracial artistic production. *The Emperor Jones* was one of the most widely performed and traveled cultural artifacts of early twentieth-century America. It was also among the most contested. Throughout this chapter, the early production history of *The Emperor Jones* serves as a case study of what I am calling "racing Broadway": the process by which intersectional and intra-racial artistic traffic between Harlem, Greenwich Village, and Broadway shaped the contours of American theatre. I use the term "racing" to refer, on the one hand, to the practice of white audiences and artists "racing up" to Harlem, where they saw—and often poached—theatrical productions and performance practices. "Racing" also refers to the ways in which African American actors changed the racial landscape of the Great White Way through their physical portrayals and performative interventions both on and off the stage. An unlikely, though central, figure linking these co-extensive projects was Eugene O'Neill. While scholars have written about the Village as a hub for theatrical experimentation and home to O'Neill and the Provincetown Players, relatively little attention has been paid to the collaborations between downtown and uptown, between the emerging modernist (and, largely white) theatre artists and the Harlem theatres. Too often, historical treatments of performers focus on their Broadway careers, thus effacing—or, as Faedra Chatard Carpenter (2014) puts it, "e-racing"—much of their body of work and half of the theatrical map. For decades, *The Emperor Jones* was a piece that resonated with a variety of black theatre artists beyond the Village and Broadway, effectively paving the way for Harlem productions, an all-black opera adaptation in midtown, and *Body and Soul* (1925), a race film by Oscar Micheaux that borrows many plot details. In spite of these innovations, many artists who stepped into Brutus Jones's boots have faded into obscurity. This essay seeks to restore their work to the historical record.

The Emperor Jones extended beyond Manhattan, playing outdoors in Pennsylvania, in black theatres in southern California, at European national theatres, and in countless productions throughout America's heartland. While some of these productions may seem obscure, they nonetheless constituted an important archive of black performers intervening in imperial representations, leaving a lasting imprint or "darkening mirror," as Stephanie Leigh Batiste has put it (2012), on American theatre and culture. Again and again, *The Emperor Jones* was the play that razed/raced barriers across America and, indeed, across the Atlantic.

The cross-racial artistic traffic along the aptly named Great White Way was more fluid than scholarly accounts have thus far documented—and *The Emperor Jones* brings these cartographies to light. Theatre scholars have not been kind to Charles Gilpin, as David Krasner has pointed out (1995: 483–96). But neither have they been good to the early Paul Robeson in juxtaposing the supposedly ornery, experienced Gilpin with the magnetic rising star, Robeson. Gilpin (see Figure 4) is frequently portrayed as the actor who refused to say "nigger" on stage, who rewrote the script while on tour, who probably drank too much, and, ultimately, whom O'Neill fired. On the other hand, Robeson appears as riding the coat tails of his Ivy-League pedigree, the one who "got" O'Neill's modernist experimentalism, who embraced white theatre, and who, early on, supposedly sold out. Neither of these narratives is entirely correct.

Gilpin challenges our understanding of authorship, having once famously declared, "I created the role of the Emperor. That role belongs to me. That Irishman, he just wrote the play" (qtd. SA 37). Indeed, it could be said that Gilpin created the play as much as O'Neill had. Yet, as often recounted in the mainstream white press, Charles Gilpin's career was supposedly a quintessential pull-yourself-up-by-your-bootstraps kind of narrative, with a trajectory from "elevator boy" or Pullman porter to Broadway star.[41] For example, with its headline "From Pullman Car Porter to Honor Guest of Drama League," the *New York Tribune* virtually ignored Gilpin's extensive work within black theatre, choosing instead to focus on his Horatio Alger story (Ford 1921: 7). Other reporters emphasized Gilpin's working-class background, noting he worked first as a printer, then as a barber. Laudatory press likewise harkened back to Gilpin's supposed humble origins. When the

Figure 4 Charles Gilpin in the 1920 production of *The Emperor Jones*. Photo by Vandamm Studio. (Billy Rose Theatre Division, the New York Public Library.)

New York Dramatic Mirror ranked Gilpin as "the greatest actor on the stage today," the writer began with the question: "What did Charles Gilpin do before he made his great success in Emperor Jones?" Answering the query was hardly necessary, but the article continued: "We are informed that New York was so unappreciative of his talents that when they sought him out, he was running an elevator in an apartment" (Bernays 1921: 641). According to O'Neill biographers Arthur and Barbara Gelb and Louis Sheaffer, Gilpin was found running an elevator at Macy's (SA 32; Gelb 1973: 445). Even the black newspaper the *Chicago Tribune* repeated the familiar elevator story while running a rave review.[42] This myth would circulate relentlessly throughout Gilpin's career.

The oft-told story of the Provincetowners "discovering" Gilpin in an elevator is not only erroneous and patronizing, but also eclipses years of

Gilpin's work as a founding member of the Anita Bush Players (later called the Lafayette Theatre Players), the leading African American theatre company in New York during the early 1910s. Though Gilpin had worked as an elevator operator sporadically when out of work from the theatre, he was a well-known actor in Harlem. Indeed, he had just finished playing a slave character in *Abraham Lincoln* on Broadway when *The Emperor Jones* opportunity arose. In other words, Gilpin had *already* raced Broadway— before playing Brutus Jones—and would continue to do so with a directorial debut on Broadway in 1926 (another underreported story, about which I will say more later). None of these accomplishments, however, would stick in the Broadway annals; Gilpin is still not credited on the Internet Broadway Database's cast listing for *Abraham Lincoln*.[43] Racial amnesia, typical treatment for black actors on the Great White Way, as Susan Curtis (2001) has shown, abounded and endures.

If many white critics ignored the fact that Gilpin was a seasoned actor before he encountered O'Neill and the Provincetown Players, the black press acknowledged it. One newspaper, for instance, highlighted Gilpin's early work as a minstrel performer with Williams and Walker before joining the Lafayette Theatre. In this account, Gilpin isn't "discovered" in an elevator; rather "the Provincetown Players found him at his home in One Hundred and Thirty-second street [*sic*] and gave him the manuscript of *The Emperor Jones*."[44] In other words, O'Neill and other Provincetowners trekked to Harlem to see the best African American performers with their sights on Gilpin.

Lester Walton, the drama critic for the black newspaper the *New York Age*, saw a performative loop between Broadway and Harlem in the wake of Gilpin's success. Walton wrote in 1920 that if Gilpin returned to the Lafayette Theatre after his Broadway success, he would be the toast of Harlem (qtd. Thompson 1972: 165). But importantly, the *opposite* would also be true: "Were the Lafayette Players to appear on Broadway, the 'Standing Room Only' sign would be very much in evidence upon their return to Harlem" (165). Given the Lafayette Players' reputation, white audiences regularly raced uptown, Walton observed:

It is beginning to dawn on the managers and actor[s] on Broadway that something worthy of more than passing consideration . . . is taking place weekly at the Lafayette Theatre further uptown. . . . Nowadays stage celebrities in goodly numbers are wending their way to Seventh Avenue and 131st Street by limousine to look upon the efforts of these colored thespians with serious eye. (qtd. Thompson 1972: 146, n1)

Not only were Harlem thespians drawing Broadway stars to see their work; many of these black companies' repertoires were poached from Broadway as well. As John G. Monroe has written in his history of the Harlem Little Theatre Movement, the Lafayette Players "performed short plays, or abbreviated versions of recent Broadway hits. . . . The plays were not about black people, and, if the actors were not light enough to pass for white, they would lighten their skins with make-up" (1984: 64). Harlem was, in other words, racing Broadway hits by extending the nineteenth-century minstrel practice of "whiting up" that Marvin McAllister has identified where black performers "interrogate[d] privileged or authoritative representations of whiteness" (2011: 1). African American artists were, in effect, dismantling the binary logic governing racial hierarchies, a practice that Carpenter has clarified as coloring whiteness: "African American artists resist[ed] the presentation of whiteness as normative and, in the process, expose[d] the fallacies associated with racial designations" (2014: 3). The interrogation of whiteness advanced by the Lafayette Players provides an important cultural backdrop in which to understand how racial barriers were at times dismantled in O'Neill's *The Emperor Jones*, not only because both Robeson and Gilpin performed with the Players, but also because it demonstrates my larger point about how theatre artists were changing the racial landscape on the stage and beyond.

When *The Emperor Jones* went on tour for almost two years from 1920 to 1922, both black and white spectators flocked to see Gilpin. It was hardly a royal tour, but there was something regal about the audiences Gilpin commanded throughout the United States, in both highbrow and lowbrow spaces—from Los Angeles to Des Moines to El Paso—even in the South until he was threatened by the Ku Klux Klan.[45] In an *Amsterdam News* interview, Gilpin recounted: "Oh, I guess I've played Jones about 2,500 times, from coast to coast, from beyond border to beyond border. In New York, on the road, at benefit performances and whatnot. And it hasn't played out its string yet" (Packard 1928: 7). Perhaps one of the most unusual venues for *The Emperor Jones* was an early manifestation of what we now call prison theatre: Gilpin performed the play in Sing Sing prison in 1923.[46] He succeeded in bringing together white and black audiences, as recounted by one Virginian reporter, undermining segregationist logic: "When the theatre was filled, by one of those unwritten laws that prevail in the South, the balcony was filled with Negroes and the orchestra with white people Gilpin appeared on the stage, and a roar of applause greeted him from the galleries."[47] What was it like for African American audiences to greet their emperor, and for white audiences to view—and perhaps to participate in—their admiration? Gilpin's own words are striking: he played Brutus Jones "from beyond border to beyond border," creating a moment of what Victor Turner (1982) might call liminality, where the performance of race is situated at a precarious threshold. *Emperor* was razing racial barriers, defying unwritten laws of segregation with thunderous applause while officially upholding them.

Gilpin loved a good comeback and so in 1926 he not only revived his role as Brutus Jones for the Provincetown Players, but also directed his own production on Broadway—a virtually unprecedented accomplishment for an African American theatre artist (Monroe 1974: 107).[48] The revival received glowing reviews in both black and white papers. The *New York Evening Post* observed that Gilpin "is at once grandiose, boastful, fearful, prayerful and cringing."[49] Gilpin was back: "The return of 'The Emperor Jones' to New York discloses to those who might have entertained any doubts of the ability of Charles S. Gilpin's [his] latent dramatic power," the *Amsterdam News* reported (Packard 1928). And, reminding its black readership of the amnesiac tendency by the white press to forget Gilpin's roots in black theatre, the article continued, "we took pride in pointing out to our readers [his latent dramatic power] years before his opportunity came to appear before exacting audiences in a sphere far removed from that of 135th street." Gilpin's career reveals not only one of many well-traveled paths from Harlem to Broadway (and back again), but also the inaccuracy of the elevator discovery narrative. Gilpin's story also serves as an example of how mythologies, exclusions, and elisions govern American theatre history, especially regarding actors of color.

In spite of paying his dues on the road for years, Gilpin had not been asked to revive *Emperor* in 1924. Instead, the role was handed to Paul Robeson. However, Robeson's assumption of the role of Brutus Jones was not really planned as a revival, and it occurred after he had already turned the role down in 1920. The 1924 staging of *The Emperor Jones* was, rather, a last-minute strategy to deal with the crisis brought on by *All God's Chillun Got Wings*, O'Neill's semi-expressionistic portrait of interracial desire. When it was reported that the white actress Mary Blair would kiss Paul Robeson's hand during the production, newspapers speculated there might be race riots. In order to assuage anxieties about possible miscegenation (and because Blair supposedly became ill), *Emperor* was performed in repertory with *Chillun* for a limited run. *Emperor* bestowed a kind of legitimacy for the shaky *Chillun* run, which opened without riots and, with the exception of barring children from performing in the prologue, provoked very little controversy after all.

When Robeson originated the role of Jim in *Chillun* and took over the portrayal of Brutus Jones in *The Emperor Jones*, he was extensively compared to Gilpin.[50] This was one of many vital "acts of transfer," to use Diana Taylor's words (2003: 2), in transmitting cultural memories from Gilpin's Brutus Jones to Robeson's. John Corbin's 1924 *New York Times* review made clear the citational tug from one actor to the other: "Paul Robeson Triumphs in Role Made Famous by Gilpin" (1924: 18). The haunting transferred from *Emperor* to *Chillun* and back to *Emperor* again. When a read-through of *Chillun* was announced in 1924, a *Chicago Defender* headline tellingly misidentified the play, playwright, and actor as follows: "Gilpin Play Read" (1924: 7). Gilpin neither wrote nor performed in *All God's Chillun*, but many *Defender* readers assumed that an O'Neill play with a black role would be his. It was not to be. In spite of this, comparisons were constantly made between the two actors, for as Marvin Carlson reminds us, former actors and productions often haunt the stage (2003: 1–15).

Gilpin not only haunted the role of Brutus Jones, but also stalked it, for he was in the audience opening night for Robeson's revival. Strangely, only the *Post* mentioned this fact: "The chief interest in the present production lies, of course, in a comparison of the skill of the new 'Emperor' and the creator of the title part, Charles Gilpin, who was in the audience to witness the debut of his successor" ("*The Emperor Jones* Reappears" 1924). Robeson's wife, Eslanda (Essie), made the following note in her diary from opening night: "Performance really fine. Gilpin was there and he and O'Neill quarreled . . . after play" (Robeson 2001: 116). It must have been a bitter pill indeed to watch Robeson perform the role that "belonged" to him, but Gilpin was far from defeated and was plotting his directorial debut.

By the time Robeson assumed the Emperor's role in 1924, he was no newcomer to the theatre, but his early theatrical work has been given little attention. He performed in the all-black hit revue *Shuffle Along* with Florence Mills and Jules Bledsoe, a revue that David Krasner has shown to be a landmark production in shaping African American theatre (and was revived on Broadway in 2016 as *Shuffle Along, or, the Making of the Musical Sensation in 1921 and All That Followed*) (2002: 248). Robeson did not confine himself to musical revues; his early work in drama is less well known but equally important. It was in the Lafayette Players' production of *Taboo*—along with white female lead Margaret Wycherly—that he was spotted by Provincetowners Robert Edmond Jones and Kenneth Macgowan, who then considered him for *All God's Chillun Got Wings*. When controversy delayed the opening of *Chillun*, Robeson went back to the Lafayette to rehearse *Roseanne* (another part he took over from Gilpin) ("Rehearsals Will").[51] Robeson's inroads into black theatre were just as calculated as his "sustained effort to become a part of the Provincetown Players," as Glenda Gill has shown (2006). In spite of this theatrical work and in addition to working on race films with Oscar Micheaux (*Body and Soul* and *Borderline*), Robeson's connections to Harlem were increasingly ignored, especially in the white press. The comparisons were made, rather, to Gilpin.

Such judgments of the two actors often focused on embodiment. While many reviews pointed out Gilpin's small stature and even baldness, many more obsessed on Robeson's physicality. Just as Gilpin faded away into obscurity, so Robeson was blown out of proportion. Taking my cue from Harvey Young, I see this discourse about Robeson's body as a manifestation of racial projections and anxieties regarding male blackness. The "black body," Young writes, is "an abstracted and imagined figure" that "shadows or doubles the real one. It is the black body and not a particular, flesh-and-blood body that is the target of a racializing projection" (2010: 7). Indeed, racialized projections infused the reviews for *The Emperor Jones*, which mentioned almost obsessively Robeson's "black body," a body that overshadowed not only white characters in the play, but also whiteness itself. For instance, the *New York Morning World* noted in 1924 that Robeson was "a fine figure of a man, possessor of an extraordinary and enviable physique and a deep, resonant voice" ("At the Provincetown" 1924).[52] The review goes on to remark upon Robeson's boxer-like physicality: "Mr. Robeson was thrice called before the curtain to receive the cheers and applause of the house. He presented such a figure in a checkered bathrobe, that one might have been pardoned for wondering just what he'd do to [boxer] Harry Willis."[53] The peculiar reference to what lurked underneath Robeson's bathrobe reveals the reviewer's queer racialized desire in more ways than one. Robeson was not only bursting out of his bathrobe—he could not be contained by prevailing discourse either. His black body was, in one sense, too large. "Big and robust" is what the *New York World* called Robeson in 1924 ("A New Emperor" 1924). While playing in London in 1925, a reviewer referred to Robeson as "a negro actor of immense height and capability" ("Eugene O'Neill's Plays" 1925).[54] Another remarked: "No praise could be too high for the performance of Paul Robeson, whose physique is as magnificent as his acting."[55] Most illustrations overemphasized Robeson's magnitude, making him appear like a goliath, dwarfing a cowering Smithers, the pathetic white English colonizer of the play. Several headlines referred to Robeson literally as a giant (e.g., "Giant Negro Actor" and "Giant-Negro Actor and His Ambition to Sing").[56] Another headline was all about numbers: "6 ft. 4 in. Negro Actor's Triumph."[57] Lloyd L. Brown, a journalist who helped Robeson write his biography, summed it up well: "There was always a largeness about Paul Robeson" (qtd. Willis 1988: 61).

Of course, Robeson *was* large, but hardly a giant. The point was not just that Robeson was tall and large, but rather that there was a *largeness about his blackness*. As the caption to the illustration put it ("Oh, the Black and White of It"), Robeson's formidable blackness pointed to—and at times subverted—epistemologies of race. These examples demonstrate in other words *not* the enormity of Robeson's physicality, but rather the immense power of racializing fantasies projected onto Robeson's body, which seemed larger than life itself. Such projections were not new, however, as Jeffrey C. Stewart (1988) points out: "the racial coding of Robeson's body size had begun long before he played Emperor Jones in 1924." In fact, as a Rutgers's football star, Robeson was billed as a "Colored Giant" on a game flier. Whereas on the football field, Robeson's "largeness" was seen as beneficial, in American public spheres it was another matter. "Throughout the plays that Robeson acts in during the 1920s," Stewart writes, "his particular body comes to signify the gargantuan threat of the Black body to civilization" (1988: 140). In a sketch that appeared in the *World*, Marcus Garvey's black nationalist publication, we see not only a "gargantuan" Robeson, but also a face drawn like an African mask, perhaps influenced by the mask from *All God's Chillun Got Wings*.[58] Resembling Garvey in this illustration, Robeson's sullen, downcast face is riveting, yet out of proportion with his large, expressionistically drawn body, a figure that could at any instant burst forth, should the arms unclasp and the eyes gaze outward. As always, the gun is strapped to the emperor, paradoxically signaling imminent danger, if not the mystical silver bullet that will be his undoing.

While Robeson was drawn as fully clothed in some print media in the role of Brutus Jones, on stage and in film he ended up almost nude by the end of the story. As Johan Callens has shown, "the racial coding of Robeson's naked (upper) body" while playing Brutus Jones was inscribed "within a racialized representational practice that played upon numerous primitivist discourses" (2004: 53). The charge of primitivism in *The*

Emperor Jones (and other O'Neill works) is a well-established critique, one that I do not intend to duplicate here. I do wish to stress how Robeson negotiated the signifying force of racializing projections. Jeffrey Stewart writes: "He, wittingly or not, became a site for the doubleness of white consciousness about the Black male body in the 1920s—that it was both a site of rejection and identification, both completely Other and one's Self" (1988: 142). Robeson had his admirers as diverse as the notorious white slummer Carl Van Vechten and the raconteur of Harlem, Alexander Gumby, both of whom devote pages in their scrapbooks to Robeson with their own sort of queer fandom.[59] Robeson would continue to have fans and detractors on both sides of the color line, a line that was crossed as well as queered, as Siobhan Somerville might say (2000: 1–14). His popular media images, such as in the film version where "those shirtless, well-oiled, muscular glimpses of him singing while shoveling coal or busting rocks in *The Emperor Jones* (1933)," were careful constructions, according to Stewart, "packaged for the gaze of an admiring public" (qtd. Callens 2004: 53). The gaze onto the black male body was not new, but Robeson's signifying force deserves particular attention.

Put another way, Robeson embodied the modernist tensions inscribed onto black men. Hazel Carby writes, "Robeson combined, in uneasy stasis and for a brief period of time, the historically contradictory elements of race, nation, and masculinity" (2009: 48–49). I would argue that *The Emperor Jones* was central to Robeson embodying these modernist contradictions and moreover that the theatre specifically allowed him the opportunity to perform, while also disidentify with, such discourses.[60] Carby continues: "To modernists' imaginings, Paul Robeson offered the possibility of unity for a fractious age, which simultaneously embodied what the dominant social order imagined to be an essential 'blackness' or 'Negroness." Building on Carby's insights (2009: 50), I'd like to highlight how Robeson undercut these racializing projections with his own performative interventions. If others were voyeuristically viewing Robeson's body, he was at least in control of some of the presentations. Robeson negotiated the primitivistic contradictions of what Kurt Eisen (2008) has called ethnographic modernism. As Michelle Stephens (2014) has written, Robeson consciously curated a powerful image of himself by posing for a series of nude photographs and sculpture. One thing is certain: Robeson knew he was being looked at and cultivated certain looks—many while performing Brutus Jones. In a 1924 production photo from *The Emperor Jones*, Robeson is "still standing," to use Harvey Young's formation, returning the gaze back at the photographer and viewer,

Figure 5 Paul Robeson in the 1924 production of *The Emperor Jones*. Photo credit: White Studio. (Billy Rose Theatre Division, the New York Public Library.)

challenging efforts to contain him (see Figure 5). He is in character both as the belligerent Brutus Jones and as a radicalized citizen. Like so many New York actors, Robeson worked on both sides of Broadway, both uptown and downtown, in productions that were consciously citing, if not critiquing, Broadway. And O'Neill's dramas were central to this performative project.

The Emperor's story does not end with Gilpin or Robeson or any single actor performing Brutus Jones. To this royal family I add Jules Bledsoe (about whom I have written elsewhere), Opal Cooper, and Wayland

Rudd.[61] Journalist Gwendolyn Bennett made a compelling case for Rudd's interpretation of Brutus Jones in 1930:

> For me there was something fearful and contemptible about the Brutus Jones of Charles Gilpin; there was something almost childlike about the rollicking Emperor of Paul Robeson; Wayland Rudd did something that was a combination of both of these with a dash of something so poignant that it wrung your heart as you lived through the part with him.[62] (1930: 271)

Rudd's powerful performance has been given scant scholarly attention (other than Barry Witham's book [2013] on Philadelphia's Hedgerow Theatre founded by Jasper Deeter, the actor who performed the original Smithers), but its importance extends to breaking the color line in spectatorship. Bennett's piece provides details:

> Inter-racial gatherings in Philadelphia are usually farces except in one or two rare instances. This was one of the rare instances. To speak of a theatrical premiere as an interracial gathering seems an anomaly. However, this particular premiere bore all the earmarks of a studied and planned meeting of the proverbial twain. (1930: 270)

As the Hedgerow production demonstrates, O'Neill's *The Emperor Jones* razed barriers on stage just as it dismantled segregationist logic in the audience.

Many actors performed Brutus Jones for over a decade, in different spheres and productions, circulating in and out of adjacent cartographies. When Gilpin originated the role of Brutus Jones on Broadway in 1920, Robeson was performing other roles in Harlem. When Gilpin went on tour with *The Emperor Jones*, Robeson was making theatre both with the Lafayette Players and in the Village, eventually taking over the role as emperor in 1924. By the time Jules Bledsoe appeared as Brutus Jones in a 1926 Harlem production, he was booed off the stage. Gilpin never gave up on the role he always claimed was his, touring throughout the United States, while Robeson performed the role in England. Gilpin directed his own production on Broadway in 1926, breaking another racial barrier. Meanwhile, Bledsoe found opportunities abroad, singing the opera version of *The Emperor Jones* to great acclaim in Europe in the early 1930s. After a memorable Philadelphia performance, Wayland Rudd would become an expatriate in

Russia, finding more meaningful roles for him there. Gilpin and Bledsoe, both of whom fought tirelessly against racism on and off the stage, would both die at early ages. Robeson was officially launched into stardom with the film version of *The Emperor Jones* (directed by Dudley Murphy in 1933) and became increasingly engaged with civil rights work. Taken together, but not collapsed as one, these productions show how *The Emperor Jones* enacted important cultural production within and beyond imperial representation. O'Neill's other so-called "race plays" (*The Dreamy Kid*, 1918 and *All God's Chillun Got Wings*, 1924) would fade into oblivion with few productions after 1925. Indeed, with the exception of Joe Mott's character in *The Iceman Cometh*, O'Neill refrained from portraying African American characters in his later works, turning instead to the vexed interiority of his own family for dramaturgical content. *The Emperor Jones*, on the other hand, was performed by almost every great African American actor. Again and again, *The Emperor Jones* has been a vehicle for staging matters of race beyond the Great White Way.

TONY KUSHNER'S O'NEILL: SEEKING MEANING ON
MARBLEHEAD NECK

Sheila Hickey Garvey

In 1973 Tony Kushner was a seventeen-year-old Columbia University undergraduate in medieval studies working part-time as a switchboard operator at the United Nations. The son of artistically gifted musician parents, Kushner was raised to love the arts. Inspired by rave reviews, the financially strapped student purchased standing-room-only tickets to see the highly acclaimed 1973 Broadway revival of Eugene O'Neill's *A Moon for the Misbegotten* directed by José Quintero and starring Jason Robards and Colleen Dewhurst. In later years Kushner would recall that he was so "devastated" by that three-hour production he returned and stood a second time (2012).

Despite this strong response, Kushner recalled "being a young nineteen-year-old and reading *Long Day's Journey Into Night* for the first time and sort of not getting it and finding it endless and pathetic and solipsistic and all sorts of embarrassing things" (2012). Kushner's opinion of O'Neill's worth remained unchanged for twenty years until he attended a Baltimore's Center Stage 1993 production of *A Moon for the Misbegotten* directed by his friend Lisa Peterson. He recalled being astonished after walking into the theatre's auditorium and

> seeing the stage painted like the sky and the front of the house and the background was the grass and the rocks and so she [Peterson] had stood the holistic world of Eugene O'Neill on its head . . . there were vaudeville sort of theatre songs maybe in it and it was done in a style that was deliberately theatricalized and it was the first time that I thought, "Oh My God, you know these are theater people or at least Jamie is at any rate. And *Long Day's Journey Into Night* is about two actors and a playwright and a failed concert pianist or somebody who maybe should have been a concert pianist. I mean there's artificiality in this; there's something going on here beyond playing naturalism." And I thought to myself, "I really should go back and take another look." (2012)

Once home in New York, Kushner revisited his college copy of *Long Day's Journey Into Night* and noted to himself that he "had spilled [it] all over with ink." He "pried it open" and read the entire play in two hours while sobbing. He put it down having concluded, "I'm wrong. This is the greatest play ever written by an American and one of the greatest plays ever written" (2012).

It wasn't Eugene O'Neill who changed, it was Tony Kushner. At the time he attended the *Moon* revival, his own world was being turned upside down much like the staging effect that startled him in Baltimore. Lisa Peterson's nonrealistic conceptualization of *Moon* was radically different from José Quintero's 1973 Broadway revival. It altered Kushner's previous notion of Eugene O'Neill as a writer indulgently bogged down in distasteful self-examination and smothered by realism. But there was something else that Kushner had come to understand about O'Neill, and that was grief and mourning.

Having recently received an Olivier Award nomination in London, in April 1993—and shortly after Kushner attended the Baltimore O'Neill revival—his play *Angels in America, Part One: Millennium Approaches* premiered on Broadway. The production won both the Pulitzer Prize and the Tony Award in 1993. The following year *Angels in America, Part Two: Perestroika* won a second Tony Award, marking the completion of the historic seven-hour, two-part epic that Kushner subtitled, *A Gay Fantasia on National Themes*. Equally important to Kushner, an openly gay man, was that he was able to have a national and international venue to voice through *Angels* a damming criticism of Ronald Reagan's administration, one that he considered unconscionably negligent in its nonresponse to the era's AIDS epidemic.

Until the success of *Angels in America*, Kushner saw himself as a completely different writer from Eugene O'Neill. Kushner's writing was Marxist and political. It required Brechtian staging techniques and other nonrealistic theatrical conventions to match and emphasize his use of mythological references, dream sequences, fantasy locations, and ghosts. Kushner's writing intermingled the temporal, the supernatural, and fantasy. But in the early 1990s Kushner's ideological and artistic beliefs about life and art were being challenged. He was catapulted to fame and became a mainstream capitalist success while many friends and fellow artists died agonizing deaths from AIDS. Survivor guilt was a logical, instinctual reaction from a humanist such as Kushner. Death entwined with tragic circumstances and success was O'Neill's way of life. In 1993, Kushner came to understand that

> one of the reason we love O'Neill so much is that those things that are overwhelming in his work—loss and grief and the accompanying devastation and the unsuccessful mourning—are in some ways a

carrot that there's some meaning to life, some purpose to human existence and that our job in some way is to discover what that might mean and to try in some way through that discovery to fulfill our purpose. And, that sense that O'Neill is haunted by throughout, that fear of failure and success that he inherited from his father and his brother. I mean the universality . . . that's why there's a dialogue between me and O'Neill. (2012)

By 1998 Kushner had begun drafting a script that he would later refer to as his *Moby-Dick* (2016). It was a screen treatment for filmmaker and Broadway producer Scott Rudin with an unspecified deadline, about aspects of Eugene O'Neill's life that fascinated Kushner. The plot would focus on an occurrence in the winter of 1912 when O'Neill, then twenty-four, unsuccessfully attempted suicide (the experience on which he based the recently recovered 1919 play *Exorcism*). This would be the core of the film's storyline and would address whether or not those who saved O'Neill's life knew what they were doing, says Kushner, "when they didn't let him go into a Veranol-induced coma and just die. I am looking at, and risk sentimentalizing, the relationship of art and life and the possibility and impact of art on life. [Saving O'Neill] was certainly something they did because they're not terrible people. Did they save him the way you would save a kindred who would have taken an overdose of drugs? Or, did something more than that happen? It's complicated. . . . So I'm delving into that. It's been difficult. That may be one reason I've taken so much time" (2016).

Yet it wasn't until 2003 that Kushner would describe himself as "coming out" publicly about his fixation on O'Neill. This occurred when Richard Eyre of Britain's National Theatre asked him to write the program notes for a production of O'Neill's *Mourning Becomes Electra* starring Helen Mirren. It was in these notes that Kushner described O'Neill's attempt to write the epic play cycle, *A Tale of Possessors Self-Dispossessed*, as "an omnivorous fiction that devours its creator" (2004: 252). This insight and Kushner's other observations about O'Neill struck such a strong chord that quotations from the program notes began to circulate. It was eventually reprinted in the *Times Literary Supplement*, *American Theater* magazine, and *The Eugene O'Neill Review*. He was invited to be interviewed onscreen for a 2006 American Experience documentary for PBS, *Eugene O'Neill*, directed by Ric Burns and scripted by Arthur and Barbara Gelb. The film project intrigued Kushner as an examination of the toll that being an artist took on O'Neill's life and paralleled his own reflections on the cost to O'Neill's personal life and health from his relentless efforts to perfect his craft.

In 2009 composer Jeanine Tesori asked Kushner if he might work with her on a new opera. The two had each received nominations for Tony Awards, his as playwright and hers as composer, for their 2004 collaboration on the Broadway musical *Caroline, or Change*. Tesori had been contacted by Francesca Zambello, the artistic director of the Glimmerglass Opera in Cooperstown, New York, requesting music for a companion piece to an already scheduled one-act opera about American painter Edward Hopper. Upon learning of Zambello's proposal Kushner's thoughts turned to his still-evolving O'Neill screen treatment that he gave Tesori. After reading it, she became very interested in working on the scenes about a terrible argument that took place in 1951 between O'Neill and his wife, Carlotta, while they were living in Marblehead Neck, Massachusetts. Her choice appealed to Kushner because focusing on that one segment of his broader O'Neill project would serve as a test to examine his ruminations on other portions of O'Neill's life. Kushner later recalled being somewhat flippant knowing he had a god-like power to create *his* O'Neill. He remembered thinking, "This is going to be a great little thing with a baritone out in the snow, alone, singing while he succumbs to hypothermia . . . a great opera set-up" (2012). However, once Kushner and Tesori began working in depth, Kushner took upon himself O'Neill's point of view, that of a frail and broken man, humbled by repeated failures, unable to write, and on the precipice of erasure through death. Kushner metaphorically titled his one-act opera *A Blizzard on Marblehead Neck* to reflect the actual weather conditions at the rocky seaside location for the opera and the real-life O'Neills' domestic crisis.

Kushner and Tesori completed their truncated version of a planned longer production in a little more than six months, just as Zambello began rehearsals. As O'Neill had done in so many of his plays, Kushner structured the plot of *Blizzard* by intermingling classical playwriting conventions with very American character types and European avant-garde stage techniques. For instance, the three classical unities of time, place, and action are loosely employed. The action covers less than twenty-four hours; unity of action is observed by including only the incidents leading up to and during O'Neill's near death from hypothermia. The unity of place convention is suggested by setting the opera solely on the grounds of the O'Neills' Marblehead Neck property. Set designer Erhard Rom resolved the problem of where to situate Officer Snow who, in the opera, finds O'Neill and saves his life. Using a shuttered overhead light,

Mark McCullough framed Snow's cramped office within the grounds of the O'Neill's modest estate. While the police officer types his post-incident report, we see the circumstances he describes recreated adjacent to him on the O'Neills' Marblehead property.

Quite obviously, Kushner's tragic hero is Eugene O'Neill, who is referred to as Kreon, Oedipus, King Lear, and other ancient classic protagonists within the libretto. In like manner, Kushner writes Carlotta O'Neill as a vengeful Clytemnestra and also a Jocasta unwittingly forced into collusion because of her husband's omissions and failures. O'Neill's three children, Eugene Jr., Shane, and Oona, are described at various moments by the Carlotta character as having been sacrificed by their Agamemnon-like father for the sake of his playwriting ambitions. Further classical conventions in *A Blizzard on Marblehead Neck* include a facsimile Greek chorus in the guise of three American theatre critics of the era, Bernard DeVoto, Louis Kronenberger, and Mary McCarthy. These reputed intellectuals of the post–Second World War era who panned original productions of several of O'Neill's greatest plays at times also serve as a trio of vengeful furies in modern guise. Besides highlighting the similarities between himself and Eugene O'Neill as playwrights, Kushner projects himself in the three critics as having once been as self-righteously judgmental as they were regarding O'Neill's larger import and contributions to the theatre. The Mary McCarthy character, in particular, serves as a window into Kushner's thinking prior to his O'Neillian conversion.

As Kushner explains, by seeing only O'Neill's weaknesses in such works as *The Iceman Cometh* McCarthy "blinds herself to what makes him so really great and protean . . . his ability to sort of rearrange the molecules of the bones of the people in the audience listening to him, which he could not do if he didn't write at such extraordinary length. . . . And what makes it a masterpiece is in part that you hear the themes so much and the hopelessness of being stuck in a rut in this terrible way" (2012). As Part I of the opera concludes, Carlotta sides with O'Neill's critics, challenging her husband to question his own ultimate worth. She repeats the word "flop," perhaps to counter O'Neill's barbs at her, in citing his failures: first as a playwright with premieres of *The Iceman Cometh* and *A Moon for the Misbegotten*, next as a father—a charge Kushner himself believes O'Neill guilty of to "an almost criminal level of license" (2012)—and last as a husband because his physical disorder has made him impotent. The betrayed O'Neill leaves the house, summoning what little physical strength and emotional dignity he can muster. Like King Lear, O'Neill escapes into a treacherous storm.

Part two of *A Blizzard* continues the Shakespearean references as Eugene O'Neill speaks lines of the character of Antigonus from Shakespeare's *A Winter's Tale*:

The storm begins, poor wretch,
That for thy mother's fault art thus exposed
To loss, and what may follow! Weep I cannot,
But my heart bleeds, and most accursed am I. (3.3.49–52)

Antigonus has been ordered by King Leontes to kill his daughter, who he believes is illegitimate. O'Neill recites Shakespeare, having been betrayed in his youth by his drug-addicted mother and then accused at the end of his life by Carlotta of abandoning his daughter Oona. Kushner further compounds parenting references by using a selection from the playwright that O'Neill learned to admire from his own father, James O'Neill, the parent who did not abandon him. During this sequence, Kushner writes O'Neill as a man who believes himself on the verge of death, pondering his past omissions and sins.

In the Glimmerglass production, scene designer Rom and lighting designer Mark McCullough echoed Kushner's artist-to-artist homage by supplying a mesmerizing and supersized full moon similar to those O'Neill describes in many of his own stage directions. Beneath this fascinating orb and wandering through a dense blizzard, the now lunatic and confused O'Neill begins to fantasize himself a wrongly accused Irish peasant, declaring his innocence before an unseen judge. In an Irish tinker's dialect, O'Neill pleads, "Not a wife-beater, I naver shtruck the drab" (Kushner 2011: 17). The kind of abusive physical action that both the O'Neills at times indulged in. Kushner enacts a version of poetic justice upon O'Neill for his bad behavior by portraying him as becoming a caricature of a plummy nineteenth-century actor, exactly the sort of stage Irishman stereotype O'Neill devoted his life to erasing from the stage. As O'Neill begins to succumb to hypothermia, he entertains another fantasy, this time of his estranged daughter Oona. A young woman appears on the stage who seems like an apparition dressed entirely in white, although her clothing is that of a 1920s Broadway chorine. Simultaneously, the "The Missing Song" is heard. As O'Neill beckons to the Oona/angel/chorine character, he refers to himself as Oedipus, while singing, "Daughter of the blind old man, where I wonder have we come to now" (Kushner 2011: 19).

In the initial writing phase, Kushner had not consciously thought of the character appearing to O'Neill was anything more than an angel; eventually, he said, "I realized that the angel was Oona and I was very moved by that. And since reading [biographer Louis] Sheaffer the first time I've always been struck that this man who was so attuned to family . . . that what O'Neill did to Oona is positively staggering" (2012). The Oedipal implications of Oona's presence in O'Neill's dream-like haze during this latter scene especially delighted Kushner when he connected the angel to Oona. In Kushner's view Oona's marriage to Charlie Chaplin, her father's contemporary, was her way of administering a Freudian sort of checkmate to her physically diminished father. According to Kushner, "I also have always loved that [O'Neill] who was such an old Freudian had overwhelming Oedipal panic because of [Oona] catching . . . probably only about one of three men on the planet who was as revered as an artist as much as O'Neill was. Charlie Chaplin was— if you wanted to do him in—Charlie Chaplin was the absolutely correct person" (2012). As the scene between the Oona figure and O'Neill continues, a bath-robed Carlotta wanders upstage singing out, "Gene! Please don't die, Gene, Gene, please come back! Geeeeeeeennnnnnne!!" Carlotta cannot find Gene and exits, as does Oona, but not before encouraging O'Neill to rest his "stone-cold, burning, broken heart." Now completely alone, the O'Neill character utters ideas expressed by the actual O'Neill, saying that he will not ask for God's forgiveness but rather forgive himself: "I hope there's a hell for the good somewhere!" Then, succumbing to hypothermia, O'Neill lies down in a bed of snow while singing, "Goodbye old moon. Drop into the sea. I don't need you anymore" (2011: 22).

In the final scene Kushner maintains his classical framework and references, but also seizes the opportunity to end with his own brand of populism, exercising the poetic license or "liberties" he states at the beginning of the libretto that he will indulge. For instance, he modifies some of the actual incidents that occurred the night of the argument between the real Mr. and Mrs. O'Neill. During that snowy 1951 evening it was their physician Dr. Dana who stumbled upon O'Neill at the spot where he had fallen, having been called there by someone unnamed, perhaps the O'Neills' houseman, Saki (Gelb 2016: 688–96). After finding O'Neill, Dr. Dana brought him back into the nearby house and called an ambulance. Since Kushner wrote an opera and not a documentary, the playwright chose to replace the actual Dr. Dana with the character of the wise and gentle Officer John Snow, who states in the opera that it was he who found "an old man who's half-alive, half-buried in a snowdrift, unresponsive, can't revive. It was minutes till my shift was finished, but so what? He was child's play to lift" (2011: 23). Kushner also gave Snow the suggestive name Christopher as the opera's redeemer, or *deus ex machina*, who finds and saves the lost, almost frozen O'Neill. Snow also serves other purposes as the opera's Brechtian observer. The Marxist in Kushner emerges as he gives his common man Snow the final word. It is Snow who holds the powerful climactic moments at the opera's conclusion while proffering commonsense interpretations of the O'Neill couple's erratic behavior: "Your heartbeat quickens when wounds demand repaying. Love and anger both make heat. Beats freezing. Or decaying. I say she went out in a blizzard to find him, nightdress, no shoes on her feet. I came lookin' for her and found him. So she did it, sorta saved him. She saved him. Now I'm beat" (2011: 25).

As did the actual Officer Snow, the operatic incarnation of his character both sees and values the O'Neill couple's humanity as distinct from their identity as historically important American figures. The real Officer Snow often visited the O'Neills in their Marblehead home to let the elderly couple know they were safe in their isolated location, but also because he enjoyed having conversations with Eugene (Gelb 2106: 686–87). Although there is no evidence to prove that the actual Officer Snow had ever attended one of O'Neill's plays, in his opera Kushner chose to give Officer Snow dialogue that implies he attended a performance of O'Neill's 1946 production of *The Iceman Cometh*. Snow sings his review of O'Neill's work, one that is in complete opposition to its critics saying, "I loved that show! Endless? Sure. So's damnation. The torments of hell are slow" (2011: 23). Kushner fictionalizes Snow's motive to highlight this character's ability to empathize with the distraught older man and his confused wife. Kushner describes Snow as "someone who's suffered. He tells you that at the beginning of the song. His sister is crazy . . . and he [Snow] sounds like someone who may have had a drinking problem . . . . So, he [Snow] really loves *Iceman* . . . he gets it. He's a very nice guy, the policeman, but whatever his suffering has been, he gets it that . . . the point of the length of *Iceman* which its critics were too clever to get" (2012).

For this spiritually uplifting conclusion Kushner gave himself the daunting task of writing Officer Snow's lyrics in *terza rima*, the three-lined rhyme scheme—ABA, BCB, CDC—that Dante used, according to Kushner, because "it's a ladder. The rhyme scheme keeps progressing forward. It never returns. It keeps climbing. And of course in the *Divine Comedy* the *Inferno* is the descent and in *Purgatory* and *Paradiso* it's an ascent up this ladder." Accordingly, Kushner wrote Snow's police report in *terza rima* to signify O'Neill's eventual ascent from his own personal hell (2012). However, he faced a problem when choosing to use this poetic form: he had no idea how his partner Tesori planned to structure her musical score for the opera as a whole, much less for any of his individual lyrics. He realized, even before showing her his lyrics for Officer Snow, that his use of the *terza rima* would present her with a challenge. Kushner recalled that the composer soon became intrigued with the form: "Because she couldn't compose in a *terza rima* form she did sort of a 50's jazzy thing where the rhymes are incredibly fugitive throughout the song" (2012).

Kushner wanted the character of Snow to serve as an American counterpart of Elizabethan groundlings, in the strong belief that O'Neill's plays appeal to all economic segments of contemporary society and more specifically to those capable of appreciating a great work of art. Kushner's theory is that O'Neill's highly sophisticated writing has appealed to those individuals O'Neill referred to as "the fog people," meaning those not wedded to a fixed aesthetic vision of the sort voiced by professional critics of *The Iceman Cometh* in 1946 and *A Moon for the Misbegotten* in 1947. Kushner believes that

> it's really O'Neill who discovered "the native eloquence of the fog people." . . . There's an intellectual difficulty in O'Neill no matter how much Bernard DeVoto sneered at it. The plays are clearly not just popular entertainment. But what's really true in O'Neill and what's astonishing in O'Neill is that he was very much in one sense his father's son. I think that all plays are this, even *Hamlet*. Even the greatest play ever written is also a work of popular entertainment. Theatre doesn't exist if a large group of people can't be held by it. (2012)

Here Kushner affirms his interest in an art-life connection and his hope that art is important. Kushner points to the existence of groundlings as evidence. For Kushner it is they or O'Neill's "fog people" who validate art because even though they are poor and perhaps uneducated, they enjoy art in theatres, cinemas, and museums. And, as they may have in Kushner's still-evolving O'Neill screenplay, the youthful playwright's derelict friends, the groundlings in his personal drama, save the life of a young man with hints of the potential for greatness.

After a brief ten-day rehearsal period, on July 21, 2011, *A Blizzard on Marblehead Neck* had its premiere to an enthusiastic reception. "The score is beautiful and singable," wrote the reviewer for *Opera Pulse*, "but not derivative or forgettable," praising the libretto as "full of quotable lines which do nothing to distract from the arc of the story." Noting that Kushner envisioned *Blizzard* as part of a three-part work, he expressed the hope that it "enter the repertory of frequently performed work of living composers" (Browning 2011). The Albany *Times Union* reviewer observed that "the music is pounding and furious while the insults, pointed and smart, zing. The pace eventually slackens, thank heavens, but the entire 40-minute opera has a power and immediacy that's rare to new works" (Dalton 2011). In a highly desired *New York Times* review, opera critic Anthony Tommasini wrote, "Though just 40 minutes, it's an intense and strangely involving work, with a brilliant libretto by Mr. Kushner and an eclectic score by Ms. Tesori" (2011: C2).

Kushner was satisfied with the results of this collaboration, and for a few years following its premiere, the Metropolitan Opera's managing director Peter Gelb was ready to commission a full-length version. However, Kushner was not able to follow up with an extended revision that could coincide with the Met's season planning schedule. However, Scott Rudin maintains interest in producing both the film and what is now planned as a Broadway musical version, which Kushner hopes to call *A Fire in the Shelton Hotel.* The title incorporates the name of the Boston hotel where the couple were staying when O'Neill died. It is also the location where they destroyed the unfinished cycle's manuscripts. Kushner envisions that the latter will occur at the set's sitting room fireplace.

Kushner offers several reasons why his O'Neill projects remain unfinished. He keeps up a busy production schedule; in 2016 alone he had two productions running in London, and unlike O'Neill, Kushner does not sequester himself, maintaining an active speaking schedule as he relishes public conversations and political discussions. His modesty is another factor. Kushner does not consider himself to be as essential to the development and advancement of American dramatic literature as O'Neill was:

In no way [do I] consider myself to be a writer of the stature of Eugene O'Neill. I mean, I think I'm a good playwright. And at this point in my life I've written at least one play which twenty-five years after its premiere seems to be enduring and perhaps it will endure on some level. But O'Neill was a genius, which is a word I think should be used to describe a very small group of people who do the things that no one else has done and who works steadily at an unbelievably high level. Writing *Angels In America* is a feat of which I'm very proud. It's not the same thing as writing *Long Day's Journey*

Into Night, *The Iceman Cometh* or even *Beyond the Horizon*. The way O'Neill's work single-handedly made a case for serious American dramatic literature and created a space for it in American cultural consciousness is kind of a protean act of creation. I felt at the time of *Angels in America* that I was thirty-three years old and a beneficiary of an accident because of the timing at a moment when the country and the world was really ready to assimilate the catastrophe of the [AIDS] epidemic. I came along at the right moment and it became a very, very big deal. It's stayed a big deal and I'm very grateful about that. But I sort of knew then that it would be the only kind of thing I'd do that would receive that sort of acclaim and I thought that my job now was not to ever try and match that but to really do good work that I feel proud of. I think my career is much more like Arthur Miller's or Tennessee Williams's (not to make the comparisons because they are superior writers). What they had to contend with having written a play like *Streetcar* or *Salesman* fairly early in their writing lives was struggling to know that the very best work they wrote was in their thirties. (2016)

Kushner adds, "The reason I haven't finished the film script or the opera could be Oedipal," in the sense that in finishing either script he "finishes" O'Neill. Evidence of Kushner's reticence to finish off O'Neill is found in the text of *Blizzard*. He wrote Officer Snow's dialogue as an uplifting conclusion to the opera and a happy ending to O'Neill's marital problems, an ending that leaves the audience relieved and O'Neill still alive.

Kushner is attracted to some of history's darker hours, as in his *Angels* plays and *Homebody/Kabul* and screenplays for the films *Munich* and *Lincoln*, and takes many years to write his versions of those events. As O'Neill understood, writing about agony takes its toll on a playwright's mind and soul. Still, Kushner insists that he will finish both the O'Neill film script and the musical. He firmly states they are not his own "omnivorous fictions" waiting to devour him. He is well aware of O'Neill's failed struggle to complete his American history cycle plays before his health gave out. Reflecting a decisive moment in his career Kushner recalls:

I gave an interview at some point where I said I was going to write a third part and a fourth part of *Angels in America* and I'll be like Walt Whitman, I'll just keep adding on sections to this one work. And I thought, "OK well, then all I'll be looking at is *Angels* characters for the rest of my life." And then I thought, "I don't really want to do that." So I just decided to cut the cord and move on, and it was sort of a liberation. (2016)

Rather than be another James O'Neill, trapped in a parasitic vehicle that drains his talents, or like James's son Eugene undertaking a lengthy and ultimately all-consuming cycle of plays, Kushner will try instead "to fulfill [his] purpose" (2016). Some, but not all of that "purpose" is to maintain an ongoing "dialogue" with the greatest of all America's playwrights, Eugene O'Neill.

CONCLUSION: O'NEILL AFTER O'NEILL

The reappearance of the long-lost *Exorcism* in 2011 was a major event for American theatre mainly because the revival of *The Iceman Cometh* and the premiere of *Long Day's Journey* had so powerfully revived O'Neill's previously fading stature in 1956. The recovered script was neither a masterpiece nor a revelatory document sending biographers and scholars rushing back to update their assessments of his life and work. It does, however, illuminate the progress O'Neill had made as an artist between writing this one-act play in 1919 and his next, and final, work in that form in 1941. *Hughie*, whose New York premiere late in 1964 was the last for a mature, completed O'Neill play,[1] was originally planned as part of an eight-part project that O'Neill conceived under the title "By Way of Obit" (LFA 437).[2]

Conjuring the dead

Most critics dismissed *Hughie* respectfully as a posthumous minor work, overshadowed by Quintero's 1956 productions of *Iceman* and *Long Day's Journey*, despite its featuring Jason Robards Jr. in the main speaking role following his triumphs in both of those major plays. In the larger context of O'Neill's career since 1914, however, *Hughie* not only offers a poignant coda to his sustained theatrical critique of modernity but also suggests O'Neill's belief in the power of theatre to conjure the dead back to the realm of the living. Set in 1928 in a rundown Broadway hotel, *Hughie* is primarily a monologue. Erie Smith, a has-been *"Broadway sport and a Wise Guy"* modeled on O'Neill's brother Jim (CP3: 832),[3] arrives in the hotel lobby after an extended drink. Daunted by the solitude awaiting in his room, he tries to engage the reticent Night Clerk in a late-night conversation, with his sexual exploits and tales of unspecified small-time crimes along with recollections of the Night Clerk's predecessor, Hughie, the deceased title character. Erie is a pathological extrovert, but his need for affirmation fails to penetrate the Night Clerk's solipsistic preoccupation, rendered in stage directions rather than dialogue, with the noisy urban world beyond the dingy tedium of the hotel lobby. As Erie gabbles on, he also makes clear that the late Hughie was a credulous listener who helped prop up his tenuous self-confidence: "I'd get to seein' myself like he seen me" (CP3: 845). He wants the new Night Clerk to do the same but the latter is more intent on the early morning sounds—elevated trains, garbage collectors, "*the obsequies of night*" (CP3: 838)—and thinks despondently, even apocalyptically, of general destruction.

The hotel building itself, like the house of *Desire Under the Elms*, is a defining backdrop for the characters' inner lives:

> *It is one of those hotels, built in the decade 1900-10 on the side streets of the Great White Way sector, which began as respectable second class but were soon forced to deteriorate in order to survive. Following the World War and Prohibition, it had given up all pretense of respectability, and now is anything a paying guest wants it to be . . .* (CP3: 831)

Like the play's two characters, this hotel "*has not shared in the Great Hollow Boom of the twenties. The Everlasting Opulence of the New Economic Law has overlooked it*" (CP3: 831). Erie has no family, no connections other than those conjured forth in his bragging recollections, and the Night Clerk, coincidentally named Charles Hughes, has a family but no sense of connection to the world or to any meaningful future—even the person with him is just "492" to him, a number in the hotel register. The play turns when, as if to demonstrate a basic human need to find some interest in life, he becomes fascinated by the image of Erie as a daring gambler, perhaps even a friend of the great racketeer of the time, Arnold Rothstein. This notion seems to fortify the Night Clerk, who abruptly speaks to Erie the dark thoughts previously audible only to the audience: "Well, you can't burn it all down, can you? There's too much steel and stone. There'd always be something left to start it going again" (CP3: 848). At first taken aback, Erie soon perceives his new Hughie. The two men begin rolling dice in the decrepit lobby, fending off loneliness and mortality with a game of craps and, as the curtain falls, the even older game in which "*a Wise Guy regales a Sucker*" (CP3: 851).

How to convey the Night Clerk's inner thoughts and perceptions from the playwright's detailed text is perhaps the central problem of staging *Hughie*. In this final one-act play O'Neill retrofitted the novelizing instincts that had ample range to flourish in his longer works back into the briefer form that launched his career. In fact, this brand of theatricality seemed to confound many critics even in 1964, as if invoking George Pierce Baker from a half-century earlier in questioning whether such a plotless work as *Hughie* should be considered a play at all.[4] Meanwhile, the American premiere of Beckett's *Waiting for Godot* and the burgeoning Off-Broadway theatre (a term presaged in O'Neill's stage directions, *"the side streets of the Great White Way"*) starting in the 1950s, along with the plays of Tennessee Williams (often adapted from his own short fiction) and such plays as Edward Albee's *The Zoo Story* (paired with Beckett's *Krapp's Last Tape* in its 1960 American premiere at the Provincetown Playhouse) had already signaled a clear shift in the American theatre that should have made O'Neill's 1941 play seem in 1964, if anything, presciently postmodern. Henry Hewes observed aptly in his review that a Broadway venue is too large for such an intimate play; less reasonably, however, without suggesting an alternative he criticized director Quintero for having the Night Clerk *"speak* the inner dialogue so carefully placed within the stage directions as ideas to be *thought"* and looked forward to "an Off-Broadway revival to fulfill this O'Neill masterpiece," presumably with some better way to convey those thoughts or perhaps cutting them altogether (1965: CR 942). Zander Brietzke notes more helpfully that "an urban soundscape creates rich production opportunities and challenges" for directors and designers, concluding paradoxically of O'Neill's career-long struggle with the expository and representational limits of the stage, "The more novelistic the play, the more theatrical it becomes" (2001: 56–57).

The Experimental Theatre, cont.

O'Neill cannot be credited as the first American playwright to adapt European stagecraft or to shift the emphasis from external plot to the characters' internal lives. Yet his work with the Provincetown Players and then Experimental Theatre, Inc., was crucial in establishing the mainstream commercial viability of drama in America that was both thematically daring and theatrically innovative, opening new paths for Sophie Treadwell, Elmer Rice, Albee, Adrienne Kennedy, Sam Shepard, August Wilson, Paula Vogel, Tony Kushner, and many others. O'Neill's insistence on pulling audiences into his own artistic orbit rather than limiting himself to smaller avant-garde productions or, unthinkably for him, playing to the crowd in larger houses helped create the persisting image of the playwright as an independent artist in an otherwise thoroughly collaborative art. Undoubtedly his emergence in the 1920s coincided with, and perhaps exploited, an emerging professional class with sufficient means and self-regard to embrace a playwright whose work could mirror their own "depth," as Joel Pfister has shown (1995). Yet the notion of O'Neill as "America's greatest playwright" persists because of the cumulative dramatic force of his career beyond the individual plays, some of them bad but almost always interesting, and the resistance to modernity he continues to embody notwithstanding the frequent archaisms in his work sometimes to the point of quaintness.

Along with the revival of his reputation in the 1950s and 1960s the posthumous O'Neill remains vital because of the rich theatricality that directors and actors continue to find in his work. He jealously guarded his texts while alive, resisting cuts by directors and liberties taken by actors in performance, but the O'Neill canon has inspired productions in recent decades that reimagine those plays in the same spirit of experimentation O'Neill himself brought to the stage in the 1910s and 1920s. A notable example, the 2005 production of *Desire Under the Elms* by Hungarian director János Szász at the American Repertory Theatre in Cambridge, Massachusetts, aggressively deviated from O'Neill's text, stripping down even the elms in its post-naturalistic, deliberately Beckettian scenic design while introducing numerous twentieth-century anachronisms into the 1850 setting. Even more radically, the Wooster Group's deconstructive take on *The Emperor Jones*, directed by Elizabeth LeCompte in 1992 and again in 2006, hewed close to O'Neill's dialogue while taking his expressionist staging to postmodern extremes, with video monitors occupying the minimalist set along with the actors in Kabuki-style costumes. In the title role Kate Valk in blackface stressed the intrinsic artifice in O'Neill's Jones, so that the audience is made conscious, according to reviewer Charles Isherwood, of "an actress fashioning, with superb precision, a simulacrum of a stereotype" and thus calling attention to the challenge such an apparently racist role presents for a male African American actor especially in the twenty-first century (2006).[5] LeCompte and the Wooster Group also tackled *The Hairy Ape* in the mid-1990s with Willem Dafoe in the lead role, intensifying its expressionism and, like the Provincetowners in 1922, bringing their production uptown—to the old Selwyn Theatre, the same uptown venue that Jig Cook and company had invaded with *The Emperor Jones* in 1921.

In a very different vein, *The Complete and Condensed Stage Directions of Eugene O'Neill,* as conceived and staged by the New York Neo-Futurists in two installments (2011 and 2014), pays farcical homage to O'Neill by playfully fracturing his famously elaborate, often unstageable stage directions in its trademark style of brisk verbal and physical slapstick. In 2017 British director Richard Jones brought his own conception of *The Hairy Ape* from the Old Vic in London to New York's cavernous

Park Armory Theatre, mounting the still-formidable work on a gigantic 140-foot diameter turntable and melding pop-art and constructivism to O'Neill's expressionist conception. Despite O'Neill's notorious authorial control, his work can be more susceptible to directorial reinvention than, say, the Beckett plays obsessively controlled by his estate despite their often minimally prescriptive directions for staging. In various Off-Off Broadway venues, for example, the Target Margin Theater, much in the Provincetown spirit, undertook a two-year O'Neill project starting in 2016 that included freely refashioned versions of *Mourning Becomes Electra* (cut to a brisk 100 minutes), *The Iceman Cometh*, and *Beyond the Horizon*, along with other less-often performed works. Beyond traditional and nontraditional stagings, O'Neill's plays are also regularly adapted to film, television, opera, and dance.

A global legacy

More traditional stage productions and screen adaptations prove O'Neill's durability on his own terms, as does his continued and extensive international reach. Robert Falls, artistic director at Chicago's Goodman Theatre, has been an especially strong proponent, directing several of O'Neill plays on his home stage and in 2009 organizing six productions on three continents under the title "A Global Exploration: Eugene O'Neill in the 21st Century," including contributions by the Neo-Futurists (*Strange Interlude*) and the Wooster Group (*The Emperor Jones*). O'Neill's devotion to Strindberg has been reciprocated over the years by the many O'Neill productions at Sweden's Royal Dramatic Theatre, including posthumous world premieres of *Long Day's Journey*, *Hughie*, *A Touch of the Poet*, *More Stately Mansions*, and a 1988 revival of *Long Day's Journey* directed by Ingmar Bergman in the centennial year of O'Neill's birth. Prior to the recent success of Belgian director Ivo van Hove with two major Arthur Miller revivals on Broadway, he took on *Mourning Becomes Electra* in Amsterdam in 1989, and then *More Stately Mansions* in New York in 1997 in what one critic called "a stunningly physical, unforgettably immediate production, as flattering to O'Neill's memory as The Wooster Group's *Emperor Jones*" (Kalb 2004: 212). The Irish Repertory Theatre in New York under the direction of Ciaran O'Reilly has embraced *The Emperor Jones* as a signature work in two major revivals in 2009 and 2017, as if to affirm the link O'Neill suggests in that play between the outsider status of Irish and African Americans. His plays are also regularly produced in China, Japan, and Russia, with video of productions from these and other countries helpfully gathered at the compendious online site eOneill.com. The Eugene O'Neill Society, founded in 1978, is likewise international in its reach, convening members from around the world at events held in various global venues, especially those significant in O'Neill's life and career.

With actors like Kevin Spacey, Brian Dennehy, John Douglas Thompson, and Gabriel Byrne joining the late Jason Robards Jr. and Colleen Dewhurst as consummate performers of O'Neill, along with incursions by other top-flight artists such as Al Pacino, Forest Whitaker, Jessica Lange, and Christopher Plummer, to name a few, the canonicity of Eugene O'Neill would seem to be a settled fact of modern American culture. His plays are standard fare in textbook anthologies for theatre and American literature courses, and certainly his work is pivotal in the history of American theatre, not for the (underrated) felicity or nuance of his style but for the lingering force of his vision and, as with Shakespeare, the currency and adaptability of his texts. The 1981 all-black *Long Day's Journey* featuring Ruby Dee as Mary Tyrone set aside the family's conspicuous Irishness in favor of a claim to trans-racial universality while still rooted in the small-city Connecticut milieu of 1912.

A continuing dialogue

Though a minor work, *Hughie* may offer the strongest hint of O'Neill's dramatic legacy. Like the play's tawdry hotel setting, O'Neill can seem dated when compared with playwrights with more contemporary themes, daring methods, or bracing, finely tuned dialogue. His earlier plays have the force of an American dramatic modernism being born, especially when considered as steps (or missteps) in a longer journey. During his last ten years after 1943 when a worsening tremor halted his writing, there were always more and even better plays in his mind to be written, and a great one, *Long Day's Journey*, locked away for a later generation. Meanwhile, he had managed to craft his last one-acter after two decades away from the form, in a retrospective key and a deliberately outmoded idiom. In *Hughie* O'Neill poses his last modernist challenge by leaving open just how to stage the Night Clerk's distracted, unspoken thoughts against Erie's compulsive banter as the unsettling modernity outside the deteriorating hotel leaves them both stranded in an uncertain night. With morning coming on, a simple game of dice breaks their shared curse, restoring Erie's lost confidence and giving the Night Clerk a way to bear the passing of time.

In the words of O'Neill's own requested gravestone epitaph, "There's a Lot to Be Said for Being Dead" (LFA 474).[6] Through his continuing dialogue with such artists as Robert Falls, Elizabeth LeCompte, and, as Shelia Hickey Garvey's essay in this volume confirms, Tony Kushner, O'Neill continues having a lot to say. Even more than the recovery of a lost text such as *Exorcism*, however exciting such events may be for O'Neill scholars, the key for theatre artists lies in finding new ways, new collaborations, and new audiences to keep his drama alive.

CHRONOLOGY

1877   Marriage of parents James O'Neill and Mary Ellen "Ella" Quinlan at St. Ann's Church in New York City.

1878   Brother James Jr. born.

1883   Brother Edmund born.

1885   Edmund dies of measles, contracted from James Jr.

1888   Eugene Gladstone O'Neill born on October 16 in Barrett House hotel, New York City (Broadway 43rd Street).

1895   Enters St. Aloysius Academy, New York City.

1902   Enrolls at Betts Academy, Stamford Connecticut.

1903   Learns of mother, Ella's, morphine addiction; renounces Catholicism.

1906   Starts first and only year at Princeton College.

1907   Sees ten performances of Ibsen's *Hedda Gabler* starring Alla Nazimova.

1909   Secretly marries the pregnant Kathleen Jenkins; leaves her to go on a gold prospecting trip to Honduras.

1910   Ships out to Buenos Aires on steamer; son Eugene Jr. born.

1911   Returns to New York City; lives in lower Manhattan flophouse, Jimmy the Priest's; sees all productions by the Abbey Players during their six-week New York run; attempts suicide.

1912   Returns to live with parents at Monte Cristo Cottage in New London, Connecticut; divorces Kathleen Jenkins; works as reporter for New London *Telegraph*; diagnosed with tuberculosis and enters Gaylord Farm Sanatorium for six months.

1913   Returns to New London; begins writing plays.

1914 Publishes *Thirst, and Other One-Act Plays*; enrolls at Harvard as a special student in George Pierce Baker's English 47 playwriting course; completes one year of the two-year course.

1916 Summers in Provincetown, Massachusetts; joins Provincetown Players; first plays to be produced, *Bound East for Cardiff* and *Thirst*; first New York productions *Bound East for Cardiff* and *Before Breakfast*.

1918 Marries Agnes Boulton in Provincetown.

1919 Son Shane born in Provincetown.

1920 *Beyond the Horizon* wins Pulitzer Prize (first of his four); father dies.

1921 Wins second Pulitzer for *Anna Christie*.

1922 Mother dies.

1923 James O'Neill Jr. dies.

1924 Moves with family to Bermuda.

1925 Daughter, Oona, born in Bermuda.

1926 Begins relationship with actress Carlotta Monterey.

1928 Wins third Pulitzer for *Strange Interlude*.

1929 Divorces Agnes Boulton, marries Carlotta Monterey in France; settles with Carlotta near Tours, France.

1931 Returns with Carlotta to New York.

1932 Moves to Sea Island, Georgia; begins planning American history play cycle.

1936 Moves to Seattle for several weeks; while there, his Nobel Prize selection announced.

1937 Builds Tao House near Danville, California.

1939 Writes *The Iceman Cometh*.

1940 Writes *Long Day's Journey Into Night*.

1943 Finishes *A Moon for the Misbegotten*, his final completed work as Parkinson's-like symptoms cripple his hands.

1945 Moves with Carlotta from California to New York.

1946 *Iceman* premiere in New York, his first new play production since 1934.

1947 *A Moon for the Misbegotten* premieres in Columbus, Ohio, with brief tour of other cities.

1948 Moves with Carlotta to Marblehead, Massachusetts (site of incident dramatized in Tony Kushner's *A Blizzard at Marblehead*).

1950 Eugene Jr. commits suicide.

1953 Dies of pneumonia in his residence at the Shelton Hotel in Boston, November 27.

1956 *Iceman* revival at the Circle-in-the-Square, New York, directed by José Quintero; premiere of *Long Day's Journey* in Stockholm, and then New York.

1957 Wins fourth Pulitzer posthumously for *Long Day's Journey*; *Touch of the Poet* premieres in Stockholm.

1958 *Hughie* premieres in Stockholm.

1962 *More Stately Mansions* premieres in Stockholm.

1976 Eugene O'Neill National Historic Site established at Tao House near Danville, California.

2011 Typescript of *Exorcism*, the 1919 play presumed lost, discovered and published.

NOTES

Chapter 1

1. As Sheaffer observes, "his apotheosis was virtually complete once *Electra* had opened" (SA 390).

2. When urging friends back in his Greenwich Village days to read Baudelaire and Strindberg, O'Neill would stress the poets' vision of a "downward path to salvation," according to fellow bohemian Dorothy Day, as if glimpses of eternal truth were available only in the fleeting, often sordid sensuality of the moment (SP 404).

3. See especially Chapter 5, "Touring the Red Light District," in *Staging the Slums, Slumming the Stage* (2014: 145–76).

4. For a more sharply contrarian view of O'Neill's cultural ascent, see David Savran, "The Canonization of Eugene O'Neill," in *Highbrow/Lowdown: Theater, Jazz, and the Making of the New Middle Class* (2009: 221–64).

5. Virgil Geddes devotes his 1934 book, *The Melodramadness of Eugene O'Neill*, to this critique.

6. For an excellent analysis of why O'Neill's melodramatic legacy matters, see Zander Brietzke (2001: 173–80).

7. See Pfister's discussion of O'Neill's professionally self-conscious photogeneity (1995: 2–10).

Chapter 2

1. Herne's biographer John Perry uses this epithet in his title, *James A. Herne: The American Ibsen* (1978).

2. See also Bogard's more critical view of Baker's effect on O'Neill (1988: 48–52).

3. See Dowling for a concise account of O'Neill's participation in the brothel charade, based on court records from the 1912 divorce trial in White Plains, New York (LFA 76–81).

Chapter 3

1. Originally envisioning his hero as an Irishman in the image of Driscoll of the *Glencairn* plays, O'Neill instead decided he should be "more fittingly, an

American—a New York tough of the toughs" with an archetypally American name, idiom, and outlook (Bryer 1982: 32).

2. For a brief and pertinent account of the Vose affair, see Doris Alexander (2005: 34–36).

Chapter 5

1. In 1918 with the war near an end, O'Neill wrote probably his very worst play, the one-act *Shell Shock* (CP1: 655–72), in which a doctor rather quickly cures an American officer of his postwar-traumatic compulsion to light cigarettes repeatedly. It is reductive and undramatic, "possibly the shortest course of psychoanalysis on record" (Bogard 1988: 99).

2. O'Neill acknowledged in 1929 that Jung's *Psychology of the Unconscious* "interested me the most of all those [books] of the Freudian school" (qtd. SA 245).

3. See also Du Bois's warning that the African American "not bleach his Negro soul in a flood of white Americanism" (1903: 4).

4. This shared sense of exclusion also created hostility between Irish immigrants and African Americans. For an insightful discussion of the link between minstrel shows and "Irish low-comedy types," see Eric Lott, *Love and Theft* (1993: 95–96).

5. See especially the book Macgowan wrote with Herman Rosse, *Masks and Demons* (1923).

6. The Gelbs argue that O'Neill "was so deeply tanned he needed no makeup" to play the sailor in *Thirst* (LMC 571).

7. In his notes to the Library of America edition, Bogard includes the variant of this final speech from the 1921 Boni & Liveright edition and its much harsher racist tone, with Smithers declaiming, 'Stupid as 'ogs, the lot of 'em! Blarsted niggers!' (CP1: 1104).

8. In his 1964 revival, José Quintero did include the epilogue, somewhat modified (Gelb 1964: 1, 3).

9. O'Neill wrote these remarks for a dinner honoring W. E. B. Du Bois, April 13, 1924, in New York (Halfmann 1987: 33).

10. These lines appear twice in the play (CP3: 203 and 215); in a third instance Con completes only the first three lines, interrupted by the Harfords' lawyer, Gadsby (CP3: 244), and finally in Irish brogue (CP3: 277). The same lines are recited in *More Stately Mansions* by Con's eventual son-in-law, Simon Harford, who recalls them as a favorite passage of his mother's (CP3: 327).

11. See, for example, the Gelbs (LMC 523).

Notes

Chapter 6

1. See "Upon the Blessed Isles," in *Thus Spoke Zarathustra* (1959: 197–200).

Chapter 7

1. Among those who give a comprehensive reading of O'Neill's writings but deemphasize the autobiographical element are two who take a formalistic approach with attention to theatrical factors: Kurt Eisen, *The Inner Strength of Opposites: O'Neill's Novelistic Drama and the Melodramatic Imagination* (1994), and Zander Brietzke, *The Aesthetics of Failure: Dynamic Structure in the Plays of Eugene O'Neill* (2001). Also noteworthy is the thematic study by Thierry Dubost, *Struggle, Defeat or Rebirth: Eugene O'Neill's Vision of Humanity* (1997).

2. Joel Pfister laid the groundwork for this perspective on O'Neill in *Staging Depth: Eugene O'Neill and the Politics of Psychological Discourse* (1995).

3. A few months working as a reporter for the daily newspaper in New London in 1912 convinced O'Neill that he wanted to be a writer. He had confidence in his own name even at that point, before he had written a single play. When someone on the newspaper staff told him that he had the job only because he was "Monte Cristo's" (meaning James O'Neill's) son, Eugene replied: "Someday I won't be known as his son. He will be known as my father" (SL 533).

4. Brenda Murphy's *American Realism and American Drama, 1880–1940* (1987) offers an excellent overview of the state of serious American drama at the time O'Neill was calculating his role as an innovator, which was itself not a new role for an American playwright in that era. Her *The Provincetown Players and the Culture of Modernity* effectively carries the history of authorship in which O'Neill emerged into the next generation.

5. O'Neill might also have considered Emma Goldman's *The Social Significance of the Modern Drama* (1914), which pointed to the as-yet ill-defined American social formation as a reason for the near-total absence of significant plays in America (5–6).

6. O'Neill began omitting the "G" from the title page and spine of his publications in the latter part of 1921, though some reviews of his plays suggest that the initial might have persisted in programs or other printings into 1923. O'Neill continued to use the middle initial on at least one signed contract from 1923. I am grateful to Alex Pettit for the results of his investigation, which he reported to me in several emails in April 2016.

7. We get a glimpse of O'Neill's father (the miner of commercial theatre gold), the abandoned wife (emblematic of his father's slighting of his mother's need for a home, something O'Neill would later stress in *Long Day's Journey Into Night*), and himself (also one who had abandoned a wife for gold prospecting

in Honduras). A provocative study of this play is Egil Törnqvist, "O'Neill's Firstborn" (1989: 5–11).

8. O'Neill grew a mustache in 1909 when he was on a gold-mining expedition in Honduras. He wrote to his parents on November 9, 1909, that he had done so "in order to look absolutely as shiftless and dirty as the best of them" (SL 19). That mustache did not endure, though it is perhaps significant that the character of the Poet in *Fog* (written early in 1914) has a black mustache. However, numerous snapshots from the early 1910s show him without a mustache as late as summer 1914. Perhaps it was then that he decided to grow the mustache, because that fall, when he was in Cambridge and studying with Professor Baker, he made no mention of growing a mustache in his many letters to his girlfriend, Beatrice Ashe. Becoming an artist (not nothing) involved creating that mask. I discuss this photograph at greater length in "Et in Arcadia E. G. O." (King 2016: 180–84).

9. After O'Neill's death, a newspaper reporter, Herbert J. Stoeckel, recalled interviewing O'Neill: "Throughout the interview it seemed as if he were wearing a tragic mask of concentrated sorrow. Then, without warning, he flashed an ear-to-ear smile, as if another mask had suddenly been superimposed. Then, instantaneously, this fleeting mask of comedy disappeared, and the mask of tragedy was donned again. One was shocked by the sudden transition" ("Memories of Eugene O'Neill").

10. See "Eugene O'Neill Talks of His Own and the Plays of Others," *New York Herald Tribune* (November 16, 1924): section 7:8, 14 (CEO 60–63).

11. I discuss the metaphor of the final curtain in relation to Irving speaking that line of Tennyson in the final chapter of *Henry Irving's "Waterloo"* (1993: 231–40, especially 233). I develop the topic further in "When Theatre Becomes History: Final Curtains on the Victorian Stage" (1992: 53–61).

12. Clark recounts the history of editions and revisions in the preface to the 1947 revised edition (v–vi). Also notable among portraits of O'Neill written by an author who had first-hand experience is Elizabeth Shepley Sergeant's "O'Neill: Man with a Mask," originally published in *The New Republic* (March 16, 1927) and later included in her collection *Fire Under the Andes: A Group of North American Portraits* (1927: 81–104).

13. I explore this argument at length in *Another Part of a Long Story: Literary Traces of Eugene O'Neill and Agnes Boulton* (King 2010).

14. Croswell Bowen, with the assistance of Shane O'Neill, *Curse of the Misbegotten: A Tale of the House of O'Neill* (1959). Bowen's daughter wrote a biography of her father that suggests that the biography of O'Neill serves autobiographical purposes for the biographer. She writes: "The shadows Eugene O'Neill cast on his family were indeed very dark. Having peered more and more closely into them, Cros[well Bowen], his disciple, had drawn so close it was impossible to know whether it was the darkness of O'Neill's life or the darkness of his own life that enveloped him." Betsy

Connor Bowen, *Croswell Bowen: A Writer's Life, a Daughter's Portrait* (2014: 227).

15. A valuable archive of shorter Gelb writings can be found, along with much else, such as the complete text of the Bogard volume mentioned below, on Harley Hammerman's website eOneill.com.

16. Sheaffer's *O'Neill: Son and Playwright* (1968) covers the years up to 1920; it is followed by *O'Neill: Son and Artist* (1973). Unlike the biographies by the Gelbs and Bowen, Sheaffer documents all his sources. The bulk of Sheaffer's research files are available for study at Connecticut College.

17. See Alexander's *The Tempering of Eugene O'Neill* (1962), *Eugene O'Neill's Creative Struggle: The Decisive Decade, 1924–1933* (1992), and *Eugene O'Neill's Last Plays: Separating Art from Autobiography* (2005).

18. I expand on this analysis of Black's biography (also on the Gelbs') in a review published in *Theatre Survey* (King 2001: 121–24).

19. Jack Nicholson played the part of O'Neill in the biopic about John Reed and Louise Bryant, *Reds* (1981), and one glimpses O'Neill in the biopic about Dorothy Day, *Entertaining Angels* (1996), but mostly the filmed depictions, including one by Tony Kushner, remain marginal or undeveloped. Plays by Lars Norèn, Jovanka Bach, Derek Goldman, Jo Morello, Herman Farrell, and others have attempted to capture his character on the stage, but the mask remains elusive, perhaps because O'Neill played himself with such subtlety and originality.

20. Albert Boni left the firm in 1919; his name lingered until 1928. "Liveright" herein sometimes identifies both the firm and its co-founder.

21. Omissions may be calculated by examining the textual notes in *Eugene O'Neill: Complete Plays*, ed. Travis Bogard (1988). This edition does not include the recently discovered *Exorcism*, performed but not published in O'Neill's lifetime. By 1924, O'Neill's nondramatic *oeuvre* comprised poems, a story, an essay, and several letters to the *New York Times*.

22. Bibliographical descriptions derive from my examination of personal copies and from Jennifer McCabe Atkinson (1974: 158–60). The bindings emphasize "the display and design of the title on the spine and front cover"; they feature ribbon gold, not imitation gold leaf, for stamped lettering. For these developments, see Douglas Leighton, *Modern Bookbinding: A Survey and a Prospect* (1935: 40, 59–60). For dust jackets, see Leighton 1935: 42–43; and Anthony Rota, *Apart from the Text* (1998: 106, 128). Neither I nor Atkinson has seen the dust jackets she reports (1974: 160).

23. See Pettit 2017.

24. See Dowling (LFA 275–76). An early *All God's Chillun* appeared in the *American Mercury* in February 1924, two months before the release of Boni & Liveright's edition.

25. For O'Neill's finances, see O'Neill to Kenneth Macgowan (SL 189). Noting *Desire*'s success, O'Neill wrote, "Helped by scandal, damn it!" (LFA 298).

For the price, see Boni & Liveright's December 14, 1924, *New York Times* advertisement (Figure 3).

26. See Liveright, "American Play Company" (Egleston 2004: 169); and Egleston (2004: 164).

27. See Eugene O'Neill, *Work Diary, 1924–43*, vol. 1, for October 3–4, 1924 (12) and October 12, 1924 (13).

28. The observation draws on Bogard's textual notes in the Library of America edition and collations by Claire Vanhoutte Pettit and me.

29. Liveright, "American Play Company" (Egleston 2004: 169). *Desire* opened November 11, 1924.

30. For the date, see Atkinson (1974: 160).

31. O'Neill, *Work Diary*, vol. 1, for July 14, 1924 (9), October 3, 1924 (12), and December 15–17, 1924 (15).

32. Like the omissions, the inclusion of two plays in the *Complete Works—The Dreamy Kid* and *Before Breakfast*—that Boni & Liveright had not previously published indicates selectivity, as distinct from the republication of plays for which the press held copyrights. The *Times* ad's notice of "The Provincetown Theater Plays" promised an unnamed play by O'Neill. The second (1925) edition of *Desire Under the Elms* appeared in that series, which had been retitled "The Provincetown-Greenwich Plays."

33. For the pre-production history, see Wainscott (1988: 171). Boni & Liveright later tried to capitalize on O'Neill's struggle to place *Marco Millions* by (inaccurately) advertising its edition as O'Neill's "first long play published before production"; the book "sold well," Egleston observes (2004: 171).

34. For these processes at that time, see Alex J. Vaughan, *Modern Bookbinding: A Treatise* (1929: 156–70).

35. See Pettit 2014.

36. Bogard notes one difference between the play as reviewed and as published (UO 149); more emerge in comparing the published text to the pertinent reviews in Bryer and Dowling (CR 59–96). Bogard infers that O'Neill revised the play "before [its] publication" eight and a half months after the premiere (UO 149).

37. O'Neill, *Work Diary*, vol. 1, for March 13, 1928 (54), September 10, 1928 (58).

38. Ibid., February 11, 1929 (65). The best account is Wainscott (1988: 243–55).

39. A month after the premiere, O'Neill had not seen the Guild's "cut version" (SL 327). He revised proofs provided by Liveright (see O'Neill, *Work Diary*, vol. 1, for March 18, 1929 [66]); these were presumably set from a typescript proximate to the copy that O'Neill submitted to the Guild in September 1928.

40. See O'Neill, "Working Days on Completed Plays," in *Work Diary*, vol. 1, 270.

41. See Monroe 1982: 139–41.

42. Unidentified clipping from a Chicago paper dated September 11 (likely 1922). Charles Gilpin Clipping File, Hatch-Billops Collection.

43. *Abraham Lincoln* ran at the Cort Theatre on Broadway from December 15, 1919, until May 1920. Gilpin is not credited as part of the cast on the Internet Broadway Database: https://www.ibdb.com/Production/View/6741 (accessed March 12, 2016).

44. "Charles Gilpin Began as Minstrel," otherwise unidentified clipping from the Charles Gilpin Clipping File, Hatch-Billops Collection.

45. Ibid.

46. "Entertains Prisoners," *Pittsburgh Courier*, June 30, 1923, 4.

47. "Black and White," March 30, 1922, otherwise unidentified clipping from the Charles Gilpin Clipping File, Hatch-Billops Collection.

48. Gilpin's production ran from November 10, 1926, through January 15, 1927, a total of about 150 performances by my calculations, though the record is sparse. Moss Hart provides one of the few accounts of this in *Act One* (1959: 98–99).

49. *New York Evening Post*, otherwise unidentified clipping from 1926.

50. The comparison of Robeson to Gilpin happened mostly after the fact. Robeson's *Emperor* was staged by the Provincetown Players and not covered extensively in the press.

51. *All God's Chillun* Clipping File, New York Public Library for the Performing Arts, Billy Rose Theatre Division. Hereafter referred to as NYPLPA.

52. From *The Emperor Jones* Clipping File, NYPLPA.

53. Harry Willis was known as the "Black Panther," a talented black boxer who, like Jack Johnson, was at the top of boxing, but never allowed to challenge white athletes for a title match.

54. From the Collection of Carl Van Vechten. Paul Robeson File, 1922–25. Beinecke Rare Book and Manuscript Library. The *Pittsburgh Courier* reprinted the London reviews for its black readership as "Robeson Wins Praise of Critics in London," *Pittsburgh Courier*, October 10, 1925, n.p.

55. This review appeared in the *London Daily Graphic* on September 11, 1925. The *Chicago Defender* reprinted it as "Reviews: Paul Robeson," *Chicago Defender*, October 31, 1925, 7.

56. "Giant Negro Actor," [London] *Daily Mail*, September 11, 1925, n.p. See also "Giant Negro-Actor on his Ambition to Sing," *Evening News*, September 11, 1925, n.p.

57. "6ft. 4 in. Negro Actor's Triumph." [London] *Star*, September, 1925. n.p. Collection of Carl Van Vechten. Paul Robeson File, 19XX-25. Beinecke Rare Book and Manuscript Library.

58. From *The Negro World* (June 1, 1924); in Alexander Gumby's scrapbooks at Columbia University's Rare Book and Manuscript Library.

59. Alexander Gumby's scrapbooks are at Columbia University's Rare Book and Manuscript Library.

60. José Esteban Muñoz describes the process of disidentification as working simultaneously within and against popular discourse (1999: 1–34).

61. See Katie N. Johnson, "Brutus Jones' Remains: The Case of Jules Bledsoe" (2015), and Michael Morrison, "Emperors Before Gilpin: Opal Cooper and Paul Robeson" (2012).

62. From the Hatch-Billops Collection, Opportunity Binder 1923–46.

Conclusion

1. This excludes early plays such as *Now I Ask You* and *Recklessness* that have been produced in recent years in smaller venues around New York or elsewhere.

2. Dowling reports that O'Neill completed one other play for this series but destroyed it in 1944 (LFA 437).

3. Reviewers in 1964 were aware of this connection, having seen Jim O'Neill as Jamie Tyrone in *Long Day's Journey*. See also Floyd (1985: 559–60).

4. The most explicit such assessment was in the *Newark Evening News*, whose reviewer called *Hughie* "not a play, but rather a short story without a plot" (Hipp: CR 931).

5. For actor John Douglas Thompson's views on this topic, including his sharp disapproval of the Wooster Group production, see Garvey (2010: 163–79).

6. The actual epitaph on his gravestone, "Rest in Peace," is more decorous but perhaps also more ironic.

BIBLIOGRAPHY

Works by Eugene O'Neill

The Calms of Capricorn: A Play, ed. Donald Gallup (New Haven and New York: Ticknor and Fields, 1982).

"Children of the Sea" and Three Other Unpublished Plays by Eugene O'Neill, ed. Jennifer McCabe Atkinson (Washington, DC: NCR, 1972).

Complete Plays, 3 vols., ed. Travis Bogard (New York: Library of America, 1988).

Exorcism: A Play in One Act (New Haven: Yale University Press, 2012).

Eugene O'Neill at Work: Newly Released Ideas for Plays, ed. Virginia Floyd (New York: Ungar, 1981).

Eugene O'Neill: Comments on the Drama and the Theater: A Source Book, ed. Ulrich Halfmann (Tubingen: Gunter Narr, 1987).

Long Day's Journey Into Night: Critical Edition, ed. William Davies King (New Haven, CT: Yale University Press, 2014).

Poems: 1912-1944, ed. Donald Gallup (New Haven and New York: Ticknor and Fields, 1980).

The Unfinished Plays: Notes for the Visit of Malatesta, the Last Conquest, Blind Alley Guy, ed. Virginia Floyd (New York: Ungar, 1988).

The Unknown O'Neill: Unpublished or Unfamiliar Writings of Eugene O'Neill, ed. Travis Bogard (New Haven, CT: Yale University Press, 1988).

Work Diary 1924-1943, 2 vols. Preliminary edition, ed. Donald Gallup (New Haven, CT: Yale University Library, 1981).

Correspondence

Bogard, Travis and Jackson R. Bryer (eds.), *Selected Letters of Eugene O'Neill* (New Haven, CT: Yale University Press, 1988).

Bryer, Jackson R. (ed.), *"The Theatre We Worked For": The Letters of Eugene O'Neill to Kenneth Macgowan* (New Haven, CT: Yale University Press, 1982).

Commins, Dorothy (ed.), *"Love and Admiration and Respect": The O'Neill-Commins Correspondence* (Durham, NC: Duke University Press, 1986).

King, William Davies (ed.), *A Wind is Rising: The Correspondence of Agnes Boulton and Eugene O'Neill* (Madison, NJ: Fairleigh Dickinson University Press, 1999).

Roberts, Nancy L. and Arthur W. Roberts (eds.), *"As Ever, Gene": The Letters of Eugene O'Neill to George Jean Nathan* (Rutherford, NJ: Farleigh Dickinson University Press, 1987).

Biographies, interviews, memoirs

Black, Stephen, *Eugene O'Neill: Beyond Mourning and Tragedy* (New Haven: Yale University Press, 1999).

Boulton, Agnes, *Part of Long Story: Eugene O'Neill as a Young Man in Love*, ed. William Davies King (1958; Jefferson, NC: McFarland, 2011).

Bowen, Croswell, *The Curse of the Misbegotten: A Tale of the House of O'Neill* (New York: McGraw-Hill, 1959).

Clark, Barrett H., *Eugene O'Neill: The Man and His Plays*, rev. ed. (New York: Dover, 1947).

Dowling, Robert M., *Eugene O'Neill: A Life in Four Acts* (New Haven, CT: Yale University Press, 2014).

Estrin, Mark (ed.), *Conversations with Eugene O'Neill* (Jackson: University of Mississippi Press, 1990).

Gelb, Arthur and Barbara Gelb, *By Women Possessed: A Life of Eugene O'Neill* (New York: Putnam, 2016).

Gelb, Arthur and Barbara Gelb, *O'Neill*, rev. ed. (New York: Harper and Row, 1973).

Gelb, Arthur and Barbara Gelb, *O'Neill: Life with Monte Cristo* (New York: Applause, 2000).

King, William Davies, *Another Part of a Long Story: Literary Traces of Eugene O'Neill and Agnes Boulton* (Ann Arbor: University of Michigan Press, 2010).

Murphy, Brenda and George Monteiro (eds.), *Eugene O'Neill Remembered* (Tuscaloosa: University of Alabama Press, 2016).

Shaffer, Yvonne, *Performing O'Neill: Conversations with Actors and Directors* (New York: St. Martin's, 2000).

Sheaffer, Louis, *O'Neill: Son and Artist* (Boston: Little, Brown, 1973).

Sheaffer, Louis, *O'Neill: Son and Playwright* (Boston: Little, Brown, 1968).

Reviews, bibliographies and reference works

Atkinson, Jennifer McCabe, *Eugene O'Neill: A Descriptive Bibliography* (Pittsburgh: University of Pittsburgh Press, 1974).

Bryer, Jackson R. and Robert M. Dowling (eds.), *Eugene O'Neill: The Contemporary Reviews* (Cambridge: Cambridge University Press, 2014).

Dowling, Robert M. (ed.), *Critical Companion to Eugene O'Neill: A Literary Reference to His Life and Work*, 2 vols. (New York: Facts on File, 2009).

Ranald, Margaret Loftus, *The Eugene O'Neill Companion* (Westport, CT: Greenwood, 1984).

Reaver, J. Russell, *An O'Neill Concordance*, 3 vols. (Detroit: Gale Research, 1969).

Smith, Madeline C. and Richard Eaton, *Eugene O'Neill: An Annotated International Bibliography, 1973-1999* (Jefferson, NC: McFarland, 2001).

Bibliography

Smith, Madeline C. and Richard Eaton, *Eugene O'Neill Production Personnel: A Biographical Dictionary of Actors, Directors, Producers, and Scenic and Costume Designers in Stage and Screen Presentations of the Plays* (Jefferson, NC: McFarland, 2005).

O'Neill criticism: Book-length studies

Alexander, Doris, *Eugene O'Neill's Creative Struggle: The Decisive Decade, 1924-1933* (University Park: Pennsylvania State University Press, 1992).

Alexander, Doris, *Eugene O'Neill's Last Plays: Separating Art from Autobiography* (Athens, GA: University of Georgia Press, 2005).

Alexander, Doris, *The Tempering of Eugene O'Neill* (New York: Harcourt, Brace, 1962).

Baker-White, Robert, *The Ecological Eugene O'Neill: Nature's Veiled Purpose in the Plays* (Jefferson, NC: McFarland, 2015).

Barlow, Judith E., *Final Acts: The Creation of Three Late O'Neill Plays* (Athens, GA: University of Georgia Press, 1985).

Bennett, Michael Y. and Benjamin D. Carson (eds.), *Eugene O'Neill's One-Act Plays: New Critical Perspectives* (New York: Palgrave Macmillan, 2012).

Berlin, Normand, *O'Neill's Shakespeare* (Ann Arbor: University of Michigan Press, 1993).

Bloom, Harold (ed.), *Eugene O'Neill*, updated ed. (New York: Infobase, 2007).

Bloom, Steven F. (ed.), *Eugene O'Neill, Critical Insights* (Ipswich, MA: Salem, 2013).

Bloom, Steven F., *Student Companion to Eugene O'Neill* (Westport, CT: Greenwood, 2007).

Bogard, Travis, *Contour in Time: The Plays of Eugene O'Neill*, rev. ed. (New York: Oxford University Press, 1988).

Bower, Martha Gilman, *Eugene O'Neill's Unfinished Threnody and Process of Invention in Four Cycle Plays* (Lewiston, NY: Edwin Mellen, 1993).

Brietzke, Zander, *The Aesthetics of Failure: Dynamic Structure in the Plays of Eugene O'Neill* (Jefferson, NC: McFarland, 2001).

Chothia, Jean, *Forging a Language: A Study of the Plays of Eugene O'Neill* (Cambridge, UK: Cambridge University Press, 1979).

Diggins, John Patrick, *Eugene O'Neill's America: Desire under Democracy* (Chicago: University of Chicago Press, 2007).

Dubost, Thierry, *Struggle, Defeat or Rebirth: Eugene O'Neill's Vision of Humanity* (Jefferson, NC: McFarland, 1997).

Eisen, Kurt, *The Inner Strength of Opposites: O'Neill's Novelistic Drama and the Melodramatic Imagination* (Athens, GA: University of Georgia Press, 1994).

Engel, Edwin, *The Haunted Heroes of Eugene O'Neill* (Cambridge, MA: Harvard University Press, 1953).

Floyd, Virginia, *The Plays of Eugene O'Neill: A New Assessment* (New York: Ungar, 1985).

Frazer, Winifred L., *E.G. and E.G.O.: Emma Goldman and The Iceman Cometh* (Gainesville: University of Florida Press, 1974).

Gallup, Donald C., *Eugene O'Neill and His Eleven Play Cycle: "A Tale of Possessors Self-Dispossessed"* (New Haven, CT: Yale University Press, 1998).

Geddes, Virgil, *The Melodramadness of Eugene O'Neill* (Brookfield, CT: Brookfield Players, 1934).

Herrmann, Eileen J. and Robert M. Dowling (eds.), *Eugene O'Neill and His Early Contemporaries: Bohemians, Radicals, Progressives, and the Avant Garde* (Jefferson, NC: McFarland, 2011).

Hinden, Michael, *Long Day's Journey Into Night: Native Eloquence. Twayne's Masterworks* (Boston: Twayne, 1990).

Manheim, Michael (ed.), *The Cambridge Companion to Eugene O'Neill* (Cambridge, UK: Cambridge University Press, 1998).

Manheim, Michael, *Eugene O'Neill's New Language of Kinship* (Syracuse, NY: Syracuse University Press, 1982).

Murphy, Brenda, *O'Neill: Long Day's Journey into Night, Plays in Production* (Cambridge, UK: Cambridge University Press, 2001).

Orlandello, John, *O'Neill on Film* (Rutherford, NJ: Fairleigh Dickinson University Press, 1982).

Pfister, Joel, *Staging Depth: Eugene O'Neill and the Politics of Psychological Discourse* (Chapel Hill: University of North Carolina Press, 1995).

Porter, Laurin R., *The Banished Prince: Time, Memory and Ritual in the Late Plays of Eugene O'Neill* (Ann Arbor: UMI Research Press, 1988).

Raleigh, John Henry, *The Plays of Eugene O'Neill* (Carbondale, IL: Southern Illinois University Press, 1965).

Richter, Robert A., *Eugene O'Neill and "Dat Ole Davil Sea": Maritime Influences in the Life and Work of Eugene O'Neill* (Mystic, CT: Mystic Seaport, 2004).

Robinson, James A., *Eugene O'Neill and Oriental Thought: A Divided Vision* (Carbondale, IL: Southern Illinois University Press, 1982).

Shaughnessy, Edward L., *Down the Nights and Down the Days: Eugene O'Neill's Catholic Sensibility* (Notre Dame, IN: Notre Dame University Press, 1996).

Shea, Laura, *A Moon for the Misbegotten on the American Stage: A History of the Major Productions* (Jefferson, NC: McFarland, 2008).

Tiusanen, Timo, *O'Neill's Scenic Images* (Princeton, NJ: Princeton University Press, 1968).

Törnqvist, Egil, *A Drama of Souls: Studies in O'Neill's Super-naturalistic Technique* (New Haven, CT: Yale University Press, 1969).

Vena, Gary, *O'Neill's The Iceman Cometh: Reconstructing the Premiere* (Ann Arbor: UMI Research Press, 1988).

Viglino, Barbara, *"Perverse Mind": Eugene O'Neill's Struggle with Closure* (Madison, NJ: Fairleigh Dickinson University Press, 1999).

Wainscott, Ronald, *Staging O'Neill: The Experimental Years, 1902-1934* (New Haven, CT: Yale University Press, 1988).

Winther, Sophus Keith, *Eugene O'Neill: A Critical Study*, 2nd ed. (New York: Russell & Russell, 1961).

Bibliography

O'Neill archives/special collections

Billy Rose Theatre Division, New York Public Library Archives & Manuscripts, New York, NY, USA.

Eugene and Carlotta O'Neill Library (1000 books from their personal collection), Long Island University, Post Campus, Brookville, NY, USA.

Eugene O'Neill Papers, Eugene O'Neill Collection, Agnes Boulton Collection of Eugene O'Neill, and Eugene O'Neill, Jr. Collection, Beinecke Rare Book and Manuscript Library, Yale University, New Haven, CT, USA.

Hammerman Collection. Private collection held by Harley J. Hammerman, MD. Accessible online: http://www.eoneill.com/collection.htm (accessed February 5, 2017).

Sheaffer-O'Neill Collection, Linda Lear Center for Special Collections & Archives, Connecticut College, New London, CT, USA.

Articles, chapters, and reviews on O'Neill

Anderson, John, "Humor Flows from O'Neill Pen, With Cohan and Guild Aiding to Make Brilliant Event." *New York Evening Journal* (October 3 1933): 12. (CR 735–36)

"At the Provincetown." *New York Morning World* (May 7, 1924): n.p.

Barlow, Judith, "No He-Men Need Apply: A Look at O'Neill's Heroes." *The Eugene O'Neill Review* 19 (1995): 110–21.

Barlow, Judith, "O'Neill's Female Characters." *The Cambridge Companion to Eugene O'Neill*, ed. Michael Manheim (New York: Cambridge University Press, 1998): 164–77.

Bennett, Gwendolyn. "The Emperor Jones." *Opportunity* 8 (1930): 270–71.

Benchley, Robert, "The Theatre: Top." *The New Yorker* (November 7, 1931): 28, 30. (CR 706–08)

Bentley, Eric, "The Life and Hates of Eugene O'Neill." *Thinking about the Playwright: Comments from Four Decades* (Evanston, IL: Northwestern University Press, 1987): 27–56.

Bernays, Edward L., "Ask Me!" *Dramatic Mirror and Theatre World* (April 9, 1921): 641.

Bowen, Croswell, "The Black Irishman." *PM* (November 3, 1946): mag.: 13–17. (CEO 203–23)

Broun, Heywood, "Beyond the Horizon by Eugene O'Neill a Notable Play." *New York Tribune* (February 4, 1920): 9. (CR 61)

Broun, Heywood, "Drama: Provincetown Players Give Fine Thrill in a Sea Play." *New York Tribune* (November 25, 1918): 9. (CR 47–48)

Brown, John Mason, "The Doldrums of Midwinter." *Theatre Arts Monthly* 10 (March 1926): 145–46. (CR 505–06)

Cahill, Gloria, "Mothers and Whores: The Process of Integration in the Plays of Eugene O'Neill." *Eugene O'Neill Review* 16 (1992): 5–23.

Callens, Johan, "'Black is white, I yells it out louder 'n deir loudest': Unraveling The

Wooster Group's *The Emperor Jones.*" *Eugene O'Neill Review* 26 (2004): 43–69.

Chothia, Jean, "Trying to Write the Family Play: Autobiography and the Dramatic Imagination." *The Cambridge Companion to Eugene O'Neill,* ed. Michael Manheim (Cambridge, UK: Cambridge University Press, 1998): 192–205.

Chura, Patrick, "'Vital Contact': Eugene O'Neill and the Working Class." *Twentieth-Century Literature* 49 (2003): 520–46.

Clurman, Harold, "Theatre." *The Nation* 183 (November 24, 1956): 466 (CR 878)

Coleman, Alta May, "Personality Portraits: No. 3. Eugene O'Neill." *Theatre Magazine* 31 (April 1920): 264, 302.

Corbin, John, "Emperor Jones Revived." *New York Times* (May 7, 1924): 18.

Cowley, Malcolm, "Eugene O'Neill: Writer of Synthetic Drama." *Brentano's Book Chat* 5 (1926): 17–21. (CEO 75–80)

Crichton, Kyle, "Mr. O'Neill and the Iceman." *Total Recoil* (Garden City, NY: Doubleday, 1960): 113–31. (CEO 188–202)

De Casseres, Benjamin, "Broadway to Date: O'Neill, Galsworthy and Shakespeare to Share the Current Honors." *Art & Decoration* 28 (March 1928): 62, 96. (CR 548)

Eisen, Kurt, "'The Curtain is Lowered': Self-Revelation and the Problem of Form in *Exorcism.*" *Eugene O'Neill's One-Act Plays: New Critical Perspectives,* ed. Michael Y. Bennett and Benjamin D. Carson (New York: Palgrave Macmillan, 2012): 113–28.

Eisen, Kurt, "Theatrical Ethnography and Modernist Primitivism in Eugene O'Neill and Zora Neale Hurston." *South Central Review* 25 (2008): 56–73.

"The Emperor Jones Reappears at Provincetown With a New Emperor." *New York Post,* May 7, 1924, n.p.

"Eugene O'Neill's Plays." [London] *Evening Standard* (September 11, 1925): n.p.

Gabriel, Gilbert W., "All God's Chillun Got Masks." *New York Sun* (January 25, 1926): 20. (CR 482–83)

Garvey, Sheila Hickey, "An Interview with the New Emperor." *The Eugene O'Neill Review* 32 (2010): 163–79.

Gelb, Barbara, "Quintero in the Square." *New York Times* (February 16, 1964): section 2: 1, 3.

Gilder, Rosamond, "Each in His Own Way: Broadway in Review." *Theatre Arts* 30 (December 1946): 684, 687–90. (CR 833)

Gill, Glenda E., "Eugene O'Neill and Paul Robeson: An Uneasy Collaboration in Three of O'Neill's Early Plays." *Laconics* 1 (2006). Available online: http://www.eoneill.com/library/laconics/1/1e.htm (accessed January 20, 2017).

Hallström, Per, "Award Ceremony Speech." Available online: http://www.nobelprize.org/nobel_prizes/literature/laureates/1936/press.html (accessed October 16, 2016).

Hammond, Percy, "The Theatres." *New York Herald Tribune* (May 16, 1924): 10. (CR 370–71)

Harrison, Hubert H., "With the Contributing Editor: The Emperor Jones." *The Negro World* (June 4, 1921): 6. (CR 132–34)

Hinden, Michael, "*The Emperor Jones:* O'Neill, Nietzsche, and the American Past." *The Eugene O'Neill Newsletter* 3 (1980). Available online: http://www.eoneill.com/library/newsletter/iii_3/iii-3b.htm (accessed November 14, 2016).

Bibliography

Hipp, Edward Sothern, "New York Stage: Robards in O'Neill Work." *Newark Evening News* (December 23, 1964): 10. (CR 931–32)

Isherwood, Charles, "An Emperor Who Tops What O'Neill Imagined." *New York Times* (March 14, 2006). Available online: http://www.nytimes.com/2006/03/14/theater/reviews/an-emperor-who-tops-what-oneill-imagined.html (accessed February 4, 2017).

James, Patterson, "New Plays: The Straw." *The Billboard* 33 (December 3, 1921): 19. (CR 234)

Johnson, Katie N., "Brutus Jones' Remains: The Case of Jules Bledsoe." *Eugene O'Neill Review* 36 (2015): 1–28.

Kalb, Jonathan, *Play by Play: Theater Essays and Review, 1993-2002* (New York: Limelight, 2004).

Kantor, Louis, "O'Neill Defends His Play of Negro." *New York Times* (May 11, 1924): section 9: 5. (CEO 44–49)

Kennedy, Jeff, "Probing Legends in Bohemia: The Symbolic Dance Between O'Neill and the Provincetown Players." *Eugene O'Neill and His Early Contemporaries: Bohemians, Radicals, Progressives, and the Avant Garde*, ed. Eileen J. Herrmann and Robert M. Dowling (Jefferson, NC: McFarland, 2011): 160–93.

Kerr, Walter, "No One Will Ever Live in It . . ." *New York Times* (November 12, 1967): section 2: 1, 5. (CR 954–57)

King, William Davies, "Et in Arcadia E. G.O." *Eugene O'Neill Review* 37, no. 2 (2016): 180–84.

Kushner, Tony, A Blizzard on Marblehead Neck (unpublished manuscript, 2011).

Kushner, Tony, "The Genius of O'Neill." *The Eugene O'Neill Review* 26 (2004): 248–56.

Kushner, Tony, Interview with Sheila Hickey Garvey. Personal interview. Hamden, CT. October 11, 2012.

Kushner, Tony, Interview with Sheila Hickey Garvey. Personal interview. Hamden, CT. July 23, 2016.

Lahr, John, "Found Pages: Introduction." *The New Yorker* (October 17, 2011): 73.

Macgowan, Kenneth, "Crying the Bounds of Broadway." *Theatre Arts Monthly* 8 (June 1924): 357, 359–60. (CR 347)

Majumdar, Rupendra Guha, "O'Neill's American Precursors." *Laconics* 1 (2006). Available online: http://www.eoneill.com/library/laconics/1/1d.htm (accessed November 2, 2016).

Meaney, Gerardine, "*Long Day's Journey Into Night*: Modernism, Post-Modernism and Maternal Loss." *Irish University Review* 21 (1991): 204–18.

Mollan, Malcolm, "Making Plays with a Tragic End: An Intimate Interview with Eugene O'Neill, Who Tells Why He Does It." *The Philadelphia Public Ledger Sunday Magazine* (January 22, 1922): 3. (CEO 13–20)

Morrison, Michael, "Emperors Before Gilpin: Opal Cooper and Paul Robeson." *Eugene O'Neill Review* 33 (2012): 159–73.

Nathan, George Jean, "A Turn to the Right." *Vanity Fair* 41 (November 1933): 66. (CR 753–55)

"A New Emperor." *New York World* (May 8, 1924): n.p.

O'Neill, Eugene, "Memoranda on Masks." UO 404-11.

O'Neill, Eugene, "Strindberg and Our Theatre." UO 387.

O'Neill, Eugene, "The Playwright Explains." *New York Times* (14 February 1926): sec. 8: 2.

O'Neill, Eugene, "A Letter from O'Neill." *New York Times* (April 11, 1920): section 6:2.

O'Neill, Eugene, "An Open Letter on the Death of George Pierce Baker." UO 419-20.

O'Neill, Eugene, "The Nobel Prize Acceptance Letter." UO 428.

Packard, Paul, "Emperor Jones Gilpin's Last Stand." *New York Amsterdam News* (July 25, 1928): 7.

Pettit, Alexander, "Comedy and Metacomedy: O'Neill's *Desire Under the Elms* and Its Antecedents." *Modern Language Quarterly* 78 (2017): 51-76.

Pettit, Alexander, "The Texts of O'Neill's *Beyond the Horizon:* Ruth Mayo, Agnes Boulton, and the Women of Provincetown." *Eugene O'Neill Review* 35 (2014): 16-28.

"Rehearsals Will be resumed about May." *World* (May 19, 1924): n.p.

Robinson, James A., "The Masculine Primitive and *The Hairy Ape*." *The Eugene O'Neill Review* 19 (1995): 95-109.

Rundle, Erika, "The Hairy Ape's Humanist Hell: Theatricality and Evolution in O'Neill's 'Comedy of Ancient and Modern Life.'" *The Eugene O'Neill Review* 30 (2008): 48-144.

Sergeant, Elizabeth Shepley, "O'Neill: Man with a Mask." *Fire Under the Andes: A Group of North American Portraits* (New York: Knopf, 1927): 81-104.

Shaughnessy, Edward L., "O'Neill's African and Irish-Americans: stereotypes or 'faithful realism'?" *The Cambridge Companion to Eugene O'Neill*, ed. Michael Manheim (New York: Cambridge University Press, 1998): 148-63.

Skinner, Richard Dana, "The Play: *Ah, Wilderness!*" *Commonweal* 18 (1933): 620. (CR 751-52)

Steen, Shannon, "Melancholy Bodies: Racial Subjectivity and Whiteness in O'Neill's *The Emperor Jones*." *Theatre Journal* 52 (2000): 339-59.

Stoeckel, Herbert J., "Memories of Eugene O'Neill." *Hartford Courant* (December 6, 1953): Sunday Magazine, 3.

Törnqvist, Egil, "O'Neill's Firstborn." *Eugene O'Neill Review* 13, no. 2 (Fall 1989): 5-11.

Vidal, Gore, "The Theatre." *The Nation* 187 (October 25, 1958): 298-99. (CR 914-16)

Westgate, J. Chris, "Rethinking O'Neill's Beginnings: Slumming, Sociology, and Sensationalism in *The Web*." *Eugene O'Neill's One-Act Plays: New Critical Perspectives*, ed. Michael Y. Bennett and Benjamin D. Carson (New York: Palgrave Macmillan, 2012): 35-50.

Wilson, John S., "O'Neill on the World and *The Iceman*." *PM* (September 3, 1946): 18. (CEO 164-66)

Woollcott, Alexander, "Through Darkest New England: 'Desire Under the Elms' a Spoon Riverism by O'Neill." *New York Sun* (November 12, 1924): 28. (CR 414).

Bibliography

Wyatt, Euphemia Van R[ennselaer], "Plays of Some Importance." *Catholic World* 129 (April 1929): 80–82. (CR 683–85)

Zapf, Hubert, "O'Neill's Hairy Ape and the Reversal of Hegelian Dialectics." *Modern Drama* 31 (1988): 35–40.

Other works cited

Adams, Henry, *The Education of Henry Adams: An Autobiography* (1907; Boston: Houghton Mifflin, 1918).

Addington, Sarah, "Who's Who in New York's Bohemia," *New York Tribune* (November 14, 1915): section 4: 2.

Arendt, Hannah, *On Revolution* (1963; London: Penguin, 1990).

Baker, George Pierce, *Dramatic Technique* (Boston: Houghton Mifflin, 1919).

Batiste, Stephanie Leigh, *Darkening Mirrors: Imperial Representation in Depression-Era African American Performance* (Durham, NC: Duke University Press, 2012).

Baudelaire, Charles, "The *Exposition Universelle*, 1855." *The Mirror of Art: Critical Studies by Charles Baudelaire*, ed. and trans. Jonathan Mayne (Garden City, NY: Doubleday, 1956): 192–219.

Baudelaire, Charles, "The Painter of Modern Life." *The Painter of Modern Life and Other Essays*, ed. and trans. Jonathan Mayne (London: Phaidon, 1964): 1–40.

Bennett, Joan and Lois Kibbee, *The Bennett Playbill* (New York: Holt, Rinehart and Winston, 1970).

Black, Cheryl, *The Women of Provincetown, 1915-1922* (Tuscaloosa: University of Alabama Press, 2002).

Bourne, Randolph S., "Trans-National America." *Atlantic Monthly* 118 (July 1916): 86–97.

Bradbury, Malcolm and James McFarlane, "The Name and Nature of Modernism." *Modernism: A Guide to European Literature, 1890-1930*, ed. Malcolm Bradbury and James McFarlane (London: Penguin, 1991): 19–55.

Brecht, Bertolt, "On the Use of Music in an Epic Theatre." *Brecht on Theatre*, ed. and trans. John Willett (New York: Hill and Wang, 1964): 84–90.

Brooks, Van Wyck, "On Creating a Usable Past." *The Dial* 64 (1918): 337–41.

Browning, David, "Can't Swim in the Sea if You Can't Reach the Water." *Opera Pulse* (July 31, 2011). Available online: https://www.operapulse.com/opera-news/2011/08/03/double-bill-at-glimmerglass-opera-review/ (accessed January 28, 2017).

Buckle, G. E., *The Life of Benjamin Disraeli, Earl of Beaconsfield*, vol. 6 (London: J. Murray, 1920).

Burton, Richard, *The New American Drama* (New York: Thomas Y. Crowell, 1913).

Canales, Jimena, *A Tenth of a Second: A History* (Chicago: University of Chicago Press, 2010).

Carby, Hazel., *Race Men* (Cambridge, MA: Harvard University Press, 2009).

Carlson, Marvin A., *The Haunted Stage: The Theatre as Memory Machine* (Ann Arbor: University of Michigan Press, 2003): 1–15.

Carpenter, Faedra Chatard, *Coloring Whiteness: Acts of Critique in Black Performance* (Ann Arbor: University of Michigan Press, 2014).

Carter, Huntly, *The New Spirit in Drama & Art* (London: Frank Palmer, 1912).

Cheney, Sheldon, *The New Movement in the Theatre* (New York: Mitchell Kennerly, 1914).

Clark, Clifford Edward, Jr., *The American Family Home*, 1800-1860 (Chapel Hill: University of North Carolina Press, 1986).

Clewell, Tammy, "Introduction: Past 'Perfect' and Present 'Tense': The Abuses and Uses of Modernist Nostalgia." *Modernism and Nostalgia: Bodies, Locations, Aesthetics*, ed. Tammy Clewell (New York: Palgrave Macmillan, 2013): 1–22.

Connor Bowen, Betsy, *Croswell Bowen: A Writer's Life, a Daughter's Portrait* (n.p.: University of Nebraska Press, 2014).

Conrad, Joseph, *The Nigger of the Narcissus* (1897; Garden City, NY: Doubleday, Page, 1914).

Craig, Gordon, "A Note on Masks." *The Theatre—Advancing* (Boston: Little, Brown, 1919): 98–110.

Croly, Herbert, *The Promise of American Life* (New York: Macmillan, 1909).

Curtis, Susan, *The First Black Actors on the Great White Way* (Columbia: University of Missouri Press, 2001).

Dale, Alan, "A Chronicle of New Plays." *The Cosmopolitan* 46 (1909): 677–80.

Dalton, Joseph, "Glimmerglass finds path through storm." *Albany Times-Union* (August 1, 2011). Available online: http://www.timesunion.com/entertainment/article/Glimmerglass-finds-path-through-storm-1681657.php (accessed January 28, 2017).

Dardis, Tom, *Firebrand: The Life of Horace Liveright* (New York: Random House, 1995).

DeKoven, Marianne, "Modernism and Gender." *The Cambridge Companion to Modernism*, ed. Michael Levenson (Cambridge, UK: Cambridge University Press, 1999): 174–93.

Diamond, Elin, "Modern Drama/Modernity's Drama." *Modern Drama* 44 (2001): 3–15.

Du Bois, W. E. B., *The Souls of Black Folk: Essays and Sketches*, 3rd ed. (Chicago: A.C. McClurg, 1903).

Du Bois, W. E. B., "What is Civilization? Africa's Answer." *The Forum* 73 (February 1925): 178–88.

Eaton, Walter Prichard, "Introduction." *Washington Square Plays* (Garden City, NY: Doubleday, Page, 1916): v–xvi.

Eaton, Walter Prichard, *The American Stage of To-Day* (Boston: Small, Maynard, 1908).

Egleston, Charles, *The House of Boni & Liveright, 1917–1933: A Documentary Volume* (Detroit: Gale, Bruccoli Clark Layman, 2004).

Eisenstadt, S. N., "Multiple Modernities." *Daedalus* 129 (2000): 1–29.

Emerson, Ralph Waldo, "Farming." *Society and Solitude* (1870; Boston: Houghton Mifflin, 1892): 131–48.

Emerson, Ralph Waldo, "The American Scholar." *Ralph Waldo Emerson: Essays and Lectures*, ed. Joel Porte (New York: Library of America, 1983): 51–71.

Emerson, Ralph Waldo, "The Transcendentalist." *Ralph Waldo Emerson: Essays and Lectures* (New York: Library of America, 1983): 191–209.

Bibliography

Emerson, Ralph Waldo, "Experience." *Ralph Waldo Emerson: Essays and Lectures*, ed. Joel Porte (New York: Library of America, 1983): 469–92.

Felski, Rita, *The Gender of Modernity* (Cambridge, MA: Harvard University Press, 1995).

Fernald, Anne E., "Tradition, Avant-Garde, Postmodernism." *Modernism*, ed. Astradur Eysteinsson and Vivian Liska (Amsterdam: John Benjamins, 2007): 155–71.

Ford, Torrey, "From Pullman Car Porter to Honor Guest of Drama League." *New York Tribune* (March 13, 1921): 7.

Foucault, Michel, "What Is Enlightenment?" Trans. Catherine Porter. *The Foucault Reader*, ed. Paul Rabinow (New York: Pantheon, 1984): 32–50.

Foucault, Michel, "Of Other Spaces." Trans. Jay Miskowiec, *Diacritics* 16 (1986): 22–27.

Freud, Sigmund, *Totem and Taboo: Resemblances Between the Psychic Life of Savages and Neurotics*, trans. A. A. Brill (New York: Moffat, Yard and Company, 1918).

"Giant Negro Actor." [London] *Daily Mail* (September 11, 1925): n.p.

Gilmer, Walker, *Horace Liveright: Publisher of the Twenties* (New York: David Lewis, 1970).

"Gilpin Play Read." *Chicago Defender* (March 8, 1924): 7.

"Gilpin's Return in Old Role Hailed by Metropolitan Critics." *New York Amsterdam News* (February 24, 1926): n.p.

Glaspell, Susan, *The Road to the Temple* (London: Ernest Benn, 1926).

Goldman, Emma, "The Drama: A Powerful Disseminator of Radical Thought." *Anarchism and Other Essays*, 2nd ed. (New York: Mother Earth Publishing, 1911): 247–77.

Goldman, Emma, *The Social Significance of the Modern Drama* (Boston: Richard G. Badger, 1914).

Gooding-Williams, Robert, *Zarathustra's Dionysian Modernism* (Stanford, CA: Stanford University Press, 2001).

Greetham, David, *Textual Scholarship: An Introduction* (New York: Garland, 1994).

Gregory, Montgomery, "The Drama of Negro Life." *The New Negro: An Interpretation* (1925; New York: Arno Press, 1968): 153–60.

Hamilton, Clayton, "Old Material and New Plays." *The Forum* 41 (1909): 444–57.

Hart, Moss, *Act One* (New York: Random House, 1959).

Havel, Hippolyte, "The Spirit of the Village." *Bruno's Weekly* 1 (1915): 34–35.

Herne, James A., *Margaret Fleming. Representative American Plays from 1867 to the Present Day*, ed. Arthur Hobson Quinn, 7th ed. (New York: Appleton-Century-Crofts, 1957): 513–44.

Hodin, Mark, "Late Melodrama." *The Oxford Handbook of American Drama*, ed. Jeffrey H. Richards and Heather S. Nathans (New York: Oxford University Press, 2014): 159–72.

Howells, William Dean, "Editor's Study." *Harper's Monthly* 83 (1891): 476–79.

Hughes, Glenn, *A History of the American Theatre, 1700-1950* (New York: Samuel French, 1951).

James, William, *Principles of Psychology*, 2 vols. (New York: Henry Holt, 1890).

Johnson, Katie N., *Sisters in Sin: Brothel Drama in America, 1900-1920* (Cambridge, UK: Cambridge University Press, 2006).

Jung, C. G., "The Relations Between the Ego and the Unconscious." *Two Essays on Analytical Psychology*, trans. R. F. C. Hull (Cleveland: Meridian Books, 1956): 131–253.

Kammen, Michael, *Mystic Chords of Memory: The Transformation of Tradition in American Culture* (New York: Knopf, 1991).

Kenton, Edna, *The Provincetown Players and the Playwrights' Theatre, 1915-1922*, ed. Travis Bogard and Jackson R. Bryer (Jefferson, NC: McFarland, 2004).

King, William Davies, "When Theatre Becomes History: Final Curtains on the Victorian Stage." *Victorian Studies* 6, no. 1 (Fall 1992): 53–61.

King, William Davies, *Henry Irving's "Waterloo"* (Berkeley: University of California Press, 1993).

Kinne, Wisner Payne, *George Pierce Baker and the American Theatre* (Cambridge, MA: Harvard University Press, 1954).

Krasner, David, *A Beautiful Pageant: African American Theatre, Drama, and Performance in the Harlem Renaissance, 1910-1927* (New York: Macmillan, 2002).

Krasner, David, *A History of Modern Drama*, vol. 1 (Oxford: Wiley-Blackwell, 2012).

Krasner, David, "Whose Role Is It Anyway? Charles Gilpin and the Harlem Renaissance." *African American Review* 29 (1995): 483–96.

Lacan, Jacques, "Analysis and Truth or the Closure of the Unconscious." *The Four Fundamentals of Psycho-Analysis*, ed. Jacques-Alain Miller, trans. Alan Sheridan (New York: Norton, 1978): 136–48.

Langner, Lawrence, *The Magic Curtain: The Story of a Life in Two Fields, Theatre and Invention* (New York: Dutton, 1951).

Lears, T. J. Jackson, *No Place of Grace: Antimodernism and the Transformation of American Culture, 1880-1920* (New York: Pantheon, 1981).

Leighton, Douglas, *Modern Bookbinding: A Survey and a Prospect* (New York: Oxford University Press, 1935).

Locke, Alain, "The New Negro." *The New Negro: An Interpretation* (1925; New York: Arno Press, 1968): 3–16.

Lott, Eric, *Love and Theft: Blackface Minstrelsy and the American Working Class* (New York: Oxford, 1993).

Lovett, Laura L., *Conceiving the Future: Pronatalism, Reproduction, and the Family in the United States, 1890-1938* (Chapel Hill: University of North Carolina Press, 2007).

Luce, Henry R., "The American Century." *Life* (February 17, 1941): 61–65.

Macgowan, Kenneth and Herman Rosse, *Masks and Demons* (London: Martin Hopkinson, 1923).

McAllister, Marvin, *Whiting Up: Whiteface Minstrels and Stage Europeans in African American Performance* (Chapel Hill: University of North Carolina Press, 2011).

Miller, Arthur, "The Family in Modern Drama." *The Theater Essays of Arthur Miller*, ed. Robert A. Martin (New York: Penguin, 1978): 69–85.

Mintz, Steven and Susan Kellogg, *Domestic Revolutions: A Social History of American Family Life* (New York: The Free Press, 1988).

Moderwell, Hiram Kelly, *The Theatre of To-Day* (1914; rpt. New York: Dodd, Mead, 1926).

Bibliography

Monroe, John G., "Charles Gilpin and the Drama League Controversy." *Black American Literature Forum* 16 (Winter 1982): 139–41.

Monroe, John G., *Charles Sidney Gilpin: the Emperor Jones* (MA thesis, Hunter College, New York, 1974).

Monroe, John G., "The Harlem Little Theatre Movement, 1920-1929." *Journal of American Culture* 64 (1984): 63–70.

Moses, Montrose J., *The American Dramatist* (Boston: Little, Brown, 1911).

Muñoz, José Esteban, *Disidentifications: Queers of Color and the Performance of Politics* (Minneapolis: University of Minnesota Press, 1999).

Murphy, Brenda, *American Realism and American Drama, 1880–1940* (New York: Cambridge University Press, 1987).

Murphy, Brenda, *The Provincetown Players and the Culture of Modernity* (Cambridge, UK: Cambridge University Press, 2005).

Murray, Timothy, "From Foul Sheets to Legitimate Model: Antitheater, Text, Ben Jonson." *New Literary History* 14 (1983): 641–64.

Nietzsche, Friedrich, *The Anti-Christ. The Portable Nietzsche*, ed. and trans. Walter Kaufmann (1954; New York: Penguin, 1959): 565–656.

Nietzsche, Friedrich, *Thus Spoke Zarathustra. The Portable Nietzsche*, ed. and trans. Walter Kaufmann (1954; New York: Penguin, 1959): 103–439.

Perry, John, *James A. Herne: The American Ibsen* (Chicago: Nelson-Hall, 1978).

Ratner-Rosenhagen, Jennifer, *American Nietzsche: A History of an Icon and His Ideas* (Chicago: University of Chicago Press, 2011).

Rice, Elmer, *Minority Report: An Autobiography* (London: Heinemann, 1963).

Robeson, Paul Jr., *The Undiscovered Paul Robeson: An Artist's Journey, 1898-1939* (New York: John Wiley & Sons, Inc., 2001).

Robinson, Marc, *The American Play, 1787-2000* (New Haven: Yale University Press, 2009).

Rota, Anthony, *Apart from the Text* (New Castle, DE: Oak Knoll, 1998).

Rudnick, Lois, "The New Woman." *1915, The Cultural Moment: The New Politics, the New Woman, the New Psychology, the New Art, & the New Theatre in America*, ed. Adele Heller and Lois Rudnick (New Brunswick, NJ: Rutgers University Press, 1991): 69–81.

Sarlós, Robert Károly, *Jig Cook and the Provincetown Players: Theatre in Ferment* (Amherst: University of Massachusetts Press, 1982).

Savran, David, *Highbrow/Lowdown: Theater, Jazz, and the Making of the New Middle Class* (Ann Arbor: University of Michigan Press, 2009).

Shakespeare, William, *A Winter's Tale. The Riverside Shakespeare*, ed. G. Blakemore Evans, 2nd ed. (Boston: Houghton, Mifflin, 1997): 1612–55.

Shaw, George Bernard, *The Quintessence of Ibsenism*, rev. ed. (New York: Brentano's, 1913).

Singal, Daniel Joseph, "Towards a Definition of American Modernism." *American Quarterly* 39 (1987): 7–26.

Singer, Ben, *Melodrama and Modernity: Early Sensational Cinema and Its Contexts* (New York: Columbia University Press, 2001).

Somerville, Siobhan, *Queering the Color Line: Race and the Invention of Homosexuality in American Culture* (Durham, NC: Duke University Press, 2000).

Stansell, Christine, *American Moderns: Bohemian New York and the Creation of a New Century* (New York: Holt, 2000).

Steen, Shannon, *Racial Geometries of The Black Atlantic, Asian Pacific and American Theatre* (London: Palgrave Macmillan, 2010).

Stephens, Michelle Ann, *Skin Acts: Race, Psychoanalysis, and the Black Male Performer* (Durham: Duke University Press, 2014).

Stewart, Jeffrey C., "The Black Body: Robeson as a Work of Art and Politics." *Paul Robeson: Artist and Citizen,* ed. Jeffrey C. Stewart (New Brunswick: Rutgers University Press, 1988): 134–63.

Strindberg, August, "Author's Note to A Dream Play." *Strindberg on Drama and Theatre: A Source Book,* ed. and trans. Egil Törnqvist and Birgitta Steene (Amsterdam: Amsterdam University Press, 2007): 94–95.

Strindberg, August, "Preface to *Miss Julie.*" *Strindberg on Drama and Theatre: A Source Book,* ed. and trans. Egil Törnqvist and Birgitta Steene (Amsterdam: Amsterdam University Press, 2007): 62–72.

Taylor, Diana, *The Archive and the Repertoire: Performing Cultural Memory in the Americas* (Durham: Duke University Press, 2003).

Thompson, Mary Francesca, "The Lafayette Players, 1915-1932" (PhD diss., University of Michigan, 1972).

"Three Men Who Rule the Stage To-Day." *New York Sun* (July 30, 1911): section 3:14.

Tocqueville, Alexis de, *Democracy in America,* trans. Henry Reeve, 4th ed., vol. 1 (Cambridge, MA: Sever and Francis, 1864).

Tommasini, Anthony, "A Summer Blizzard at Glimmerglass." *New York Times* (August 3, 2011): C1.

Turner, Victor, *From Ritual to Theatre: The Human Seriousness of Play* (New York: Performing Arts Journal, 1982).

Vaughan, Alex J., *Modern Bookbinding: A Treatise* (Leicester: Raithby, Lawrence & Co., 1929).

Westgate, J. Chris, *Staging the Slums, Slumming the Stage: Class, Poverty, Ethnicity, and Sexuality in American Theatre, 1890–1916* (New York: Palgrave Macmillan, 2014).

Williams, Raymond, *Modern Tragedy* (Stanford, CA: Stanford University Press, 1966).

Williams, Tennessee, *The Glass Menagerie* (1945; New York: New Directions, 1966).

Willis, Deborah, "The Image and Paul Robeson." *Paul Robeson: Artist and Citizen,* ed. Jeffrey C. Stewart (New Brunswick: Rutgers University Press, 1988): 61–80.

Wilson, Garff B., *Three Hundred Years of American Drama and Theatre: From Ye Bare and Ye Cubb to Hair* (Englewood Cliffs, NJ: Prentice-Hall, 1973).

Witham, Barry B., *A Sustainable Theatre: Jasper Deeter at Hedgerow* (New York: Palgrave Macmillan, 2013).

Woolf, Virginia, "*Mr. Bennett and Mrs. Brown*" (London: Hogarth, 1924).

Worthen, W. B., *Modern Drama and the Rhetoric of Theater* (Berkeley: University of California Press, 1992).

Young, Harvey, *Embodying Blackness: Stillness, Critical Memory, and the Black Body* (Ann Arbor: University of Michigan Press, 2010).

Zangwill, Israel, *The Melting-Pot: A Drama in Four Acts* (New York: Macmillan, 1909).

NOTES ON CONTRIBUTORS

Sheila Hickey Garvey is professor emerita of theatre at Southern Connecticut State University. She has received numerous awards from the Kennedy Center American College Theatre Festival for her direction of university productions. She received the New England Theatre Conference's Moss Hart Award and is a lifetime elected member of NETC's College of Fellows. As the resident director of Connecticut's Greater Middletown Chorale she staged Felix Mendelssohn's *Elijah* and the world premiere of the oratorio *Letter from Italy, 1944*. A documentary narrated by Meryl Streep featuring Dr. Garvey's direction of *Letter from Italy* won a 2016 regional Emmy Award. Garvey has also acted with Long Wharf Theatre, the Williamstown Theatre Festival, Allenberry Playhouse and the Weathervane Theater. She is past president of the Eugene O'Neill Society and has published articles in the *Eugene O'Neill Review, Theatre Survey, New England Theatre Journal, The Recorder, Coup de Théâtre, A Critical Companion to Eugene O'Neill*, and *Jason Robards Remembered*, which she also edited.

Katie N. Johnson is professor of English and an affiliate of film studies and women's, gender, and sexuality studies at Miami University of Ohio. She is the author of *Sisters in Sin: Brothel Drama in America* (2006), *Sex for Sale: Six Progressive-Era Brothel Drama Plays* (2015), and numerous articles and book chapters on theatre, performance, film, and U.S. culture. Johnson is a board member of the Eugene O'Neill Society and Performance Review Editor of the *Eugene O'Neill Review*. She is working on her next book project, *Racing the Great White Way: A Counter History of Early Broadway*.

William Davies King teaches at the University of California, Santa Barbara. His critical edition of *Long Day's Journey Into Night* was published by Yale University Press in 2014, followed in 2016 by an expanded multimedia edition. He is the author of *Henry Irving's "Waterloo"* (winner of the 1993 Callaway Prize); *Writing Wrongs: The Work of Wallace Shawn; Collections of Nothing; "A Wind Is Rising": The Correspondence of Agnes Boulton and Eugene O'Neill*, and *Another Part of a Long Story: Literary Traces of Eugene O'Neill; and Agnes Boulton*, and has edited Boulton's *Part of a Long Story* and a collection of her short stories. He is at work on a critical edition of *The Iceman Cometh* and a book about the Tao House context of the writing of *Long Day's Journey*.

Alexander Pettit is professor of English, University Distinguished Teaching Professor, and affiliated faculty in women's and gender studies at the University of North Texas. His essays on O'Neill have appeared in *The Eugene O'Neill Review, Journal of American Drama and Theatre*, and *Modern Language Quarterly*. Cambridge University Press published his critical edition of Samuel Johnson's *Early Works* in 2011.

INDEX

Note: O'Neill's works are entered under their titles, with sustained discussions in **bold type**. Other works are listed under their authors' names.

Index

Index

Index